COMPOSITION – PERFORMANCE – RECEPTION

Composition – Performance – Reception

Studies in the Creative Process in Music

Edited by

Wyndham Thomas

Ashgate

Aldershot • Brookfield USA **• Singapore • Sydney**

Published by
Ashgate Publishing Limited
Gower House
Croft Road
Aldershot
Hants GU11 3HR
England

Ashgate Publishing Company
Old Post Road
Brookfield
Vermont 05036–9704
USA

British Library Cataloguing-in-Publication data

Composition – performance – reception : studies in the
creative process in music
   1. Creation (Literary, artistic, etc.)   2. Composition (Music)
   3. Music – Performance   4. Music and society
   I. Thomas, Wyndham
   781.1'7

Library of Congress Cataloging-in-Publication data

Composition – performance – reception : studies in the creative process
in music / edited by Wyndham Thomas.
     ISBN 1–85928–325–X
     1. Music—Psychology.   2. Creation (Literary, artistic, etc.)
I. Thomas, Wyndham.
ML3830.S92 1998
781'. 1—DC21   97-4992
                   CIP
                   MN

ISBN 1 85928 325 X

Printed on acid-free paper

Typeset in Sabon by Raven Typesetters, Chester and printed in Great Britain by
The University Press, Cambridge.

Contents

Acknowledgements

The editor gratefully acknowledges the financial assistance of the Universities of Bristol and Southampton (pre-publication costs); South West Arts and the Department of Music, University of Bristol (commission fee); The Colston Research Society (symposium costs). Permission to reproduce music examples has been given by Boosey & Hawkes Ltd, Faber Music Ltd, Novello & Co. Ltd, Peters Edition Ltd, PWM Edition, Schott & Co. Ltd and Universal Edition Ltd. Details are provided in the list of examples. The Royal Opera House Covent Garden kindly gave permission to reproduce the photograph of Tanya Moisevitch's set design ('The Shore') for the 1947 production of *Peter Grimes*. Permission to reproduce record sleeve art-work has been given by Siegfried Lauterwasser, Stockhausen-Verlag, Deutsche Grammophon Gesellschaft, EMI Records, EMI Classics, Philips Classics, and Decca Record Company. Again, details are provided in the list of illustrations.

In thanking all contributors to this volume, the editor would like to add special thanks to Adrian Beaumont who set the music examples using *Score* and to Margaret Peirson who assisted with the administration of the 1994 Colston Symposium. Rachel Lynch of Ashgate Publishing has provided expert advice and sympathetic support.

List of Examples and Illustrations

Examples

Example 3 and 4 are reproduced by kind permission of Schott and Co. Ltd. **Examples 5** (Copyright 1956 by Hawkes and Son (London) Ltd.) is reproduced by permission of Boosey and Hawkes Music Publishers Ltd, 1997. **Examples 6 and 7** are reproduced by kind permission of Universal Ltd. **Example 11** (Copyright 1926 by Robert Lienau, Berlin) is reproduced by Permission of the Publishers. **Examples 12 and 14–18** are reproduced by kind permission of G. Schirmer Ltd. on behalf of G. Schirmer Inc. **Examples 21–24** are reproduced by kind permission of Faber Music Ltd. **Examples 25, 26, and 28–34** are reproduced by kind permission of PWM Edition.

Illustration

The Photograph of Tanya Moisevitsch's set ('The Shore') for the 1947 production of *Peter Grimes* is reproduced on page 25 in Raymond Warren's chapter by permission of the Royal Opera House, Covent Garden. The photographer is unknown.

Details of all other illustrations are included in the Notes for Chapter 8 by Nicholas Cook.

Notes on Contributors

Adrian Beaumont was born in Huddersfield in 1937 and received his musical education at University College, Cardiff, where he gained a first and an MMus. He also studied composition intermittently with Nadia Boulanger and received his DMus from the University of Wales in 1972. He has been on the staff of the University of Bristol since 1961 and is currently Reader in Composition. He has composed in all genres except opera (over twenty of his works have been broadcast on BBC Radio 3) and is at present writing a book that explores Liszt's relationships, social and musical, with a variety of other significant composers.

Susan Bradshaw studied at the Royal Academy of Music in London with Harold Craxton (piano) and Howard Ferguson (composition) and afterwards in Paris with Pierre Boulez. Widely known as both a versatile pianist and as a writer and broadcaster on music (mainly that of the twentieth century), she has published extensively on contemporary European composers and translated several books on Boulez – one in conjunction with her long-standing piano duo partner, Richard Rodney Bennett. She has taught composition, history and performance techniques (both at undergraduate and postgraduate levels). She currently teaches piano at Goldsmiths College, University of London.

Bojan Bujic is Reader in Music and Fellow of Magdalen College, Oxford. His research interests encompass music and literature in sixteenth and early seventeenth-century Italy and links between philosophy and music in the nineteenth and twentieth centuries.

Eric Clarke was appointed as Professor of Music at the University of Sheffield in 1993, having previously worked in the Music Department at City University, London. He originally went to Sussex University to read for a degree in Neurobiology but transferred to Music, graduating there in 1977. This was followed by a masters degree in analysis, aesthetics and the sociology of music and doctoral studies with Henry Shaffer in the Psychology Department at Exeter University. His principal interest is in the psychology of music, with a particular focus on performance and the study of time and rhythm. He has published widely and holds a number of important posts, notably those of Director of the Centre for Research in Music Performance and Perception at Sheffield and Chair of the Society for Research in Psychology of Music and Music Education.

Nicholas Cook is Professor of Music and Dean of Arts at the University of Southampton. His publications range from aesthetics to computer applications and from Beethoven to popular music, but he is best known as a theorist. Recent books include *Analysing Musical Multimedia* (1998) and *Music: a Very Short Introduction*, both from Oxford University Press.

Jane Davidson is a performer and academic. As a scholar, she writes on psychological aspects of music: social interaction in music performance, body movement, musical expression, and the emergence of musical skills. She is a Lecturer in the Music Department at the University of Sheffield, Editor of *Psychology of Music*, and serves on the Editorial boards of several other journals. As a performer, she has sung many operatic and oratorio roles and produced a range of Music Theatre works, from originally devised pieces to the standard opera repertoire at the Edinburgh Festival and elsewhere.

Jonathan Harvey is one of the most distinguished British composers of his generation, with many commissions and *Prom* performances to his credit. He has held University posts at Southampton, Sussex (as Professor) and Stanford, USA. He is the author of numerous articles and a book on Stockhausen. His involvement in electro-acoustic music has been trail-blazing in this country and he spends regular periods working at IRCAM in Paris. *The Riot*, commissioned for the 1994 Colston Symposium, is the subject of Adrian Beaumont's chapter on the Reception of New Music.

Charles Rosen is an internationally distinguished pianist and musical scholar. He has held Professorships at the State University of New York, Chicago University, Harvard, Oxford and Bristol and is the author of a number of acclaimed books – *The Classical Style, Sonata Forms, The Romantic Generation*, and a monograph on Schoenberg. His many recordings have included the late Beethoven Sonatas and the major keyboard works of Schumann, Debussy and Schoenberg. He has worked closely with the composers Igor Stravinsky, Elliott Carter and Pierre Boulez.

Robert Saxton was born in London in 1953 and began composing at the age of six. After encouragement from Britten, he studied with Elisabeth Lutyens and with Robin Holloway and Robert Sherlaw Johnson at Cambridge and Oxford Universities respectively. He was the recipient of the Fulbright Arts Award to the USA in 1985 and is currently Head of Composition at the Guildhall School of Music and Drama and a Visiting Fellow in Composition at the University of Bristol. He has fulfilled commissions for many organisations and individuals, including the BBC Proms, Rostropovich, LSO, ECO, Opera North, London Sinfonietta and the Nash Ensemble. Seventeen works are available on CD and current commissions include pieces for the Chilingirian Quartet, LPO, RPO and BBC3 (*The Wandering Jew*, a millennium radio opera).

Adrian Thomas is currently Professor of Music at University of Wales, Cardiff. Formerly, he held the Chair of Music at Queen's University, Belfast and served for several years as Head of Music, BBC Radio 3. He is a composer and a noted authority on Polish music. His book on Górecki was published in 1997.

Wyndham Thomas is a Senior Lecturer at the University of Bristol and has been Head of the Department of Music since 1990. He is a composer and has research interests in musical structure in medieval and modern music. He has published articles on various aspects of medieval motets and is the editor of *Robin and Marion Motets* (3 vols) and the liturgical dramas in the *Fleury Playbook*. He was the Director of the 1994 Colston Symposium and is editor of this volume.

Stephen Walsh is Reader in Music at the University of Wales, Cardiff, and a well-known writer and broadcaster on music. A Cambridge graduate, he worked as a music critic in London, principally for the *Observer* and *The Times*, before going to Cardiff in 1976. He has published books on Schumann, Bartok and Stravinsky, has translated Boulez, and co-edited the *Viking/Penguin Opera Guide*. He is at present working on a full-scale biography of Stravinsky.

Raymond Warren was Professor of Music at the University of Bristol from 1972 to 1994. Best known as a composer, his works include operas, oratorios, symphonic and chamber music, cantatas and songs. He is author of a book, *Opera Workshop*, published by Scolar Press in 1995. He is still active as a composer and is currently Senior Research Fellow in Bristol's Department of Music.

Preface

The older one gets as a composer the more one realises that one inhabits a 'cloud-cuckoo land', to quote Milton Babbitt, in which many of one's most precious intentions and designs are woefully missed by the listener. This is not actually a dispiriting realisation for two reasons. First, it is a gradual realisation that music is in some sense bigger than oneself and, secondly, there is a symbiosis in which one changes; there is a give and take in which the audience feedback becomes unconsciously or consciously influential and formative. One ingests the audience's disregard of complex pattern in favour of their perception of big gesture, for example. It may be only a slight swing, but it is a significant one accompanying the dawning realisation. It is not exactly that you start writing *for* an audience, more that you begin to perceive things differently to yourself. Your position is perhaps less of the one who puts minute dots on paper and more of the one who is fed streams of sound; or perhaps it is that the crack between these two acts is closed, making one act alone.

The Colston Symposium brought together many specialists with a common, holistic aim – to see the slippery artefact we call music as one continuum, one act: an act within which we specialise but lose the sense of the whole at our peril. Wyndham Thomas had the vision to see that many conferences are too specialised or else too loosely diverse. A really interesting focus should promulgate variety which never loses the central heart. To include a commissioned work for first performance and first reception was characteristic of his perspicuity – creation, interpretation and reception in immediate dialogue. Being chosen for the role of pig-in-bacon-factory myself was a salutory experience: I lost some of those feelings of shyness under scrutiny and enjoyed learning how my distinguished colleagues received and my distinguished performers interpreted. This ingestion was valuable, at least for me. But the wider issues aired and gathered together in this volume all related to that particular experience and one left those extraordinary days feeling that music is both in essence more complex and more mysterious, the relation to language, reason and world-view more intricate and subtle than one had ever thought. I hope such thoughts will now reach many people.

Jonathan Harvey

Introduction
Wyndham Thomas

Where does a composer find inspiration? How are musical ideas formulated and communicated? How does a performer know exactly what the composer intended and can the listener be sure that he is hearing what the composer wanted him to hear? How do contexts, modes of presentation and fashions affect the way that music is evaluated? In what ways do analysis and music criticism contribute to understanding? Should we believe what the history books say?

These are some of the questions that are regularly asked about the creative process in music. This book will supply some of the answers – or, at least, answers by some of the participants since the questions themselves imply an exploration of a complex chain-reaction which is no more capable of definitive explanation than any other sphere of artistic endeavour. What can be accomplished in general terms is an examination of the varying roles of composers, performers, listeners, critics and theorists, and the interaction between them. More specifically, the series of essays which follows will be illustrated with case-studies – as in Raymond Warren's consideration of the dramatic and psychological problems in opera composition, Susan Bradshaw's *A Performer's Responsibility* and Adrian Beaumont's account of the reception of a new work.

Written by distinguished specialists in their own fields, these chapters have grown out of papers given at the 1994 Colston Symposium at the University of Bristol. Under its title of *The Intention, Reception and Understanding of Musical Composition*, the conference deliberated on the fundamental issues raised above and, in particular, focused attention onto a newly commissioned work by Jonathan Harvey which received its first performances at a public recital given by Het Trio of Amsterdam as part of the proceedings. Clearly it is not possible to recapture the extraordinary atmosphere of that occasion,[1] but Adrian Beaumont's essay, *Expectation and Interpretation in the Reception of New Music: A Case Study*, does provide a vivid account of the different stages in the progress of Harvey's *The Riot* from conception to performance and contrasts the anticipation which preceded the concert with the audience's reaction to it. Subsequent discussions with the performers and the composer are also recorded. Although largely concerned with a specific experience, this essay none the less addresses basic questions about how we approach first hearings of compositions (whether new works or old compositions newly discovered).

A comparable starting point is taken by Bojan Bujic in his chapter on aesthetics. However, his forty-year-old memory of a contemporary Yugoslavian composition leads him to search out philosophical and psychological guide-lines for describing such an experience – outlining on his way many of of the significant theories of perception from the German Idealist Philosophers to Boulez and Nattiez. Evaluating, or forming an opinion of a musical experience, is also the theme behind Stephen Walsh's essay on Stravinsky and the Press. Walsh, of course, was for many years one of Britain's leading music-journalists and he is all too aware of the onerous responsibilities of the profession. His analysis of the destructive notices that Stravinsky received in his home-land after his Parisian successes with Diaghilev exposes the misuse of criticism as an establishment weapon. The effects on Stravinsky (his growing sense of isolation and his hostility towards the press) were long-lasting and (Walsh suggests) components in a vicious-circle of insecurity and over-assertiveness which characterised the composer to the end. By examining the competence as well as the political stance of critics (including English and American), Walsh provides a further gloss on the crucial aesthetic divide between tradition and innovation. Many a composer other than Stravinsky has been pilloried or misunderstood because critics based their reviews on inappropriate precepts or expectations – although even misguided reviews can become indispensable tools in the study of Reception Theory, as Walsh demonstrates.

Ultimately, all music commentaries, whether critical, analytical or philosophical, are destined to become part of the documentation of Music History. Stephen Walsh's multi-faceted essay, indeed, represents a significant contribution to the social history of music (in addition to its other virtues) and this is equally true of Adrian Thomas's contextual study of composition in Poland during the decade following the Second World War. As he traces the impact of politics on composers from Lutosławsky (a.k.a. Derwid) to Baird, Thomas deals with the important subjects of creative motivation and artistic integrity; with the technical and aesthetic compromises forced on composers by a policy of mass communication and social realism (*socrealizm*). 'The trio of composer, performer and listener [he writes] had become a quartet – and we all know who the other party was!' Clearly, political ideology inhibits in a way that enlightened patronage and free societies do not. Yet, even in a democracy, we are susceptible to the dictates of fashion and marketing. Nicholas Cook, in his essay on *The Domestic Gesamtkunstwerk*, reaches beyond the commercial packaging of record sleeves to examine their aesthetic significance and to evaluate some as indicators of musical reception. Composers and performers are projected as icons to be revered (if not worshipped); associations of art and music are explored; a fascinating interface of popular and 'classical' cultures is revealed in the marketing of Madonna and Ferrier, the Beatles and Stockhausen. Such links between the visual and the aural are naturally more permanent in the presentation of recorded music (and film), but they are an essential feature of concert performance too, albeit rarely documented. Some of the examples of conductors given by Cook (Toscanini, Klemperer, Bernstein) are relatively well known to us from photographs, if not from life. Each one projected highly individualistic body-language which stamped personalised authority onto interpretations of an essentially mainstream repertoire. Those present at the Colston Symposium (and many others, of course) will be able to recall the equally characteristic composure of Charles Rosen playing Schumann's *Davidsbundler* and Het Trio's more animated ensemble in their programme of twentieth-century works. This aspect of communication is dealt with in a chapter on '*The Body in Performance*' by Eric Clarke and Jane Davidson, who provide an invaluable theoretical framework to a case-study in which two (out of six recorded) performances of Chopin's *Prelude in E minor*, op.28, no. 4, are analysed with particular attention to the relationship between body movement, expression and structure. This is a rapidly developing area of investigation and the co-authors are leading figures in what is both an experimental science and an exciting new contribution to creative music-making.

In another related essay, the pianist Susan Bradshaw rehearses some of the problems faced by performers in interpreting the musical score – 'translating what may be seen into what ought to be heard'. Her sharply-focused studies of passages from sonatas by Beethoven (op.2, no.1) and Berg together with Chopin's *E flat Nocturne* (op.1, no.2) highlight the need for performers to bypass editorial additions in search of the structural evidence communicated by music as originally notated. By employing acute analytical observations herself in discussions of melodic and harmonic phrasing, she strengthens the case for the creation of a new style of performance-orientated analysis which would draw attention to 'a multiplicity of enriching relationships'. Perhaps no better example of the analytically adroit or contextually sophisticated performer can be found than Charles Rosen who contributes an essay dealing (conversely, perhaps) with *Freedom of Information in Twentieth-century Music*. Drawing on his own experiences, for example, in making authoritative recordings of works by Stravinsky, Carter and Boulez, Rosen discusses *inter alia* the productive relationship between performer and composer – questioning in essence the presumption that the composer invariably knows best how to achieve his objectives.

Most composers today would recognise the wisdom in Rosen's essay, although not all might accept his views unreservedly. The problem of producing a score that is both faithful to the composer's intentions and helpful to the performer's understanding of them is time-consuming – and often only attainable after consultation between the two parties. Certainly an appreciation of the potential (and limitations) of a performing medium is an essential prerequisite for any composer – especially, as Raymond Warren points out, a composer of opera. It was no whim on Wagner's part that he coined the term *Gesamtkunstwerk* (total work of art) to describe the future cooperation between all the arts in a theatrical context, and, although not all composers may aspire to his (probably unattainable) aims, all need to be aware of the constraints and possibilities of the dramatic and scenic elements in this most taxing of mediums. Warren writes from first-hand experience, but also as the author of a study of opera techniques which analyses, as he does here, the coordination of physical and musical gestures within short and long-term structures. By comparison, Robert Saxton's chapter is concerned with the very nature of composition itself – with the ideas, philosophical concepts and (most importantly of all) a consideration of the relationship between content and form (which generates the impulse to begin). In a way that composers have rarely permitted before, he takes us into his own personal world of cross-cultural associations, dreams, visions and imagination, and then leads us from what he terms 'detection' to 'confection'; from the intangible to the tangible. Other composers may work differently (or think they do) but Saxton allows us an insight into the process which no generalised 'method' could ever achieve. My own contribution, *Composing, Arranging and Editing*, attempts to paint a somewhat broader picture of the varying roles of composers as makers, finders and re-users of musical ideas. The practice of quotation (or self-quotation) is as old as documented music itself – as is the arranging of existing works for new forces. I draw on examples from the Middle Ages to the present century to illustrate such creative re-cycling of material and discuss its many purposes from the basic appropriateness of a borrowed plainsong or chorale to the more profound aim of establishing a relationship with the distant past (as in Schoenberg's use of the Bach motif in his *Variations for Orchestra*, op.31). The essay also touches on the aesthetic implications of editions and arrangements made by composers from Mozart to Stravinsky.

In a sense, the eleven chapters in this book could be read in any order without affecting the cumulative experience. Performers might choose to start with Bradshaw, Rosen or Clarke/Davidson; historians or critics with Adrian Thomas or Walsh. The old cliché, that the whole is more than the sum of its parts, is true in this case regardless of how the parts are assembled. However, there is a certain logic in starting with the chapters on composition (as printed) and following through to reception. This is the recognised sequence in the creative process – although it could be argued that the listener (and possibly the analyst too) reverses this order as he searches out his own creative/recreative route to identify the spark which fired his imagination. The process is a chain-reaction *and* a cycle. The success of the Colston Symposium was that it initiated discussions that have continued up to this publication. If this book stimulates more questions and more responses, it, too, will have succeeded in its aims.

Wyndham Thomas, University of Bristol

Note

1. Het Trio's 1994 Recital at St George's, Brandon Hill, Bristol, was subsequently broadcast on BBC Radio 3. The recital included two performances of Jonathan Harvey's *The Riot*.

1 The Process of Composition from Detection to Confection

Robert Saxton

The title of this essay describes a journey leading from the general to the specific. I use the word 'detection' in the title to clarify the distinction between my role as a composer and that of an analyst who analyses a 'found' object – the composition. However much analysts engage in abstraction or deconstruction, they do not face the same problems as the composer. I am not making a judgement, simply stating a fact, and it seems important to me that such a distinction be made. The reasons will, I hope, become clear as I proceed. The term 'confection' in the title may seem unusual – even frivolous – but the *Shorter Oxford English Dictionary* gives the definition of 1477 as: 'mixing, compounding', and this, I think, makes clear that I use the word justifiably to illustrate that the process of composition traces a path from the intangible to the tangible. Composition is the act of forming – but what is formed and from what?

I am frequently asked three questions by listeners: Where does your inspiration come from? When starting a piece, what do you think of first? Would I understand your music? In the space of five seconds I have been confronted with the fundamental issues of creative work, both at a philosophical and a practical level. If I break these questions down, I find that the following questions have been posed: What is 'x' – the unknown factor – which impels me to begin a piece, either conceptually or practically, perhaps both simultaneously? What is an idea? Do I think in any conscious sense at all at first? What does 'first' mean in this context? Do I write music which bears some relation to what the questioner knows, likes and which operates within certain boundaries relating to the gestures of the music's surface, which the listener hopes will be (partially) familiar?

So, where do I begin? Indeed, *when* do I begin? There is a story concerning the great French mathematician Henri Poincaré, who had spent a good deal of time on a particular mathematical problem. Here is his description of what occurred next:

1

I left Caen, where I was living, to go on a geological excursion ... the incidents of the travel made me forget my mathematical work. Having reached Coutances, we entered an omnibus to go to some place or other. At the moment when I put my foot on the step, the idea came to me without anything in my former thoughts seeming to have paved the way for it, that the transformations I had used to define the Fuchsian functions were identical with those of non-Euclidean geometry; I didn't verify the idea; I should not have had time as, upon taking my seat in the omnibus, I went on with a conversation already commenced ... on my return to Caen, for convenience sake, I verified the result at my leisure.

This passage is quoted in *The Emperor's New Mind*[1] by the Rouse Ball Professor of Mathematics at Oxford University, Sir Roger Penrose. In the same chapter, Penrose also cites Mozart's description of his own creative process in the following terms: 'I think that it is indeed likely that we are "wrong" about our perceptions of temporal progression; an extreme example is Mozart's ability to 'seize at a glance' an entire musical composition 'though it may be long'.[2] 'One must assume', continues Penrose, 'that this "glance" contained the essentials of the entire composition, yet that the actual external timespan, in ordinary physical terms, of this conscious act of perception could be in no way comparable with the time that the composition would take to perform.' Penrose then turns his attention to the incomplete final Fugue of Bach's *Art of Fugue* and poses the question as to how the composer conceived the whole. Although it fades out and although we cannot know exactly how Bach would have completed it, we do nevertheless have a real sense of implied completeness, or unity of conception in a global sense. Again, we must be aware that Bach's inner 'hearing' of this fugue is not the same as the time taken to perform or to write it. Penrose relates this to mathematical thought with regard to the indication of the black-hole picture, for which he shared the 1988 Wolf Prize in physics with Stephen Hawking. Here is Penrose's description of the process:

I did not know of any mathematically definable criterion for a 'point of no return' (not using spherical symmetry), let alone any statement of proof of an appropriate theorem. A colleague had been visiting from the USA and he was engaging me in voluble conversation on a quite different topic as we walked down the street approaching my office in Birkbeck College in London. The conversation stopped momentarily as we crossed a side road, and resumed again at the other side. Evidently, during those few moments, an idea occurred to me, but then the ensuing conversation blotted it from my mind! Later in the day, after my colleague had left, I returned to my office. I remember having an odd feeling of elation that I could not account for. I began going through all the various things that had happened to me during the day, in an attempt to find what it was that had caused this elation. After eliminating numerous inadequate possibilities, I finally brought to mind the thought I had had while crossing the street – it was the needed criterion – that I subsequently called a 'trapped surface' – forming the solution of a proof of the theorem that I had been looking for. Even so, it was some while before the proof was formulated in a completely rigorous way.[3]

My own experience is that this is exactly what happens regarding musical composition, and I am particularly interested by Penrose's statement that he formulated his proof in more than one stage. A piece may come into the composer's mind not only as a totality, but also with certain details. If the latter are 'in focus', then they might well open the door to the route which the music will take in time. However, there can be simultaneously an inner sense of momentum and an aural/visual musical idea which is static, almost as though it were bounded by a frame. Certainly, in Penrose's terms, an outline is what is in the process of forming, and the first task is to find a way of drafting it. The absolutely fundamental issue is to attempt to go to the core of what is being heard, sensed and – as I have already said – visualised as well. There are as many ways of beginning work as there are composers, but today there is no universally agreed-upon grammar. Any experienced composer will certainly have formulated a general method of procedure, but this is not the equivalent of a pre-ordained system in the Hindemithian sense. To what extent am I, at this stage, aware of how the piece will be perceived by a listener or, indeed, a player? Clearly, the answer is: in a general way. It is the forming of a coherent process and shape in time that will eventually be transmitted to others, but at the conceptual stage this unfolding cannot be a factor in real time and, as such, is not yet as a listener will experience it. Charles Wuorinen has written a book called *Simple Composition*[4] (incidentally, it is no more simple than Morley's *A Plaine and Easie Introduction to Practicall Musicke* is either 'plaine' or 'easie'). At one point, Wuorinen remarks that the most basic error made by student composers is to think of composition as 'slowed-down listening'. With this statement, he opens the door to the real issue of how a composer composes and it is, I hope, clear that the above examples of creative thinking lead to the crux of the matter.

Let us suppose that I am beginning work. I am hearing sounds and colours in my mind's ear. I sense the shape, the progress of the piece as a whole, and I hear and see the rise and fall of the lines. I also have an overall sense of what is possibly best described as the music's harmonic orbit – its internal tensions, internal rate of change and its inner energy. Imagine that you are at the desk. There, in front of you, is the famous and daunting blank sheet of paper. You can hear a rushing sound – torrents of notes; the most obvious next move is to write them down. But what are they? Where do they lead? Cast your mind back to your student days, incarcerated on a summer's day in the aural examination, when hearing four parts of a simple chorale suddenly seems impossible – you are nervous, the room is too hot, the sound reproduction is below standard, you can't hear the tenor line clearly. In this situation, your position is reactive – aural detection is required. This is a different process from that of writing counterpoint around a given *cantus firmus*, a procedure which is concerned with building, with creating, with growth and completion, not with detection.

In his book *Counterpoint*,[5] the celebrated Palestrina scholar Knud Jeppesen quotes Heinrich Wölfflin writing about the visual arts in the Renaissance as follows: 'In this type of classical arrangement the separate parts assert an independence, regardless of how closely they may be bound up in the whole. The independence is not the aimless one of primitive art; each separate detail is conditioned by the whole without, however, ceasing to be an entity'. Jeppesen continues: 'In baroque painting, for example in Rembrandt and Rubens, the unity is no longer a result; the artist begins with unity and works towards multiplicity … what Wölfflin says about baroque painting may well be applied in the field of music in the art of Bach'.

What I mean by the 'conception' of composition is the process which covers everything from the initial desire to write a piece to the 'aural detection' stage. This may last for a day or a year and obviously is not temporally an ordered hearing of the music's progress. This is, maybe, the period of overall planning, for creating a framework, but a framework flexible enough to allow real invention with, and out of, the basic material once Stage Two has begun. Stage Two is the task of composing the music through, which is not necessarily the same as literally through – composing in terms of detailed voice-leading and other factors. At this stage, I move from an aerial or global hearing and view of the piece to a temporal one; I am walking along a road, rather than memorising its width and contour from the air. In other words, I am composing sequentially – time becomes linear, as opposed to the 'frozen time-frame' of Stage One. Wuorinen has a point in relation to this: he advocates planning a time-frame for an entire piece. In his book he points to such a procedure as a way of achieving a more global and practical approach to Babbitt's 'time point' system than he, Wuorinen, thinks possible if one adheres literally to Babbitt's methods, which he criticises by implication as being too localised and structurally myopic. Once the structure has boundaries, I can maintain a temporal flow or succession of events as clearly and as logically as I wish, without any part of the whole appearing in its final form. However, I may well not wish to create such a time-frame; it is literal and, perhaps, too concerned with one dimension to be of any use. It can also be argued that it charts time-flow chronometrically and, as we have already established, musical time may not fit such pre-compositional plotting. A perceptive composer might argue that the potential conflict between such a time-frame and the more elusive, flexible nature of musical time and harmonic tension is exactly what should be tackled as a problem to be solved. For example, counting out the frame in regular pulses or note-lengths poses the immediate problem of whether or not that regularity is to be perceived aurally and continually and how, for example, this works with regard to the changes of tempo and metre at other levels of the music's structure. In conjunction with the music already in the composer's mind's ear, the issues are already complex enough to create a rounded and multi-dimensional argument.

So, the moment of conception of a piece is rarely definable. At first, it is often difficult to know exactly what is being conceived. Shapes, sound or sounds, the filling out of a particular space, both vertically and horizontally, are at issue and this is why I have avoided so far the word 'idea'. This is a problematic matter for a composer to discuss because of the very nature of music when considered in relation to 'pure' philosophy.

How direct is the connection between Conception and Idea? Plato used the word '*eidos*' to denote 'Form and Idea', and both are connected with the Greek word, meaning 'to see', but in this case, seen by an intellectual vision. This is also true of the Euclidean definition of a line – a line has no breadth, height or direction and so, a line is an 'Idea'. It has length, defined as that which lies evenly between its ends, but where are the ends? There is, incidentally, a difference between Greek and modern concepts, because Euclid always thought of a line as a segment, not unlimited – the latter may be extended infinitely, whereas a segment is finite. Now, since music exists as geometry, as a form of aural algebra (in terms of collections or sets and their operations), as an intangible aspect both of, in and about Time, and as an expression of human activity, specifically as dance and song, emanating from, and appealing to, both body and voice, it is obvious that to define the conception of a particular piece in terms of an Idea or even as a group of Ideas is nigh impossible. Only in the purest Platonic sense could we say this – the inner, intellectual vision just 'is'; we can no more touch or feel it, than we can Euclid's Line and yet the music is going to touch us, both physically, emotionally and spiritually.

As a composer, it is my task to attempt to capture the 'Idea' with my aural and intellectual butterfly-net and, if I am really honest with myself, I must not, cannot, rest until that fundamental 'Idea' is realised to the best of my ability – and yet, the 'Idea' is as intangible as that of the unportrayable God in Judaism.

I had pondered setting up a time-frame for my piece; it is not, to my mind, yet a musical or formal idea. Here we have the problem of form as framework as opposed to the process of forming which, as I inferred earlier, is inseparable from the harmonic dimension. Since we cannot literally hear a particular span of music in its entirety – as we can observe a painting or a sculpture – form, in any plastic sense, must be meaningless, but if the entirety, the wholeness, which is to be created makes musical sense with regard to time and the passing of time, then to equate the process of forming with the Idea may have meaning. My time-frame is, then, merely a method of calculating duration which, devoid of content, is numerology in time – no more, no less.

I have uncovered something of the music to be written; I have a sense of its inner momentum, its harmonic character and the overall duration of the piece. I therefore have a feeling for the proportions and, above all, like Penrose and the solution of his equation, I experience a sense of elation – of wanting to start work.

Is the next stage 'detection', is it to do with formulating musical material, or is it both? I can hear the beginning of the music in my mind's ear and begin to write it down. But does what I notate scan correctly when considered in relation to the whole? The situation is now becoming complex because I have not been able to construct a plan in any detailed sense, for the simple reason that it is impossible to précis what does not yet exist. In reality, what happens is that either I know that what I have composed is 'in scale', or I am aware that the proportions of the piece will not be exactly as I had planned because of the nature of the harmonic rhythm, phrase-lengths, texture, register and perceived rate of succession of my initial musical sounds. Do I alter this or is it an '*idée fixe*'? For all my planning, surely I owe it to the musical material to develop and transform its hidden secrets. Do I do this by developing its internal structures or by imposing external methods? The answer is, of course, that I do both. Kant's ideas concerning space and time are important here: if we do have an innate 'a priori' sense of forms of space and time, then the Idea and Form in time are not mere constructs, but a filling-out of archetypal and paradoxically tangible realities. However, great advances have been made since Kant's time regarding non-Euclidean space by mathematicians of the calibre of Gauss, Riemann and Lobatchevsky in the nineteenth century, and such suppositions regarding space and time as those held by Kant must be treated as, at best, of interest rather than being thought of as either truthful or correct. The act of composing is particularly intriguing in this light; rather than formulating analytical ideas about the 'realness' of reality, it traces a path from the intangible imagination to the tangible reality of a created work. In order to create this temporal unfolding it is necessary to ponder the problem of how to draft the music, and here a post-Schenkerian approach can be useful. To attempt to make a contrapuntal framework as a consequence of having examined one's basic material is more subtle and flexible than a literal time-frame. The factor with which it does not deal is the division of a time-spectrum, rather does it explain extension and prolongation which will be musical-proportional and time-defining elements. Freedom to expand and realise the fundamental compositional impulse is limitless and an expanding outline can be sketched which will act as a contrapuntal and harmonic foundation for the elaboration and transformation of material.

Before I write my music down, I am, possibly, in the state described by the great seventeenth-century British philosopher John Locke, in relation to the mind at birth, as 'white paper, void of all characters'. This is perhaps a negative definition of empiricism, in that the implication is that one is observing, but observing nothing. In a Platonic or idealistic sense I am aware of what might be, but I have to make it tangible.

I do, of course, have a repertoire of technical possibilities stored in my memory bank and, as a result, whatever my material is, I am going to apply to it methods of development which are not necessarily, but only contingently, justified. I am more likely to proceed by means of received methods than I am to invent an entirely new set of procedures. Obvious though this may be, it is of importance because it brings up the matter of technique. The latter is not a compilation of categories – fugue, passacaglia and others – nor is it system, but method. It is the trained memory's store-house, a repertoire of possibilities. For a composer, there exists continual two-way osmosis between the material itself and applied methods of treating the 'received' musical ideas. Whilst composition and the resultant work are not concerned with 'logic' in the sense that professional philosophy defines or requires, it seems to me that there is (latent, manifest or both), a tangential relationship here between the process of composing and certain procedures defined in philosophy. For example, in tonal practice (as Schoenberg or Schenker would have accepted it) the premise of expectancy, surprise or resolution is akin to the famous problem of induction in which the question as to 'whether the sun will rise tomorrow' is posed. We believe it will, because it always has done, but we can never be certain that this will continue to occur. When we listen to, and compose, tonal music we do so against, or in conjunction with, the near-certainty that specific root progressions will occur; the resolution of harmonic tension may be delayed, but we are as certain that it will happen as that the sun will rise in the morning. It is these deep concepts and sensibilities which make nonsense of superficial stylistic issues. If the premise is clearly defined, then the musical argument can begin; in the case of tonal practice the premise was largely pre-ordained, being 'a priori' in relation to specific pieces, but this is not to deny, of course, the uniqueness of the individual work during that era. The post-tonal environment has seen the invention of various methods, but none of these has constituted an overall body of practice. The result of such a situation is that each work has to define its premise, but it is only the unfolding of the music which reveals that premise at every level, and although any experienced composer knows his/her general premise seemingly intuitively, this remains very much an individual matter at the end of the twentieth century. There are other fascinating issues which arise from these considerations; a musical argument proceeds from a statement (be it an interval or a complex web of ideas), but when and how does it become an argument and by what means is it propelled? In creative work, development and transformation are, obviously the result of imagination and choice, but, once again, philosophical terminology may be useful. Accepting that Kant's analytic/synthetic distinction concerns the *truth* of propositions in strictly philosophical terms, I propose that the initial statement of a musical idea is – on its own terms – a proposition. If, for example, a beginning does not merely lead to an eventual close, but contains the ending within it, we may be able to define the structure as 'analytic', since its unfolding reveals what is already present. Ian Stewart, in *The Problems of Mathematics* (1987), says of axiomatic systems that the ultimate test is consistency, not truth, an attitude which seems equally valid for composition and its thought-processes.

At this juncture, I rejoin Professor Penrose's street-crossing experience because most of the detailed development and continuity in any piece which I write is achieved instinctively. I am not proposing that a composer is, or should be, an inspired or uninspired, improviser. Not at all. But when I really know my material to the extent that it haunts me all the time – even when I'm talking to someone – then my subconscious works out much of the music's progress; I know my own game-rules, which hopefully encompass expectancy and surprise. The first movement of Beethoven's 'Eroica' Symphony may be remarkable as the thing in itself, but it enhances any one's appreciation of it to be aware of Beethoven's expansion of first-movement sonata proportions, an achievement possible only because he knew his premise. In *The Classical Style* Charles Rosen, discussing the use of long-range sequence in development sections after Beethoven , says: 'It is one of the first stages in the complete systematisation of the sonata and no device was more abused by nineteenth-century symphonists, for whom it became almost a substitute for composition.' This is a most accurate description of what happens when a true process of forming, or moulding, is replaced by formal methods which neither emanate from the original material, nor, as a result, belong in terms of both clock and musical time to the sense of inevitable tension and resolution, ebb and flow which have, until recently, seemed so essential to the occidental musical experience. It is important also to consider the differences in terms of approach and result between 'geometric' and 'narrative' composition. For example, Dunstaple's *Veni Sancte Spiritus*, Bach's Two-part Invention in D minor and the second movement of Webern's op. 27 Piano Variations are what might be called 'formal' or 'abstract', but 'geometric' seems both literally and descriptively more accurate. 'Narrative' composition (which in no way infers 'extra-musical' ideas, although I shall deal with this issue later) developed out of the internal drama of the sonata and was brought to its height by Wagner, Mahler and, from different traditions, Debussy and Sibelius. 'Narrative' composition unfolds by means of transformation of material and relatively long-range tension and resolution procedures. The overall process is concerned with a journey unfolding in time (and allows diverse material to be included by opening the door to inclusiveness, as in Mahler), whereas the 'geometrical' approach has a tendency to articulate and divide time in a manner which makes us particularly aware of symmetry and non-symmetry and which favours exclusivity of material within a work. The distinctions which I make here go beyond the over-used Classical/Romantic labels. Schumann's small character pieces are part of a larger narrative conception in the piano cycles and Berlioz remains hard to categorise because he was a narrative composer who worked episodically, as exemplified in *Harold in Italy*. Many works, of course, achieve a synthesis: the second movement of Berg's Chamber Concerto, the opening movement of Bartók's Music for Strings, Percussion and Celesta and, perhaps most profound of all conceptually, *Mondfleck* from Schoenberg's *Pierrot Lunaire*. The reason, I think, why the sonata principle, in conjunction with the large-scale fugue, has been so important in Western music is that it can encapsulate both approaches simultaneously. Possibly the greatest master of this synthesis, from strophic song to late sonata, was Schubert.

I have covered the issue of what lies behind my conception of a piece; something impels me to start work and, like a mathematician, I find that it is always a problem – often of the relationship between content and form – which generates the impulse to begin. This leads me to my fundamental musical idea and, before I am aware of it, I am composing. Conception and detection are still lingering, but are now part of the move towards the mixing and compounding stage – the real composing.

In the early and mid-1980s I wrote several pieces which are concerned with darkness and light (I choose pieces at least a decade old because I can consider them more objectively than recent work). Combined with this, I suppose, the Idea in the all-embracing sense, was a desire to create music with a real sense of forward motion and which, as a result of attempting to be dynamic, had to achieve its ending, rather than merely to arrive. This is difficult for me to express in words because I felt – and still do feel – this so strongly that I am not aware of having any control over this aspect of any of the pieces in question. Let me go back to the 1960s. For some reason, I was attracted in my early teens to a poem by the great seventeenth-century Welsh poet Henry Vaughan, called 'The World'. This poem contains complex ideas about the Church, but its opening, as with all good metaphysical poetry, presents an unforgettable, shining conceit:

> I saw Eternity the other night,
> Like a great Ring of pure and endless Light,
> All calm, as it was bright.
> And round beneath it,
> Time in hours, days, years,
> Driven by the spheres
> Like a vast shadow moved, in which the world
> And all her train were hurled ....

I set the whole poem for voice and either violin and or cello (I don't remember which) and this is, fortunately, lost. A few years later, when I was in my mid-teens, I attempted another setting, this time for tenor and piano, in a manner deriving from Tippett's song cycle, *The Heart's Assurance*. Then in 1982, in response to a commission from Oliver Knussen for a piece for the St Paul Chamber Orchestra in the USA, I returned again to Vaughan's poem. Being perhaps a little wiser at the age of nearly thirty, I decided to write a purely orchestral piece. But did I decide in any conscious sense? After all, these lines had haunted me at some level for seventeen years and what had dawned on me – I now see in retrospect – was that they portrayed verbally the music I was sensing, both in terms of sound and structure. I had had to wait until an appropriate treatment of the larger Idea was both conceptually and technically within my reach. I was intent on making the music seem to grow naturally and I knew at once that it could, ideally, have no end – there could be no cadence. Of course, the piece had to end; the commission was for a work of no more than fifteen minutes! Here was the challenge, the problem to be solved; I realised that the image of a ring (or circle) in conjunction with eternity was my structural passport. In mathematical philosophy, a fine distinction can be made between a circle's endlessness and the concept of infinity which is the province of the theory of series rather than geometry, although, in our post-Cartesian world, such a distinction is, perhaps, too literal. At this point, conscious decisions began. The striking paradox of eternity and circularity coincided with the first sound of the piece, which I heard and wrote down (Ex.1):

Ex. 1   Saxton: Initial idea for a composition (composer's copyright).

It is, of course, a hexachord, which is a combination of two symmetrical trichords or, if you prefer integer notation, a (0,1,4) trichord combined with a (0,3,4) trichord. Ten years later I would have pursued the numerological aspects thoroughly; for example, the simple inversional relationship between (Ex.2):

Ex.2   Saxton: Idea developed (composer's copyright).

gives the sum dyads (taking E as 0): 60, 51, 24, sum: 6 6 6. Any relationship between the tritone and the symbolic number of the Beast is unintentional!

The above example (0,3,4) takes F sharp as 0 and, re-counting with E natural as 0, (0,3,4) maps onto (2,5,6) at t=2. I have considered the hexachord as a whole, with E as 0 in calculating the dyad sums.

Anyone familiar with George Perle's stimulating article, 'The First Four Notes of *Lulu*',[6] and with Babbitt's work on combinatoriality, will be aware of the kaleidoscope of possibilities hidden in this basic material. This is not the moment to pursue such matters, but had I composed the piece this way consciously, there could be no doubt that everything would have followed from the initial hexachord as part of a numerologically justifiable process. Of course, this would not necessarily guarantee a satisfactory overall musical result. I haven't actually written an orthodox serial piece since 1972, but as I've said already, I do have yardsticks and these are, by and large, the result of that training. So, I was aware at once of the register and spacing of my hexachord, with its tritone between the highest and lowest notes of each trichord. The music winds its way downwards to the same hexachord stated one octave lower, depicting, I hope, the endless and eternal, while at the same time, being as circular as music can be, arriving at the same chord with its ambivalent tritone axis. Movement, if such there be, is purely registral and is effected by octave transfer of notes. Intertwined with this representation of Vaughan's stream of light, woodwind, celesta and trumpet play melodic fragments and figurations using complementary pitches. There is an atmosphere of stillness, of suspended time and unity, in that the total chromatic is slowly rotating without octave duplication and within a harmonic orbit derived from the opening hexachord. At a conscious level I certainly did not compose forwards in a manner which would make the life of an analyst satisfying in terms of note-counting, but there is, I believe, a conjunction between my instinctive development of the basic material and conscious working-out at the long-range architectural level. This was an aspect of *The Ring of Eternity*[7] which came to me at once; I knew that the piece would be in two large paragraphs, lasting about seven minutes each, and that the overall span would be achieved by an effect of continual acceleration. I say 'effect' because the perceived increase in speed is not so much graded by means of decreasing time-spans and increasing tempos in a systematic way, but rather by a gradual increase in activity on the surface. The harmonic rate of change remains consistent throughout so that, towards the end, the conjunction of surface activity and slower background is heard to be a manifestation of the same source material. What was heard at the outset as foreground is now perceived as background to the quick music, but the latter is obeying the same rules (and I use the word on purpose) as the background and, as a result, there is no real background/foreground conflict. Just as the circle is complete and, therefore, unending, so the music cannot end; but, as eternity also implies never-ending Time, so the piece, moving, inevitably, in one direction, blows itself up internally. Total chromatic saturation is ended by a deafening tam-tam crescendo – the equivalent of white noise, or light so bright that it is aurally blinding. The foreground/ background issue that I have mentioned here is not the same as in tonal practice. The premise is extremely limited. My detection stage was a combination of intense concentration on the little hexachord plus a sense of the scansion of the whole structure. My desire was to derive the maximum from the minimum.

In *An Introduction to Mathematics* by Alfred North Whitehead, Bertrand Russell's collaborator on the celebrated *Principia Mathematica* (1910–1913), Whitehead makes the following statement:

> It is a profoundly erroneous truism, repeated by all copy-book writers and by eminent people when they are making speeches, that we should cultivate the habit of thinking of what we are doing. The precise opposite is the case. Civilisation advances by extending the number of important operations which we can perform without thinking about them. Operations of thought are like cavalry charges in battle – they are strictly limited in number, they require fresh horses and must only be made at decisive moments.[8]

We only need replace 'civilisation' by 'composition', I think, to see the relevance of Whitehead's remark to creative work, both historically and within each work – that is, in a wide context as well as within individual compositions. The ratio of conscious to unconscious in creative work is, of course, unfathomable, but I know, for my part, that what I have called Stage Two, the detailed composing out of initial material and realisation of the Idea, is usually more unconscious, or subconscious, than Stage One, in which I attempt to define for myself the premise and its consequences.

In 1985, I wrote a piece called 'The Circles of Light'.[9] The title refers to the twenty-eighth Canto of 'Paradiso' in Dante's *Divine Comedy*, but I certainly did not read Dante and then decide to make that particular passage the basis for my piece. I remember a feeling of growing energy, inevitable forward movement and, at some level, this became an image of darkness and light opposed, striving towards almost unbearable brightness which only just avoids being dragged down to the depths of darkness. I say this became an 'image', but this certainly was not literal in a pictorial way. I began with low opening sounds from which I developed a slowly moving background duration scheme and which led to the required problem to be solved. I knew instinctively that I was not dealing with a single span as with *The Ring of Eternity*; but what was the music that was emerging? I had written low sounds bounded by the lowest tritone on the piano, A natural and E flat, and I could hear and sense the music's progress, just as though I was watching a great circle beginning to rotate. It took me several weeks to achieve the first thirty bars or so, which build up to a cadence and then fall back at once to the depths. Slowly, it dawned on me that this was the beginning of a movement which would have a flickering, active, almost hyperactive surface, but which must have a slow rate of harmonic change beneath this. I realised that this music would increase in tension in various ways, the most important aspect being a gradual increase in the rate of harmonic activity which would be released into a fast dance. Although I kept Dante's wonderful description of the hierarchies of angels and sparks flying off the Circles in my mind, I cannot say that this was a visual image in front of me at any juncture; what really absorbed me was the realisation of my responsibility towards what was clearly becoming a symphonic structure; I had a first movement which had found release in what I now realised was a scherzo, which, in itself, was creating more harmonic, rhythmic and, therefore, structural tensions. I was also aware of the importance of the opening boundary tritone; in retrospect, I had used the implication of this interval's non-invertibility in the first movement, but now, consciously, its architectural possibilities loomed large – interlocking tritones related to the circle of fifths, pitch centres which might or might not function as quasi-tonics and, above all, the ending of the entire piece became clear, no longer merely as a sensation, but technically. Since the first low sound had been a tritone cluster, so the music would fly off into infinity on the piccolo, with a note-group which would outline the highest E flat/A natural tritone on that instrument. We have ascended – one kind of progress – but the nature of the interval implies that we may well be where we began, but experienced from beneath now, rather than above. Our ears have led us upwards. I wasn't concerned with real-life geometry or mechanics here, but with the paradox of apparent directed energy conflicting with symmetry and circularity. Once this was established, the remainder followed very fast and, perhaps unpredictably, with more direct reference to Dante. For example, the scherzo, in three unequal parts with regard to length, arrives on a D octave to begin its third section. My harmonic practice at that time resolved E flat/A on to D and A/E flat on to A flat – a shadow of the Neapolitan sixth, I suppose, although I arrived at such cadences instinctively and not by recalling bygone harmonic practice. However, in the light of what I said earlier in this essay, it is obvious that there is a mixture of instinct and acquired knowledge at work, a conjunction of the 'a priori' and the empirical. Anyway, we are dealing here with technical procedure and that is, for the most part, empirically arrived at. The D octave which I just described stands for Dante – incidentally, Dante played such games in the *Divine Comedy* himself – and the linked, slow and sustained third movement begins with a dense chord bounded by E flat/A which pincers on to a middle-register D once more. The slow music needed to be the most intense in the piece – in visual terms analogous with focusing light so intensely on paper that it burns a hole in it. The listener hears a slow continuum with melodic lines based on the tritone emerging and then disappearing, but the construction (and that is what it most definitely is) consists of two superimposed rhythmic canons based on the numbers three and nine – three for the Trinity and nine for the angelic orders. The relationship between basic conceptions and levels of realisation – from conscious to sub-conscious – is clearly complex, and I have illustrated this by demonstrating how I began to write and then proceeded with a large-scale structure. I am certain that the deepest levels of both pieces which I have mentioned are related to their literary points of departure; sound is not only physically fundamental in the universe – we know about the Big Bang, after all, because scientists can track distant pulses – but is also the surface manifestation of concepts of time, direction, force, energy, darkness, light, space and human emotions and rituals as embodied in dance and song. Vaughan's poem and Dante's vision of the Divine Presence created a resonance in me in relation to aspects of each poetic extract which I then attempted to realise so that music, word and imagery were perceived to be unified at the deepest level – but this fundamental level, the true Idea, is the ultimate instinctive, archetypal region and is, for me as a composer, the area which I cannot analyse. I believe that Dante, Michelangelo, Galileo, Kepler, Spinoza, Newton, Bach, Einstein and Schoenberg are united by these aspirations and sensibilities. In short, a small number of 'a priori' ideas unite the varied manifestations which are the perceived work of artists, scientists and philosophers.

This is why, in our increasingly materialistic and media desensitised world, it is more important than it has ever been for what my colleague Nigel Osborne has called 'the community of thought' to face up to its responsibilities. We are here concerned with the reception and perception of music at a time when there is the widest chasm known since the Renaissance between 'High Art' and so-called popular culture. The new factor which has emerged since the 1970s is a disbelief in any kind of historical inevitability, resulting in what can be described as 'cultural amnesia'. By and large, the current corporate-sector mentality is not a viable replacement for the Church or a responsible intelligentsia and a vacuum has been created which has, temporarily I hope, been filled by the vague, rootless cultural time-travelling of so-called 'post-modernism'.

I am not waving the banner for any ideology, but I cannot ignore the historical fact that neither Bach nor Immanuel Kant travelled beyond the geographical borders within which they were born and worked; serious thought and worthwhile (let alone 'great') art do not seem to grow from a global melting-pot, but from a few profound Ideas – in the fundamental Platonic sense – which are then developed in an organic way. Schoenberg wisely said 'one must learn from the masters, but one then takes the essence and creates something new. One must not imitate.' This is not a plea for a return to Herder-like concepts of national identity; that led to Hitler. I am only asking for a responsibility towards the depths of our heritage. Here lies the way to universality. I believe passionately that creative artists should get on with the business of creating; but to do so requires a feeling for, a knowledge of one's premise in relation to one's training.

In his inaugural lecture as Thomas Wharton Professor of English Literature at Oxford University, Terry Eagleton made the following point:

> Post-modernism, taking its cue from its mentor Friedrich Nietzsche, offers an audacious way out of the impasse; forget about ontological grounds and metaphysical sanctions, acknowledge that God – or the superstructure – is dead, and simply generate up your

values from what you actually do, from that infinitely proliferating network of conflict and domination to which Nietzsche gives the name of will to power. Such a strategy promises to overcome the performative contradictions of advanced capitalism – the disabling discrepancies between fact and value, rhetoric and reality, what we actually do and what we say we do, which are themselves a source of ideological instability. But it exacts an enormous cost, which these social orders are quite properly too prudent to pay (the social orders are those of capitalism here); it asks them to forget that the role of culture is not only to reflect social practice, but to legitimate it. Culture must not simply generate itself up from what we do, for if it does one will end up with all the worst kind of values ... if you erode people's sense of corporate identity, reducing their common history to the eternal now of consumerist desire, they will simply cease to operate effectively as responsible citizens.[10]

I began by quoting Sir Roger Penrose, and it seems to me that there really is no gulf between art and science at a serious level of thought and intention. A burning desire to discover, to enlighten, to be enlightened, to enhance quality of life for anyone open to such matters is common to both areas, but if the majority have no interest in any of this, then society, and those who organise it, cannot and must not blame physicists or composers. I am aware that for example Heisenberg, the physicist, and the poet T. S. Eliot supported fascism in 1939, and the issue of artistic/scientific vision is a complex and troubling matter when it comes into conflict with moral and ethical issues. Artists are expected to communicate in a way not expected of their scientific colleagues and I have no argument with this at all; but I am not prepared to cease to ponder the issues which I have raised and to play the populist card by adopting superficial aspects of an ephemeral vernacular (itself frequently based on a false premise) in order to please or, at worst, pacify a listener who has no interest in my premise. I spend a good deal of my time working with students, and I believe in doing so; but when I am composing, I cannot consider consciously the shortcomings of our education system and its related problems and consequences, for the very reasons which I have, I hope, made clear; I am a minute part of a vast body of thought and practice which has seen many manifestations over the past five thousand or so years, from the ancient Hebrews' biblical codes to the present. In his book *The Sleepwalkers* (1959), Arthur Koestler tried to analyse how and why Europe emerged from the Dark Ages into the light of the Renaissance and the Enlightenment. We ignore the past five centuries of European thought at our peril. Yes, it nearly went under in the Nazi camps and, yes, Europe is now facing up to the collapse of the Soviet bloc, but beneath the surface of history lies the real Idea, as the ancient Greeks knew. Because only one per cent of the population of Britain goes to Church regularly surely does not invalidate Christ's teachings or St Augustine's writings? At the end of his apocalyptic novel, *The Wandering Jew*, the former East German dissident Stefan Heym has a most moving and beautiful scene in which Christ and the Wandering Jew, who he has condemned to wander the earth until the Second Coming, are united; here is the end of it (the translation is Heym's own, and the Rabbi referred to is Christ):

We are falling, the Rabbi and I. My eternal brother, says he, do not you leave me. And I leaned my head on his breast, as I had done at his last supper, and he kissed my brow and put his arm about me and said that I was like flesh of his flesh and like a shadow which belonged to him, and like his other self. And we united in love and became one. And as he and God were one, I too became one with God, one image, one great thought, one dream.[11]

Let us remember that Albert Einstein spent many years working on his 'unified field theory'. He never solved the problems of this task, but in 1918, speaking at Max Planck's sixtieth birthday, he said;

> the supreme task of the physicist is to arrive at the universal elementary laws from which the cosmos can be built up by pure deduction. There is no logical path to these laws; only intuition, resting on sympathetic understanding can lead to them ... the longing to behold harmony is the source of the inexhaustible patience and perseverance with which Planck has devoted himself ... to the most general problems of our science ... the state of mind that enables a man to do work of this kind is akin to that of the religious worshipper or the lover; the daily effort comes from no deliberate intention or programme, but straight from the heart.[12]

Across the cultural spectrum, conception and detection are unified. When I discuss composing music I have to cover the wide field that I have covered; it is not sociological issues or trends which guide or even affect the premise of my argument. It is only at the level which is at once the most simple and the most complex that the whole process begins and to which, in the end, perception and reception can be related. My role as a composer is to compose, just as an astronomer surveys the heavens. It is all part of humankind's adventure, but who receives or perceives what, and how, is not, ultimately, my problem. I can always face up to my responsibilities to myself and to my Idea, but any other category of responsibility is related to issues over which I have no control. I mix and compound – not to confound, but to share my excitement and the thrill of inventing and thinking; if society at large doesn't wish to join artists and scientists on the journey, that is its affair, not ours.

Notes

An earlier version of this chapter was published in *The Musical Times* (October, 1994) as 'Where do I Begin?'

1. Sir Roger Penrose (1989), *The Emperor's New Mind*, OUP, p. 541.
2. Penrose, op. cit., p. 547. I am indebted to Professor Nicholas Cook of the University of Southampton for pointing out to me that Mozart's letter from which this extract comes is now known to be fake; this is revealed by Maynard Solomon in 'On Beethoven's Creative Process: a Two-part Invention', *Music and Letters*, vol. 61, pp. 272–83. However, as Penrose finds a resonance with the idea expressed, the overall argument is, in my opinion, unaffected.
3. Penrose, op. cit., pp. 543–44.
4. Wuorinen (1979), *Simple Composition*, New York, Longman.
5. Knud Jeppesen (1931), *Counterpoint*, Hansen – reprinted Dover Edition (1922/ trans. G. Haydon).

6. George Perle, 'The First Four Notes of *Lulu*', in *The Berg Companion*, ed. Douglas Jarman (1989), Macmillan, pp. 269–89.
7. Robert Saxton, *The Ring of Eternity*, Chester-Edition. First performed at the Henry Wood Promenade Concerts in 1983. Recorded on EMI (CCD 7 49915 2).
8. Alfred North Whitehead (1948), *An Introduction to Mathematics*, OUP, pp. 41–2.
9. Robert Saxton, Chamber Symphony: *The Circles of Light*, Chester-Edition. First performed 1986. Recorded on EMI (CCD 7 49915 2).
10. Terry Eagleton (1993), *The Crisis of Contemporary Culture* (Inaugural Lecture as Thomas Warton Professor of English in the University of Oxford), Clarendon Press, Oxford, p. 7.
11. Stefan Heym (1984), *The Wandering Jew*, Holt, Rinehart and Winston, New York, p. 297.
12. Quoted in: Banesh Hoffmann and Helen Dukas (1975), *Einstein*, Paladin/Granada, p. 222.

2 The Composer and Opera Performance

Raymond Warren

If the relationship between composer and performer in concert music is complex, and other chapters in this book will no doubt have testified at least that much, how much more complex is it in opera where, enmeshed with the purely musical colloquy between conductor, orchestra and singers there is a notionally triangular relationship in the extra-musical dimension in the theatre. I will argue that at the apex of this triangle is the composer, normally represented by a conductor who can be assumed to be closest to his musical intentions. At another vertex is the producer and those who work for him, who have to accept the score and creatively re-think its essential drama so that it is viable in the theatre. The producer's work is of course done in cooperation with the singers at the third vertex, who in turn have their own understanding of the score (with some submission to the interpretation of the conductor) and of the drama (with some submission to the ideas of the producer) and on that basis must project their roles to the audience through their own stage personalities. It is this triangle, so characteristic of opera, that I wish to explore here.

This is a big subject and I can only take a few aspects of it, with no claim to be comprehensive or even systematic. I shall consider in a general way the tensions that can arise when the different disciplines come together and look at how some of those tensions were worked out in two particular cases: productions of Britten's *Peter Grimes* (1945) and Tippett's *King Priam* (1962). Among my concerns is the nature of the consequences for the others when, as in *King Priam*, the composer employs an innovative technique to solve a musico-dramatic problem, and the difficulties for them when, consciously or not, he puts himself on the stage. I referred to the composer as being at the apex of the triangle, the dominant partner, because I believe opera is primarily a musical form. In the final amalgam the music defines and dominates in those crucial areas of structure, mood and pace; the pace not only of the action on the stage but also of the changing emotions of the characters. It follows, then, that for an operatic experience the music must be

17

respected or at least not contradicted by the dramatic interpretation. In the spoken theatre an ironic effect can be achieved by acting or producing against the words, but if this were done against music the resulting irony, however dramatically effective, would be essentially un-operatic. Just wherein lie the interpreters' legitimate operatic freedoms is one of my areas of inquiry.

However, before going into that, I would like just to touch on the wider issue of opera composition in general, which has never been a subject for study in the same way as other branches of musical composition: one cannot buy a book on it as one could on orchestration, or symphonic form. Obviously for the composer it is a very specialised activity, not only because musical forms must be dictated by the dramatic intent (unless of course the librettist can allow the creative process to be engineered the other way round), but also because the theatre has its own musical ambience, so that, for instance, pacings are different, and the musical density called for when the visual dimension is added is not necessarily that of the symphony or oratorio. It is not surprising that opera has tended in the past to attract its own specialist composers and that (with the notable exceptions of Handel and Mozart) the great masters who have crossed the divide have not on the whole sat equally happily on both sides.

The composer's relationship with the librettist is a big area not to be pursued here: for those wishing to make a study of it the classic source is no doubt the celebrated Strauss–Hoffmannsthal correspondence,[1] but since *Peter Grimes* is on our present agenda, I must add that I am indebted to the valuable work which has been done by Philip Brett[2] and others on the genesis of that opera. Nor do I intend to go into the relationship with the conductor, though *King Priam* does in fact provide a rather rare example of a disagreement with the composer, to which reference will be made later. Perhaps I might just quote what the conductor in question, John Pritchard, had to say in general terms about his function at rehearsals in relation to the producer and singers:

> ... when the production is still trying to find its shape ... to apply a little touch of the rein, to stop singers being pushed too far, to weed out anything which goes against the score.[3]

A difficulty in thinking about the composer in the theatre arises from the different interpretative expectations in the musical and theatrical worlds. To the musician the score is normally treated as sacrosanct and so the conductor's and singers' musical freedoms in opera would only extend to comparatively minor licence in matters of tempo, dynamics or articulation – big matters to a musician, of course. Since the notes are sacrosanct the singers can exercise only a limited freedom over the inflections of their phrases, and their performance has to embrace an assimilation of the mood, atmosphere and affection of the supporting (or even sometimes dominating) orchestral accompaniment. In these respects the opera singer enjoys much less freedom than the speaking actor whose text, while defining syntax and assonance, leaves free the timings, pace, pitch and stress. The distinction can go deeper still as can be shown in a well-known example.[4] Shakespeare's *Hamlet* can be understood as the tragedy of a man unable to make up his mind, and can be given an overall interpretation to that effect. Yet there is evidence in the words that he is basically a resolute man rendered irresolute only in the single matter of avenging his father's death. Again he may be played as a melancholy man or as someone not habitually so, but plunged into unwonted gloom by that death. A freedom of a different kind can be exercised by the gravediggers in the same play, who can project themselves as comic characters or, quite the reverse, as giving a simple but serious comment on the human condition. It would seem to be part of Shakespeare's art that his text should leave room for such discrepancies, and so leave room too for the creative response of the actors in resolving or balancing them. No opera composer would bargain for liberties of this order: an operatic Hamlet would find that the big issues would already have been determined by the composer and the main characterisation enshrined in the structures of the music.

But if the singer has less space than the actor, very real freedoms still remain. These are most in evidence in passages where the music itself is not strong, as in the recitatives of classical opera which allow almost as much variation of pace and stressing as spoken dialogue. The constraint still exists, of course, that there must be consistency with all those passages where the music is strong, and in earlier opera this generally meant the arias. In *opera seria* these posed a particular inter-pretative difficulty for the singer because of the way in which they were con-structed. Each aria would have one main affection so that the character was built up facet by facet over the whole opera, leaving the singer with the problem of maintaining a credible consistency and integrity. This is a crucial problem for any singer nowadays studying classical opera and indeed it spills over to some extent into later opera. It is curious that, so far as I know, none of the eighteenth and early nineteenth-century manuals on opera addressed the issue at all. What can certainly be said is that the modern singer will find the freedoms allowable in the recitatives helpful in establishing the full character quickly and so projecting a more rounded entity at each successive stage. The same interpretative principle will often apply to passages of lesser and greater musical intensity in operas not so rigidly constructed. The reconciling and balancing of facets of character which appear separately is of the essence of interpretation in the spoken theatre too, a general difference being that music usually moves more slowly than words so that in opera the individual affections are projected more consistently over longer stretches of time.

It is these longer passages of strong music which dominate the characterisation of most operas (*Pelleas et Melisande* is a notable exception), and most differences of interpretation are no more than a matter of differences of balance between them. We may for example find Callas's reading of the role of Tosca frenetic, Rysanek's impetuous and Behrens's filled with moral fervour,[5] but the power of the music with which each of these aspects (and many others) is articulated means that none of them can be dismissed entirely from any interpretation. Paradoxically the hardest roles for the singer to interpret are generally not those like Tosca with breadth and richness but the narrow ones where the music, in concentrating on a single character trait or mood, seems to cramp the style of the singer in projecting the character as fully human at all. The role of Hecuba in *King Priam* is a case in point and will be discussed later.

There are times in opera when the musical experience is so strong as almost to pre-empt any visually interesting manifestations of the drama. A famous example is the virtuoso coloratura of the distraught Lucia, taking up the drama of that role into a musical experience in which it is arguably the virtuosity of the singer rather than the musical composition *per se* which holds the stage. On the other hand, in the final trio of *Der Rosenkavalier* it is rather the composer who holds the stage, and the singers again need to do little more acting than to maintain their stage positions and let the music take over: some producers may even prefer to make this explicit by bringing the singers to the front of the stage away from the other associations of the drama for the moment. *Tristan and Isolde* has music of this intensity (and a correspondingly slow dramatic pace) for such a large proportion of its length that Wagner even went so far as to advise Nietzsche, who was about to see the opera, 'off with your spectacles, you are only to listen to the orchestra'.[6] Only a very self-effacing producer would fully endorse that! However, there are more dramatic times, even in *Tristan*, when the singer will want to act more freely, unless, like Jon Vickers in the title role, he is deliberately acting in a restrained way throughout in order to project an inward, introspective character. One general approach to stage movement, favoured by the producer Jean-Pierre Ponnelle, was consciously to choreograph the music. Dent took a rather similar view, though from another angle, seeing it as a sort of deception in which the singer will 'time every gesture so as to make the audience think that it is his inward emotion which causes the orchestra to play the appropriate musical phrase'.[7] Most singers, I think, would prefer to think of their acting as a more instinctive reaction to the inner meaning of the music.

The producer who comes to opera, as many do, after experience of the greater freedoms of the spoken theatre will often feel a tension between the overriding musical presence and the dramatic innovations which he would feel to be his legitimate contribution to the performance. One such common contribution is to use visual means to highlight the big issues which the opera addresses and to suggest the relevance of these to situations nearer the experience of the audience. Transposition of historical period can often be achieved without affecting the essential thrust of the music, as in Kupfer's 1980 WNO production of *Fidelio*, updated to a context of twentieth-century fascism, or Miller's shifting of *Rigoletto* to the downtown New York of the 1950s. These both make the point that the macabre events of the operas could well happen in our own day. Trouble for producers often comes when a good idea, perhaps even justifiable from the libretto, is not consistent with the music, or distorts its essential thrust. For an example of this we might compare possible productions of Mozart's *The Marriage of Figaro* and the Beaumarchais play on which its libretto is based. There are undertones of revolution in the play which can be picked out in such a way that the comedy is given a certain irony by being played against a threatening background. Many of these undertones were duly taken over by Da Ponte in his adaptation, but Mozart was generally not interested in them at all, and indeed the moment in the play where, arguably, Figaro most openly menaces the Count occurs in the opera in a secco recitative virtually unnoticed by the composer.[8] The musical drama is not about this at all. Its very fully human characters are involved in personal problems which lead to a significant reconciliation at the end, and to put this into a context with more than the faintest suggestion of political revolution is to contradict the music.

We should distinguish between what the singer is to do when the music refers to him or her, as in a solo aria, and the greater liberties which are possible when it does not. Tippett, having stated his premise from the composer's point of view that 'in opera the musical schemes are always dictated by the situations' goes on to put this problem clearly:

> ... if one character is winning and one is losing it is rarely that music can express both these characters' emotions at once. There has to be a decision as to whose? and for how long? ... In *Don Giovanni* there is an embarrassing place where Dona Elvira has to be on the stage listening to Leporello's entertaining (but from Elvira's point of view insufferably tactless) list of the Don's amorous conquests. As the music is all Leporello's we do not know whether Mozart imagined Elvira as speechless with fury or proudly insensitive. No amount of stage production can ever remove the dramatically equivocal problem caused by the operatic decision in music.[9]

He might have added that the hapless Elvira must in practice settle for one such reaction (there are many more possibilities from which to choose, including sheer disbelief) and hold on to it against the over-riding power of the music without upstaging Leporello, who must, of course, be dominant because his is the music. A similar problem was neatly solved in the 1983 ENO production of Handel's *Giulio Cesare*, and the example helps to define the limits of music's tolerance of what goes against it. Cleopatra's aria '*Non disperar*' is a mocking of her younger brother Ptolemy's claim to the throne which she regards as hers. Since he is on stage throughout the aria his reactions to her upbraidings are clearly of dramatic importance, even though the music of the aria necessarily ignores them. John Copley, the producer, put Cleopatra in strong positions at first, singing from a throne, to emphasize her royal claims, and then moving downstage. However, in the reprise of the aria he placed her at the back of the stage and Ptolemy at the front so as to draw attention to his gestures of anger. I suggest that what made such an extreme staging musically as well as dramatically acceptable was at least in part the fact that this was the da capo, going over what had already been heard before. In that context the dramatic variation of positioning came alongside the expected musical variation of the reprise and in a sense matched it. It should also be noted, though, that the primacy of Cleopatra and her music was re-established in the positioning at the final ritornello of the aria when she came downstage and right around in front of him as she swept imperiously off for her obligatory exit.[10] We shall look later at a different kind of solution to a similar problem caused by the operatic decision in the staging of *King Priam*.

Although the above Handel production probably went beyond the staging conventions of the eighteenth century, one could still feel that Handel himself, in having chosen to keep Ptolemy on stage, would not have been totally surprised by the interpretation. Sometimes, though, stagings can make points which are neither connected to the music nor against it, but outside it in a way that the composer could not be expected to have foreseen. This probably happened at the beginning of Act III of *King Priam*, when Sam Wanamaker, the first producer, placed the three women, Hecuba, Andromache and Helen, in exactly the same positions as their respective husbands had occupied in the previous scene. I do not know whether Tippett approved of the *alter ego* implications of this (I suspect he may well have done so), but I would infer from the absence of musical correspondences between the two trios that he was probably surprised. Ponnelle in his 1981 production of *Tristan and Isolde* wanted to project the end of the opera as a dream fantasy in which Tristan dies alone with only the illusion of being in Isolde's arms. feeling that Isolde's vocal lines in the last act are very much part of the symphonic fabric he proposed that she should sing from the orchestra pit. Again one could argue that the interpretative intention was not against the score and the suggested positioning not illogical. However, what mattered this time was not whether Wagner would have approved but that the soprano singing the role of Isolde refused to co-operate, and insisted on singing her 'Liebestod' on the stage – a reminder that the producer is constrained not only by the score but also by the singers, and must work out his stagings in the ways best suiting their own understanding and personalities.[11] There can easily be personal clashes here, something a composer would more rarely meet in the concert world. One way of lessening this danger is for the producer to have a meeting with the whole cast before the first rehearsal to discuss the general approach and this can give the composer an interesting insight into how the work is generally understood at that stage. Wanamaker, in the first rehearsals of *King Priam*, adopted the unusual tactic of having the singers speak their parts in rhythm against a piano reduction, presumably to give them a sense of the dramatic pace as a basis for the fuller musical realisation to come.

The discussion so far could be drawn together by referring back to the composer/conductor–producer–singer triangle and briefly considering how it often works in practice. Each of them will almost certainly have ideas and expectations formed as the result of homework done on the score before they first meet and, however experienced they are, they will probably be surprised by insights and revelations from the others when the opera begins to take on a life of its own on the stage. The hardest role in the stage rehearsals is probably that of the singers, for it can too easily happen that, in trying to take in the dictates of conductor and producer (unless those two are unusually close in outlook across their different disciplines), they find themselves caught up in a kind of compromise interpretation which can act as a barrier to the exercising of their own artistic integrity. As the earlier quotation from John Pritchard suggests, it is often (though by no means always) the conductor who takes the more defensive conservative line against the radicalism of the producer.

This is perhaps a convenient moment to pause and enquire how our two chosen composers viewed their working relationships with their operatic interpreters. It is evident that they adopted very different attitudes, though, as we shall see, the deeper issues were often remarkably similar. For Tippett on this level it was all comparatively simple. He avoided the difficulties of collaboration with a librettist by writing his own text and, after some early consultations with the production team, it would seem that he put the score into their hands without interfering at all: an unusually self-effacing approach. He wrote in his autobiography that at the time of his earlier opera, *The Midsummer Marriage*:

> ... I was fairly clear that the composer should come to rehearsals to help sort out the production. But I soon learnt the limits of intervention: moreover the many explicit directions I had given in the libretto were absurd, because they were unrelated to any particular stage. It's always a delicate matter how much freedom a composer should allow the producer and designer in matters of staging. My view now is that one must trust them, for they have a technical knowledge of lighting and other presentation techniques far beyond that of the average composer. My inclination, with all succeeding operas, has been to consult them well in advance, and not appear at rehearsals until the last moment, and only then at their express invitation.[12]

Britten was much more typically involved with his interpreters at every level throughout the preparations for the first production of *Peter Grimes*. Not only was he directly concerned with the rehearsals himself but, as it were from the other direction, his principal singer, Peter Pears, had been concerned with the planning of the work right from the outset and had already written words which were used by Mantague Slater, the official librettist, when that appointment was eventually made, and well after that time too. As late as a few months before the first performance Britten wrote in a letter that he and Pears were 'pretty well rewriting his part'.[13]

Eric Crozier, the producer, also contributed to the later planning stages before the completion of the score. Indeed it was within the final fortnight, when the rehearsals were being held in the theatre, that cramped conditions in the wings forced Crozier to require an extra minute or so of music to accommodate a scene change during the Act I Storm Interlude, a section of music which had already given the composer much trouble in the composition. Crozier later recollected that Britten

> ... was always very sensible about practical matters, but he looked very glum indeed when faced with this demand. I was, he said, like someone who brings a huge block of stone along to an architect when he has just completed a cathedral and tells him to fit it in somehow. But finally he agreed.[14]

There were some interesting similarities in the first stagings of the two operas, involving productions on both big and smaller stages; and in both cases too the producer and set designer had to take account of a certain tension between foreground and background in the description of which the composer was personally involved.

In *Peter Grimes* there is the play of the Borough characters and the force of the sea through (or against) which they have to lead their lives. Britten wrote that his earliest attraction to the story, when he was living in America in 1941, was the background, his nostalgia for his native Suffolk and his childhood memories of the sea:

> My parent's house in Lowestoft directly faced the sea and my life as a child was coloured by the fierce storms that sometimes drove ships on to our coast ... In writing *Peter Grimes*, I wanted to express my awareness of the perpetual struggle of men and women whose livelihood depends on the sea ...[15]

The first production was given on the comparatively small stage of the Sadler's Wells theatre in Rosebery Avenue, and Kenneth Green's main set stressed the intimacy of a village centre bounded by pub and village hall, the presence of the sea being potently suggested by the outline of a lighthouse. Eric Crozier, after quoting the words Grimes sings in Act I, 'I am native, rooted here ... By familiar fields, Marsh and sand, Ordinary streets, Prevailing wind', goes on to explain that his aim as producer was

> ... to evoke those ordinary streets, the curious distinctive shapes and textures and juxta-positions of Aldeburgh buildings and the particular quality of light that bathes them, and also to recreate something of the life that had filled the town in the early years of the nineteenth century. Kenneth Green and I attempted, by what might be called selective realism, to express the truth of that particular place and its people. ... Some critics felt that the visual idiom of the designs did not match the idiom of the music. There may have been some truth in this. But in the circumstances, remembering the element of risk inherent in staging a new opera for the reopening of Sadler's Wells, we were probably right in our approach, which was, in any case, what the composer wanted.[16]

When, a few years later, Guthrie produced the work at Covent Garden he felt:

> that in the vast dimensions of Covent Garden intimacy was out of all question and that the majestic sweep of the score, the evocation of the sea and its ineluctable influence on the destinies of the characters, could be interpreted better by a simpler, more spacious setting. Tanya Moisewitsch designed a superb set using the entire width and depth of the Covent Garden stage. A horizontal cloth surrounded a single enormous set piece suggesting a jetty. This worked splendidly for the scenes of storm and stress; but I must admit it was rather implausible and overwhelming to the moments of intimate and would-be humorous conversation.[17]

Britten, despite the tenor of his earlier remarks quoted above, did not approve of this shift of emphasis from the first production. In a conversation recorded by Ande Anderson, when Guthrie defended his approach because 'the sea made these people what they were', Britten replied 'No, these people would be the same wherever they were'.[18]

In thinking about this we should perhaps consider the evidence of the score itself. The most powerful expressions of the sea come mostly in the interludes when the curtain is down, but the sea music does in fact spill over into the following scenes on many occasions and in many ways. Britten's innovative re-thinking of techniques culled in part from Verdi and Wagner enabled him to project the presence of the sea throughout the first ten minutes or so of Act I Scene 1[19] and, as

Tanya Moisevitsch's set design for Britten's *Peter Grimes*

the storm approaches, much of the later sections of the scene too. What Britten is able to do (and a producer much less easily) is so to modify the sea's presence that it can function perfectly as an accompaniment to the sharply focused interplay of the Borough characters. After the storm interlude which follows this scene, Britten does the same thing again but by a somewhat different method, the brilliant use of percussion rolls enabling the storm from the sea to continue through almost the whole of the pub scene too. With such forceful and insistent sea imagery one can see why Guthrie may have found the original set rather inadequate, though perhaps one should not condone his cutting out some of the verismo passages he found so incongruous on his imposing stage set at Covent Garden. It should be said in passing that, while the cutting of the text is a common practice in the spoken theatre, and in classical opera too, in a through-composed modern work like *Peter Grimes* the musical implications would normally rule it out unless the changes were very minor indeed (as in this case) or the composer was called in to do some re-writing. Guthrie's changing of a few words was perhaps the less contentious in that there was arguably no contradiction to the sense of the music.

There are times in *Peter Grimes* when the foreground and background coalesce, notably in the final section of Act I Scene 1 when (following the pathetic fallacy of the comparable storm scene in *Rigoletto*) Grimes' feelings of grim determination and anger are at one with the growing storm. If on the smaller stage one was aware of the storm's reinforcing his every feeling, on the bigger stage and seascape set one felt his comparatively smaller figure to be almost overwhelmed by it. Guthrie was the producer at the Metropolitan in New York when Jon Vickers took the part of Grimes and between them they changed and indeed arguably enlarged the role. Vickers had a bigger and rougher voice than Pears and, as Peter Conrad noted, transformed the part from 'an ineffectual dreamer, a misfit but no menace' into a more robust character, closer to the ruffian of Crabbe's poem. Through him the soliloquies became 'declarations of defiance' and in the Act I Scene 1 storm positively 'invited the blasts of the tempest'.[20] This, of course, was fully in scale with Guthrie's enlarging of the stage to a more universal dimension and it provides an instance of a fruitful alignment of the visions of producer and singer. Britten is said not have liked this development of the character. Ultimately, I think, its validity has to be measured by its compatibility with the music. Vickers' singing, consistent with his acting, did stretch the natural lyricism of some of the music almost to breaking point, so that one felt the dramatic validity was greater than the musical. If this is so then it is at the very limit of the singer's legitimate operatic freedom.

King Priam experienced a comparable staging problem but the other way round, in that it was written for a first production in Covent Garden and only later, in the Kent Opera production, had to be re-thought for staging on a smaller scale. Moreover, unlike *Peter Grimes*, which was conceived for a traditional opera staging, it employed new techniques of lighting taken over from the spoken theatre to effect quick scene changes. Shortly before the first performance Tippett, like Britten, referred to the background of the opera, speaking of:

... the resonances that sound in all of us when we speak of Troy [which] arise from generations, centuries of European concern with that immortal story.[21]

The short prelude to the opera, beginning with echoing pairs of trumpets in high seconds, seems to evoke the general atmosphere of heroic war. In the original production the set, by Sean Kenny, confirmed this interpretation. It was visible during the prelude and, as *The Times* critic wrote, 'the monumental masonry evoked the heroic grandeur of the epic story'.[22] When, in the Kent Opera production the stage and set were small, there was no attempt to evoke such grandeur, the critic Andrew Clements describing the sets as 'lean and effectively functional'.[23] In that context the opening music was taken to refer to the troubled mind of Hecuba, whose entry follows immediately. This may not have been exactly what the composer had in mind but the musical legitimacy of the interpretation is, I think, confirmed by the use of similar fanfares (with the brass muted) to accompany Hecuba's later references to her disturbing dream.

One of the outstanding qualities of the *Iliad* story is that the characters in it are very sharply drawn: they are archetypal, larger than life, as befits those who in some cases are descended from the gods; indeed the gods themselves become involved in the conflict. Tippett made a bold decision that the distinctions between the characters should be as close as possible to the absolute and this he achieved by an innovative technique in which each person not only has unique musical material but unique scoring too, with the division of the orchestra into characteristic small units.[24] Thus Hecuba will sing with just the violins, playing furiously in unison, and no one else shares that sound except on one occasion Priam when he allows himself to be dominated by her will. I should like to look at how this technique affects the singers in both dialogue and monologue.

Firstly in dialogue. It is clear that in a conversation between two characters each accompanied in this way the music will consist of alternating, sharply differentiated blocks of sound. It might seem an obvious way to structure an operatic dialogue but it has not been generally adopted in the past: of all the great composers it was perhaps Monteverdi who came closest to it.[25] If the characterisation is sharp the resultant mosaic musical form can seem stiff and lacking in overall continuity, which is no doubt the intended effect in the first scene when Hecuba, having just heard the prophecy that Paris, her new baby, will bring about the death of her husband Priam, bullies Priam against his fatherly instincts to have the child put to death.

What kind of a person is Hecuba? The blocks of music allocated to her in the score would suggest she is essentially a proud and imperious woman whose primary concern is for her husband as monarch of Troy. Janet Price, who played Hecuba in the Kent Opera production said[26] she found it difficult to make her convincingly human at all, as distinct from archetypal. Should she, for instance, show any feelings of remorse for the death of her child, or warmth towards her husband? The problem stems partly from Tippett's ruthless excision (in both libretto and music) of anything not directly relevant to his main dramatic purpose, to explore Priam's two choices and their consequences: he even avoided a love scene between Paris and Helen! There is nothing new about this, of course, for the history of operatic adaptations is full of cases of simplified or deleted characters, and full of problems for singers trying to round them out.

The problem set by Tippett for Hecuba can be expressed in musical terms, that once the prophecy is revealed, and that is very early in Act I, almost all her part is accompanied by the violin figure referred to earlier, the first appearance of which is shown below.

Ex. 3   Tippett: *King Priam*, Act 1, Scene 1, Figs 35–36.

To sing against such an accompaniment makes any suggestion of human warmth virtually impossible: the composer is surely ruling it out. Indeed John Pritchard, who conducted the first performance in 1962, thought it altogether too much for a singer to have to contend with, and (I quote from Tippett's autobiography):

> ... reduced the impassioned rhetoric for all the violins ... to a feeble single instrument; it took years to persuade conductors to have this played by the full section of the violins

the way I intended – Roger Norrington, in fact, was the first to do so in Nicholas Hytner's superb Kent Opera realisation of 1984.[27]

Janet Price has certainly shown in the theatre that it can be performed as the composer intended and with a powerful effect of forceful tension. However, earlier in the scene before the prophecy she felt she could show a restrained humanity in the way she looked at the baby (to the music for solo oboe which had earlier been established as referring to the baby) and later clasped Priam's hand as she told him of her dream (to the brass fanfares but now muted) and this led a critic to refer to her as 'a nicely balanced, unusually sympathetic Hecuba'.[28] One interesting consequence of this early hint of warmth is that her later unyielding hardness is understood to be not just a character trait but a supreme effort of will. Whether the composer had such a possibility in mind is unlikely, in that his simplification of the three leading women of the opera, Hecuba, Andromache and Helen into archetypes (they later appear as Athene, Hera and Aphrodite), does have the effect of throwing into sharper relief the more vulnerable humanity of Priam, and he of course is the real subject of the opera. However, (Janet Price told me) Tippett himself did not disapprove of her interpretation and indeed was in general happy to accept such insights brought by each new singer into a role.

Andrew Shore, who sang Priam in the 1995 ENO production which, like the first production, was on a big stage, also felt that a problem in the role was to reconcile the human and the archetypal.[29] In this case, though, there is music for each of these aspects and the difficulty is to project them both as parts of one integrated personality, a dilemma which Shore felt to be inherent in the very character itself. Again the difficulty was acute in the 'block' dialogue of the first scene, and almost explicitly so because after the oracle and Hecuba's immediate reaction to it (described above) he is given a line which encapsulates the whole problem.

Ex. 4   Tippet: *King Priam*, Act 1, Scene 1, Figs 42–43.

(Ex. 4 concluded)

In this music the lower strings, violas and cellos, are as soft and warm as Hecuba's violins were hard and cold, and she, of course, must 'freeze' in a hard attitude while he sings. Shore understood the phrase as a prayer for guidance. If this is a legitimate interpretation it neatly by-passes a dilemma in the music itself in that Tippett (intentionally?) puts the two rather similar chords, the augmented sixth on 'father' and the dominant seventh on 'king' the wrong way round. For if it is Priam's role as king that decrees that the good of the state should take precedence over a life, then that is the word which should be given the more fearful augmented chord (certainly that would be the meaning in Schubert whom Tippett actually quotes in his next opera) and his fatherhood given the gentler chord. It is as if Priam's thoughts are not yet in focus, a reading confirmed by the next musical block in which, with no preparation in either words or music, he takes over Hecuba's violins and orders the child to be killed. The sheer stiffness of this extraordinary volte-face projects Priam clearly enough as an immature man: presumably he is only in his early twenties at this time. He must surely make some big gesture at this point, perhaps a turn towards Hecuba, to give credence to his sudden change of heart in accepting her resolution to have the baby killed. However, even here Shore did find one mitigating feature in the character, that whereas Hecuba's vocal line had gone up to a shrill high note at the end of the phrase 'let the child be *killed*', Priam's repeating of the words finishes by going down instead of up; indeed he repeats the last two words descending even further to a bottom G sharp. The effect of this is to suggest a real, if ineffectual, humanity which even the frenetic violins don't quite obscure. The stiffness of the scene was probably one of the factors leading Tom Cairns, the producer of the 1995 ENO staging, to have the whole scene played behind a gauze so as to suggest a certain distancing from reality. Although Priam's character has no later contradictions as difficult to interpret as those in the first scene, it does indeed change considerably over the course of the opera and presents a challenge to the interpreter trying to project a single person. Shore felt he could best make sense of the whole if he understood it as taking in a whole life span, developing and changing as Priam gets older. Such a consciousness of the age of the man at each stage is not always to be found in the music itself, but again, I understand, the composer did not disapprove. It is a problem of character integration similar to that of the *opera seria* arias, though more acute. Not all of the block-form dialogues in the opera are as stiff as this. In a later scene, when the adult Paris asks Helen to go away with him, the musical phrases overlap in a more supple way to give a greater sense of continuity and harmony between the two characters.

For an example of the block technique in monologue we can take Priam's second choice which, unlike the first, is made in a way which is true to his real nature. Unknown to him, the baby Paris was not in fact killed and some dozen years later he meets the youth when out on a hunting expedition. This time the man himself speaks at the deepest level. After the initial shock, there is joy that his son is alive, fear for himself and then the triumphant decision to let the boy live and to accept his own inevitable destiny. These reactions are unusually wide for a comparatively short passage of opera but Tippett uses the same technique to build up blocks within a monologue so that a whole rich character is revealed in a cogent and economical way. This time the singer knows exactly what is expected of him, to integrate through his stage personality what is a linear progression in the music, a very common operatic situation that might be encountered in an accompanied recitative in classical opera. Tippet wrote later of how, in the first production, the producer coped with the problem of the operatic decision – what to do with the other characters on stage during this monologue:

> Wanamaker was quite ready to freeze everyone else on the stage into immobility allowing Priam to sing from within the stage grouping, and then by stage lighting to extract Priam's *mind* as it were, out of the group in order to allow him a special relation to the audience.[30]

Britten could have done with some of this lighting expertise in the first production of *Peter Grimes*. In reply to a letter from Rutland Boughton, who had criticised the darkness of the night in Act III Scene 2, he ruefully pointed out that 'there should have been a spot on Peter all through the scene'.[31] In this opera too, excisions made in the course of composition have left a legacy of problems for performers who have to flesh out their roles through their own stage personalities. In the early drafts of the libretto the character of Grimes was transformed from the ruffian of Crabbe's poem to something more complex and subtle. Yet alongside this Britten seems almost systematically to have removed any specific motivations to account for Grimes' attitude to life and why he was regarded as an outsider. One instance of this which can be traced from the various drafts was an obsessive father fixation, probably based on the incident in Crabbe's poem where his father appears to him in a dream.[32]

A good deal of attention has been given to Britten's expunging any references to Grimes being a homosexual. In earlier drafts there were indeed such references and at one point the lovely aria in the hut scene as he dreams of a future life with Ellen 'and she will soon forget her schoolhouse ways' was addressed to the boy 'and you would soon forget your workhouse ways'.[33] This would certainly account for much in his character that would be otherwise unexplained, his feelings of guilt, why he is regarded as an outsider and even why he seems hesitant in his relationship with Ellen, rejecting Balstrode's advice to marry her at once. But in the final version of the work Britten surely made this particular view of the character of Grimes quite untenable because the music itself does not allow it. One need only mention the force and heartfelt sincerity of the passages when he sings of his love for Ellen; 'Your voice out of the pain...', 'There's the jersey that she knitted': and of course the phrase referred to earlier, and which is now addressed to Ellen. For this reason I think Jon Vickers was right to refuse to play Grimes as a homosexual.[34] The composer may not have liked Vickers' interpretation of the role, but would surely have endorsed this much.

A further attraction of homosexuality as an explanation for Grimes is that his alienation from society can then be seen as a projection of Britten's own similar position; and since in the 1940s it was very difficult to be open on this subject he may well have felt similarly inhibited against allowing it to be a factor in the opera. But it does not follow that in these more liberal times we now have a licence to do so. If Britten is, in a sense, putting himself on the stage then it is the more general aspect of alienation that is depicted and the opera in this respect is no more than an allegory: he was able to address the issue of homosexuality in a much more direct way by the time of *Death in Venice* in 1973. However fully Britten is projecting himself into the role of Grimes, Vickers is surely right to feel that the performer has no licence to show greater personal knowledge of the composer than is strictly compatible with the words and music of the role itself.

The idea of the composer putting himself on the stage goes back perhaps to *Die Meistersinger* and certainly to *Capriccio*. Of course a good opera composer can empathise with all of his characters and one would not stop to ask whether Mozart reveals himself most as Don Giovanni, Figaro, Don Alfonso or Papageno: musically speaking he can be any of them and many more. But that was before the Romantic revolution made self-expression a prime motivation for music and, by Wagner's time, for opera too. Sometimes the composer may halt the drama and, in a more limited sense, come on stage to comment on the action. If that is what Mozart does in a comic way at the end of *Don Giovanni*, then Beethoven does it more seriously in the finale of *Fidelio*.

In the D minor Interlude in Act III of *Wozzeck* Berg seems to emerge from his role as narrator and to speak personally in directing our feelings towards sorrow and pity for his hero. It is in a sense near to this that Tippett himself also comes on stage towards the end of *King Priam*, taking the form of the god Hermes, to explain his role as composer. The music here, scored for flute, harp and piano, is more gentle and lyrical than almost anything else in the opera and, like the *Wozzeck* interlude, it is an imposition on the story rather than an intrinsic part of it. What he has to say expresses the ideal, I imagine, for most opera composers in defining the real justification for music's unnatural intrusion into drama at all: as a go-between, like the god himself, bridging the gap between the world of action and its inner meaning. It is the function of singers and producer to share in this activity right across its whole range and, in giving the action a fully human theatrical dimension, to lead the audience into that inner world.

> Do not imagine all the secret of life can be known from a story.
> O but feel the pity and the terror as Priam dies. . . .
> O divine music,
> Melt our hearts,
> Renew our love.[35]

Notes

1. Tr. Hammelmann and Osers (1952), *The Correspondence between Richard Strauss and Hugo von Hoffmannsthal*, Collins.
2. Philip Brett (1983), *Benjamin Britten: Peter Grimes*, Cambridge Opera Handbooks, ch. 3.
3. Quoted from John Higgins (1978), *The Making of an Opera*, Secker and Warburg, p. 181.
4. The example is used in Tyrone Guthrie (1961), *A Life in the Theatre*, Hamish Hamilton, ch. 2.
5. These examples are taken from Peter Conrad (1987), *A Song of Love and Death*, Chatto and Windus.
6. From a letter to Nietzsche dated 25 June 1872, quoted in Dietrich Fischer-Dieskau (1974), *Wagner and Nietzsche*, tr. J. Neugroschel (1976), Sidgwick and Jackson, p. 91.
7. E.J. Dent (1940, rev. 1949), *Opera*, Penguin.
8. Figaro's 'Why not, I never dispute what I don't know' in the recitative immediately before the finale of Act III. Geraint Evans in his justly famous interpretation of the part is mistaken, I believe, in making a big gesture of defiance here: see William Mann (1977), *The Operas of Mozart*, Cassell, p. 421, footnote.
9. Michael Tippett (1959), 'The Birth of an Opera' in *Moving into Aquarius*, Routledge, pp. 58–59.
10. The action can be seen on the video film (1984) of the production.
11. How Peter Hall did this in a production of *Don Giovanni* can be followed in some detail in John Higgins (1978), op. cit.
12. Quoted from Michael Tippett (1991), *Those Twentieth Century Blues, an Autobiography*, Hutchinson, p. 218.
13. From a letter to Ronald Duncan of 24 February 1945, reprinted in Mitchell (ed.) (1991), *Letters from a Life, The Selected Letters and Diaries of Benjamin Britten, 1913–1976*, Vol. 2, p. 1243.
14. Quoted from Eric Crozier 'Staging First Productions I' in David Herbert (ed.) (1979), *The Operas of Benjamin Britten*, Hamish Hamilton, p. 26.
15. 'Introduction' in *Peter Grimes: Benjamin Britten*, Sadler's Wells Opera Books, 1946, John Lane The Bodley Head.
16. See Eric Crozier (1979), 'Staging First Productions I' in Herbert (ed.). op. cit., p. 26.
17. Quoted from Guthrie (1961), op. cit., ch. 16.
18. Quoted from Brett (1983), op. cit., p. 97.
19. The figurations of the first Sea Interlude may reappear with new harmonies or the harmonies with new figurations.
20. Quoted from Conrad (1987), op. cit., p. 346.
21. Quoted from Michael Tippett (1980), *Music of the Angels*, Eulenberg, p. 227.
22. From *The Times*, 31 May 1962.

23.   Andrew Clements in *Opera*, December 1984, p. 1383.
24.   It is an interesting coincidence that a very similar technique was used by Henze in *Elegy for Young Lovers*, whose first performance was a year before that of *King Priam*.
25.   As in the duet in *L'Incoronazione di Poppea*, Act III Scene 3, where Nero accuses the innocent Drusilla. The two characters have very different music and possibly would have had different continuous scorings too.
26.   In a private interview with the author.
27.   Michael Tippett (1991), op. cit., pp. 221–22.
28.   Andrew Clements in *Opera*, December 1984, p. 1384.
29.   In a private interview with the author.
30.   Quoted from Tippett (1980), op. cit., pp. 233–34.
31.   The letter is dated 29 August 1945 and reprinted in Mitchell (ed.) (1991), op. cit., p. 1336.
32.   George Crabbe (1809), *Peter Grimes*, XXII, p. 290 seq.
33.   The point is made in Brett (1983), op. cit., p. 78.
34.   See interview in *Opera* XXXIII (1982), pp. 364–65.
35.   From Act III, Interlude 3, in Michael Tippett (1962), *King Priam*, Schott.

3 Composing, Arranging and Editing: A Historical Survey

Wyndham Thomas

My title juxtaposes three activities, all of which result in a performable musical product. At first sight, it may seem that this is their only link; that they have entirely separate functions; that their ordering is hierarchical, even. However, it can be argued that composing requires the use of editorial skills; that the editor becomes in effect a surrogate composer; that arranging is an aspect of composition, albeit one that is often denigrated. This is not to say that editors and arrangers have to be composers (though many have been) or that composers always communicate their intentions adequately through their finished scores (otherwise there would be no need for editors). Rather, the interrelationships which do exist point to a common purpose – that of communicating musical ideas and commenting on them. It is the aim of this essay to investigate these objectives and to explore the ways in which existing material or inherited traditions have been used in the developing craft of composition. Central to this will be a broader definition of composing, which takes into account earlier practices, and a survey of the work of composers as arrangers and editors.

The perception of composition as a fundamentally *written* art in which the composer exercises total control over his output, asserts his authorship through the printed score or its electronic equivalent, and is rewarded for his efforts by commissions and royalty payments is a relatively modern one which has its roots in the development of commercial publishing and concert promotion. With its implications of ownership and individuality, this stands in sharp contrast to the view of composition in earlier centuries when the processes of *finding* and *making*[1] were carried out within a predominantly oral tradition in which it was often difficult to separate the roles of composer and performer.[2] Those familiar with the Bamberg and Montpellier collections of thirteenth-century motets will be aware of the many variant readings to be found – some works with newly invented or highly ornamented *triplum* parts, others as three-voice versions of two-part 'originals' – and all constructed above a borrowed melody (*cantus prius*

35

factus). This essentially additive process was itself derived from earlier polyphonic models (Notre Dame *clausulae*) and, in turn, led into the fourteenth- and fifteenth-century isorhythmic motet, the motet-chanson and the cyclic mass. The re-use of existing material (*contrafactum*) was a legitimate technique of the period. Although resulting in some blurring of authorship (especially before *c*.1300), it demonstrated that composition was an organic process concerned with the past and the present while contributing to the future. The quotation of music and texts from the public domain also enabled composers to pay compliments and to make veiled references to associated meanings – as in the well-known thirteenth-century motet, *Mout me fu gries/Robins m'aimme/Portare*,[3] in which an optimistic *rondeau* (also used in Adam de la Halle's *Jeu de Robin et Marion*) accompanies a lament for a lost love above a fragment of plainsong from the Feast of the Finding of the Holy Cross which combines associations of grief (memories of the Crucifixion) with pleasurable anticipation (for the Resurrection).[4] The short piece is a sophisticated commentary on the joy and sadness of sacred and secular love and has implications infinitely more subtle than those expressed in the conventional *pastourelle* verses that are being sung.

Music's ability to communicate generalities in terms of mood or states of being has long been acknowledged. Boethius's anecdote about Pythagoras using a spondaic melody to calm a jealous youth who had become 'wrought up by the sound of the Phrygian mode'[5] is an early example of its therapeutic powers which are now being exploited successfully in a clinical context. Medieval composers also saw polyphony as a potent symbol of natural order, following Pythagoras again in the emphasis given to the *perfect* harmonies of the octave, fifth and fourth. By the early fourteenth century, the harmonic proportions of 2:1 (diapason or octave), 3:2 (diapente or fifth), and 4:3 (diatessaron or fourth) had been incorporated into the temporal and structural characteristics of motets and mass movements, thereby extending the specific symbolism of number into a repertoire already enriched by allusive melodic quotations. Such architectonic qualities abound in the works of Philippe de Vitry and Guillaume de Machaut (where the use of hocket – the fast alternation of notes in the upper voices – often signals the conclusion or repetition of a tenor pattern) and it is clear that they and their contemporaries regarded music as a medium for demonstrating mathematical (and, by analogy, theological) truths as well as being a vehicle for narrative (as in the formulaic *lais*). Examples by later composers, such as Dunstaple and Dufay, show that this tradition continued at least up to the mid-fifteenth century – a period described by Rob Wegman as something of a watershed between medieval *making* and modern *composing*.[6]

A comparison between Dunstaple's *Veni Sancte Spiritus – Veni Creator Spiritus* and Dufay's *Nuper rosarum flores* demonstrates how the two composers drew on existing material and conventions that were appropriate to their needs (celebrating Whitsun and the consecration of Florence Cathedral, respectively) and then constructed complex sounding-symbols of the Holy Trinity, on the one hand, and the archetypal biblical Church, on the other. In the case of Dunstaple's motet,[7] the borrowed hymn (*Veni Creator Spiritus*) is presented on two distinct levels of perception: an incomplete fragment is used as a slow-moving isorhythmic tenor, and the four lines of the complete melody are ornamented and sung one-by-one in the top voice at the start of each sub-section (one-and-a-half times in total). Furthermore, the lines in the top part are sung to the words of the Whitsun Sequence, *Veni Sancte Spiritus*, not to the original text which instead is used by the newly composed contratenor. The overall structure is based on two principles: exact replication (each of the three main sections has two rhythmically identical halves) and diminution (the three sections reduce in a 3:2:1 proportion). These principles can also be observed in the melodic relationship between the thrice-repeated tenor and the top part's paraphrase of the plainsong. The overall proportions embody harmonic perfection and the 'completion' of the Trinity through the gift of the Holy Spirit (signified in poetic and musical quotations). Margaret Bent[8] hints that the *eleven* notes of the chant that are used in the tenor talea (the repeated rhythmic pattern) might themselves be symbolic of the eleven apostles who remained to receive the Holy Spirit. Dufay's motet[9] uses a similar method of composition, although his model is architectural rather than doctrinal. Like Dunstaple, he has duets to announce the appearance of the borrowed tenor chant in each of the four sections of the work; the chant is specific to the occasion (*Terribilis est locus iste* is the Introit of the Mass for the Dedication of a Church); and the structural proportions (6:4:2:3) reveal perfections, in augmented and reversed relationships. However, the two motets differ in their function and symbolism. *Nuper rosarum flores* sets a new text (possibly by Dufay himself) which celebrates the building of the cathedral, comments on its dedication to the Virgin Mary, and records the role played by Eugenius IV in the consecration. For many years, the coincidence of the completion of Brunelleschi's dome with Dufay's presence in Florence (as a member of the papal choir) led to the belief that the motet attempted to mirror the proportions of the cathedral itself – indeed, the *two* tenors that present the chant canonically at the fifth might be seen as representing a foundation in an architectural as well as a musical sense; or, as Charles Warren suggests,[10] the double shell of the dome. It has now been convincingly argued[11] that the motet's proportions are derived not from the approximate proportions of the Duomo but from the exact measurements of the Temple of Solomon (1 Kings, 6) which would have been well known to Dufay (and possibly to the Florentine architects). Whereas Dunstaple's motet can be seen as a timeless testimony to Christian faith (though linked to a single feast), Dufay's work is very much a document of Man's achievement which draws on biblical as well as liturgical associations and which is as much concerned with the context of worship as with faith itself. What unites the two works is a compositional procedure which monumentalises inherited components and their associations in a new framework.

In a literal sense, this process could be termed a *rearrangement* of material but this would be to confuse construction with transcription (or *reconstruction*) such as is found in the keyboard intabulations of songs by Dufay and his contemporaries located in the mid-fifteenth-century Buxheim Organ Book. These (together with their counterparts in the earlier Robertsbridge and Faenza manuscripts) provide us with some of the first examples of arrangement in the modern sense. Significantly, the keyboard pieces are identified by their original first-line titles (often in very approximate transliterations) and hence are linked to their original composers rather than to the arranger. The actual techniques used in this repertoire vary from the lightly embellished but basically literal transcription from one medium to the other (as in the intabulation of Dufay's *Franc cuer gentil*) to the highly decorated version of the same composer's *Se la face ay pale*.[12] In the latter example, Dufay's tenor is preserved unchanged (as it is in his eponymous Mass) although the extent of ornamentation in the top part necessitates a slower overall tempo than in the original *ballade*. There is an important connection here with the quasi-improvised figurations found in the *basse-danse* arrangements in the Buxheim Organ Book (and elsewhere) – and one that reveals a continuing dependence on the additive process of invention found in earlier vocal polyphony. The known traditions of improvisation in dance music suggest that there could well have been a symbiotic relationship between performing and composing at this time – as, no doubt, there was in improvised discant.

Clearly, there is a substantial difference between the two extremes of arrangement described above, but each in its way identified a route for future compositional developments. The imitative texture of *Franc cuer gentil* can be seen, in its keyboard guise, as a prototype for the later *canzona* and the extensively ornamented *Se la face ay pale* as a precedent for keyboard variations and the broken consort repertoire. Each represents a creative process, although this is perhaps more obviously the case in the transformation of texture that results from high levels of passage-work and ornamentation. Thomas Morley's *First Booke of Consort Lessons* (1599)[13] is of major significance in this respect since, not only is it the first publication of chamber music to specify precise instrumentation, it affirms the artistic status of the arranger himself through the overall quality and consistency of the arrangements. Using a selection of material by his contemporaries (including Byrd and Dowland) and himself, Morley demonstrates how to make divisions on repeated dance sections with the lutenist usually taking the most prominent role while the other instruments either fill in the harmonies (pandora and cittern) or outline treble, alto and bass lines derived from the original models (treble viol/violin, flute/recorder, and bass viol) – although they sometimes join in with variations, too.

If the title of Morley's publication implies a didactic purpose or a method, then this might also suggest the need for an increasingly professional role for the arranger (who may well have been a performer, too). Earlier publications, for example Attaignant's seven books of keyboard transcriptions of 1531, are often uneven in quality leading Gustav Reese[14] to conclude that they may have been produced by the members of an *atelier* (workshop) rather than by identifiable arrangers – and there seems little doubt that the hint of professional inferiority sometimes attached to arranging dates from around this time. However, this is not to say that the *canzoni* of Girolamo Cavazzoni (1542), Andrea Gabrieli (1577), or

Claudio Merulo (1592) are other than accomplished contributions to an expanding repertoire of keyboard music, and it is examples such as these (and Morley's) that stimulated a mainstream of creative arrangements in subsequent centuries. Monteverdi's five-part arrangement of Arianna's lament, '*Lasciatemi morire*', in his *Sixth Book of Madrigals* (1614) is a notable instance of a composer responding to the success of a piece in one medium (his opera of 1608) by widening its availability in another (and adding substantially to its harmonic expressiveness in the process). Composers were themselves celebrated (as in the case of Palestrina) by a minor industry of arrangements (by Anerio and Soriano) and parody masses – a tradition that dates from the fifteenth century and represents yet another genre in which reworking of existing musical ideas is an accepted compositional technique. In more senses than one, composers in the seventeenth century kept alive the spirit of the past through perpetuating style as well as technical procedures. *Stile antico* was consciously cultivated in Rome (probably as a tribute to Palestrina, its greatest exponent) but it also infiltrated other centres and (by way of Fux's *Gradus ad Parnassum*)[15] the works of much later composers as, for example, in the Masses of Michael Haydn. The fact that many of today's composers acknowledge the benefits of a training in sixteenth century counterpoint is a fascinating reflection on the inherent qualities of Palestrinian style and the educational value of mastering the technical disciplines of the past. No less a composer than Beethoven recognised the need for such a discipline in an area detached from contemporary practice and there can be little doubt that a similar training has been of great benefit to the editors of early music as well.

The extent to which musical arrangements became an integral part of mainstream composing can be illustrated by a brief examination of the output of J.S. Bach and Handel, both of whom made considerable use of self-borrowing as well as adapting material from other sources. Norman Carrell[16] is one of a number of scholars who have provided invaluable documentation of the complex cross-references in Bach's works, pointing out the many reworkings of keyboard pieces, the re-use of instrumental compositions in the cantatas (and the reverse), and the substantial number of arrangements of works by other composers – from the illustrious (Corelli, Vivaldi and Albinoni) to the lesser known (Raison, Fischer and Prince Johann-Ernst). Many of these latter transcriptions (of Vivaldi especially) would have been made as part of Bach's own musical studies (in which copying out scores by accredited masters would have been seen as a normal educational activity) and most show a continuation of the traditional process of written ornamentation (which may reveal something of the *unwritten* tradition of embellishment in contemporary performance practice). In particular, Bach's extensive use of Lutheran chorales in his cantatas, passions and organ preludes establishes a link with the older traditions of plainchant *cantus prius factus* writing and demonstrates a comparable meeting-point between the craftsmanship of the composer and his musical inheritance. Basil Lam[17] has drawn attention to the extent of Handel's borrowings from other composers (much, it would seem, has still to be documented) but a single example of self-borrowing must suffice now to illustrate the reworking of existing material in a new context. The Double Concerto in B flat Major (No. 27 in Chrysander's edition), dating from the last decade of Handel's life, makes much use of music from previously composed works; quotations include the opening chorus of *Messiah* ('And the Glory of the Lord') and the chorus 'See from his post Euphrates flies' (from *Belshazzar*) – itself based on an earlier Handel duet. It is tempting to conclude that such blatant re-cycling of material carries implications of a lack of originality, but a more realistic assessment would be that it was initiated by lack of time, since composers such as Handel and Bach were frequently required to produce new works at short notice – whether for commercial, political or liturgical reasons. Composers, perforce, were obliged to become arrangers if they were to meet the increasingly demanding requirements of the patronage system or to survive in the relative insecurity of the free-market system chosen by Handel.

It was for similar reasons that the impecunious Mozart undertook his arrangements of four of Handel's oratorios.[18] Baron Gottfried van Swieten, a Viennese diplomat, was passionately fond of the music of Handel and Bach and organised performances of their works at the large hall of the court library and various private residences, none of which possessed an organ. Mozart, who had already arranged five fugues from Bach's *Well-tempered Clavier* for String Quartet (K. 405 – possibly for van Swieten's soirées in 1782/83), was engaged (as Joseph Starzer before him) to produce alternative parts for the missing continuo. *Messiah*, the best known of these arrangements, was completed for March 1789 and is still recognised as an acceptable alternative to Handel's original scoring when conditions dictate. Such arrangements are significant indicators of a keen (and growing) interest in music of the past which gained in momentum as the nineteenth century unfolded – as is witnessed in Mendelssohn's historic performances of Bach. In one sense, at least, Romanticism was concerned with a rediscovery of the distant past – not merely with the icons of the eighteenth century, but with the idealised culture of the Middle Ages (Romanesque or German, *romanisch*). If this is more immediately apparent in literary or poetic works (Scott and Tennyson, for example), it is mainly because the musical depiction of the past was mostly couched in the idiom of the present (the nineteenth century, that is). Thus, the medieval legend of Tristan is portrayed by Wagner using a musical vocabulary that looks forward to the twentieth century rather than back to the thirteenth century of Gottfried von Strassburg. Even arrangements of traditional folk songs (by Brahms, for example) are set in the harmonic idiom of the present, albeit touched occasionally with flavours of modality. It was left to a new breed of scholar–musicians, schooled in the notational practice of the Middle Ages, to revive interest in the musical fabric of the periods that inspired the novels and libretti of the Romantic era. Foremost among these was Edmond de Coussemaker, whose edition of medieval treatises (1864–76) supplemented a much earlier set of *Scriptores*, edited by Martin Gerbert (1784), and who published some of the earliest transcriptions of twelfth- and thirteenth-century music – notably, liturgical dramas (1860) and the complete works of the trouvère Adam de la Halle

(1872).[19] The compositional by-products of this surge in musicology will be assessed later, but it is worth noting that the revival of interest in post-Palestrinian music also gained force in the mid-nineteenth century, especially in the pioneering editorial work of Friedrich Chrysander who devoted most of his life to a biography and an edition of the works of Handel. Although neither of these vast enterprises was completed, the contribution of Brahms should be recorded. He assisted in these and other projects by realising figured bass parts and editing the clavier works of Couperin for Chrysander's *Denkmäler der Tonkunst*. Brahms is known to have had a deep interest in earlier music. He possessed the autograph score of Mozart's G minor Symphony (K.550) and revised Mozart's *Requiem* for a new edition of his works. He was also involved in the complete edition of Chopin's works and he edited music by Schubert, Schumann and Bach. Perhaps the most significant of his many tributes to earlier composers (which include sets of variations on themes by Handel and Haydn) is his use of Bach's chaconne theme from Cantata 150 in the finale of his Fourth Symphony – where a section in sarabande rhythm provides a further hint of his assimilation of earlier manners.[20]

However, it is probably the extensive output of Franz Liszt that best illustrates the nineteenth century's metastatic position between the heritage of the past and the innovations of the 'new music' of the 1900s. Indeed, his famous Sonata in B Minor of 1852 has acquired a tardis-like significance in that it draws on the structural precedents of Schubert's *Wanderer* Fantasy and the finale of Beethoven's Ninth Symphony to create a monothematic four-in-one-movement form which simulates narrative[21] and which was destined to be adopted by many later composers – amongst them Arnold Schoenberg, notably in his Chamber Symphony no.1, op.9, (1906) and the Phantasy for Violin and Piano, op.47 (1949). Liszt's numerous arrangements and transcriptions (which include the Schubert and Beethoven works mentioned above) attest to his willingness to learn from his predecessors and his contemporaries. As a virtuoso pianist, of course, he was ideally placed to disseminate orchestral and operatic works in a more easily accessible medium and it is clear that (although many transcriptions are literal) in some cases a substantial amount of recomposition is carried out. Charles Rosen[22] has drawn attention to Liszt's ability to create a coherent cycle out of a selection of individual songs (as in his transcriptions of six of Chopin's *Chants Polonais* from op.74) and to his masterly concealment of one of Chopin's rare miscalculations in the song, 'My Joys'. Arrangement – or paraphrase, as it might more accurately be termed – reaches new peaks of artistic and aesthetic significance in Liszt's operatic transcriptions. Rosen comments with characteristic perspicacity:

> This ability to reformulate a musical idea in terms of new styles of performance, and to reorder material according to various dramatic scenarios made Liszt the only true master of the opera fantasy. ... The finest ... juxtapose different parts of the opera in ways that bring out a new significance, while the original dramatic sense of the individual number and its place within the opera is never out of sight.

and, with specific reference to *Réminiscences de Don Juan* (1841):

It is not simply the melodies of Don Giovanni that Liszt transcribed but the dramatic situations and the sense of the whole opera.

The title, *Réminiscences de Don Juan*, must be taken not as a series of isolated memories but as a synoptic view of the opera, in which the different moments of the drama exist simultaneously: what Liszt reveals is the way in which they are interrelated. He combines material from different parts of the opera freely.[23]

This sort of creative arrangement, therefore, acts as a commentary on the original as well as transferring it from one medium to another. At first sight, this might seem to have many historical precedents (in Renaissance paraphrase technique and Baroque chorale-cantatas, for example) but there is a fundamental difference in time-scale in that the earlier processes are mostly concerned with creating larger structures out of their borrowed material whereas Liszt (in his opera paraphrases) is necessarily aiming at an abbreviated version of his. It is tempting to suggest an analogy with present-day film-trailers or recordings of opera highlights, but this would be to debase Liszt's intellectual (as well as musical) assimilation of his chosen repertoire. At his best, his ability to focus attention onto the core of an opera's action is a revelation of its message rather than a mere substitute for its length. In his *Don Giovanni* paraphrase, he uses the 'statue' music to frame variations on 'Là ci darem la mano' and ultimately to undermine the spirit of the 'Champagne' aria. Fate is omnipresent. Perhaps he learnt this from Mozart's Overture – if so, it was a lesson well digested.

Not all of Liszt's arrangements aspire to such lofty heights, of course, and many are as much concerned with pianistic colouring and technical display as with demonstrating the sort of insight described above. Yet, the sheer breadth and catholicity of his taste are evident in the long list of his transcriptions, which includes works by a great many of his celebrated contemporaries (Berlioz, Verdi, Tchaikovsky, and Wagner, for example) as well as by lesser known composers and by himself. That he was also aware of music before Mozart can be seen in his arrangements of Bach, Arcadelt and Lassus; it is also clear that baroque techniques such as fugue and chorale-variations were influential in the development of his own compositional style as in works such as his threnodic Variations on *Weinen , Klagen, Sorgen Zagen*[24] or the celebrated organ show-piece, Fantasia and Fugue on *Ad nos, ad salutarem undam.*

It was, perhaps, as inevitable that the greater accessibility of early music would revive interest in pre-tonal compositional methods as it was that composers should be drawn into editorial activities. Equally, the transcription and dissemination of editions of folk-songs in the nineteenth century contributed to a growing realisation that major/minor tonalities could be enriched by the characteristic qualities of the modes. Certainly, the dramatic quotation of themes with strong liturgical associations (such as the 'Dies Irae' sequence) enabled composers like Berlioz, Liszt and Saint-Saëns to draw on precise textual associations within purely instrumental contexts. A tradition of compositions based on the BACH motif sprang up (no doubt stimulated by Bach's own musical autograph in *The Art of Fugue*) and the use of cryptograms became common-place. Schumann's fascination with themes derived from names and places is well documented as is Brahms' symbolic use of the FAF (*Frei aber Froh*) motif in his Third Symphony – and both enjoy the same ancestry in works such as Josquin's Missa *Hercules Dux Ferrariae* (which derives its *cantus firmus* from the solmisation syllables present in the name of the composer's patron). Similar dedicatory gestures can be found in music of the so-called Second Viennese School. Alban Berg identified the three main figures of the Schoenberg circle in the introductory bars (and main themes) of his Chamber Concerto of 1925 by using the musical pitches found in their names – Arnold Schönberg;[25] Alban Berg; Anton Webern (where B = B flat, H = B natural and S = E flat). Schoenberg himself quoted the BACH motif in his Variations for Orchestra (op.31) as though to acknowledge his line of descent and Webern used the same four-note cell as the basis of the note-row for his String Quartet (op.28), probably on account of its intervallic economy. More recently, composers such as Shostakovich have personalised their output by incorporating their musical 'signatures' into their material or (as in Lutosławski's *Musique Funèbre*) using cryptograms to convey a musical tribute (to Bartók).

The increased awareness of the past has, of course, manifested itself in the so-called neo-classical movement in music of the twentieth century. Although it is most commonly associated with Stravinsky's output between *c*.1920 and *c*.1950, many other composers (notably Hindemith, Bartók and, surprisingly, Schoenberg) have made use of the structures, techniques and manners of earlier music – and not just of the classical period. Schoenberg's Suite for Piano (op.25), for example, uses baroque dance forms (*Gavotte, Musette, Minuet* and *Gigue*) as convenient formal restraints in what was his first completely serial composition – coincidentally finished in 1923, the same year as Holst's bitonal Fugal Concerto (another unlikely fusion of linguistic innovation and neo-classical structure). Yet it is Stravinsky who best exemplifies the artistic movement which was rather unkindly categorised by Constant Lambert as the 'Age of Pastiche'.[26] Stimulated, no doubt, by Diaghilev's artistic 'time-travelling',[27] Stravinsky had cooperated in a number of theatrical projects involving the orchestration, re-orchestration and completion of works by earlier composers even before the aesthetic landmark of *Pulcinella* in 1919.[28] His output over the next thirty years or so was characterised by similar excursions into the worlds of the baroque ritornello and concerto, the classical symphony and sonata, and the set pieces of eighteenth-century opera.[29] He incorporated music by Tchaikovsky into his ballet, *The Fairy's Kiss* (1928), he aped the gestures of Verdian Grand Opera in sections of *Oedipus Rex* (1926/27), and (like Milhaud and Satie) made cross-cultural references to jazz, rag-time and popular dance in works as diverse as *The Soldier's Tale* (1918) and the *Ebony Concerto* (1945). No single work better demonstrates the extraordinary stimulus of the past than *The Rake's Progress* (1948/51) – acknowledged by the composer as having been written under the direct influence of the 'Italian-Mozart style'[30] – and, indeed, it is traditionally viewed as the culmination of an era; what Stephen Walsh terms 'more of an end than a beginning'.[31] But Stravinsky was still fascinated by the structural potential and technical tricks of earlier music. The

Ex. 5   Stravinsky: Arrangement of J.S. Bach's Choral-Variations on Vom Himmel hoch;
         Variation 1, bb. 1–6.

Ricercare of the Cantata (1951/52), the Dirge-Canons of *In Memoriam Dylan Thomas* (1954), and the palindromic outer movements of *Canticum Sacrum* (1955) provide ample evidence of this as does his arrangement of Bach's Choral-Variations on *Vom Himmel hoch* which was undertaken as a companion piece to *Canticum Sacrum* for its first performance at St Mark's, Venice in 1956.[32] Example 5 shows how Stravinsky's orchestration of Variation 1 preserves the contrapuntal fabric of Bach's organ piece but adds continuo-like arpeggiate accompaniments (on flutes, harp and oboes) which partly obscure the harmonic clarity of the original in a manner not far removed from his earlier practice in *Pulcinella*. Elsewhere in his arrangement, Stravinsky departs substantially from Bach by transposing Variations 2–4 and writing a new canon at the seventh in Variation 3.[33]

Whether we approve of Stravinsky's aesthetic stance or not, there can be no denying that, in this arrangement and other similar works, he is presenting us with his reconsideration of existing repertoires and a re-creation of the past in terms of the present. His neo-classical works (and *The Rake's Progress* in particular) might

(Ex 5. concluded)

have something of the flavour of Shakespeare in modern dress, but few would question the contemporary force of comparable theatrical products such as Bernstein's *Romeo and Juliet* allegory in *West Side Story* – or doubt the dramatic validity of Stoppard's *Hamlet*-inspired, *Rosencrantz and Guildenstern are Dead*. Schoenberg's typically waspish satire in his short cantata, *Der neue Klassizismus* (op.28, no.3),[34] does less than justice to the neo-classical aesthetic (and, by implication, to Stravinsky's compositional integrity) and fails to take into account his own arrangements and exercises in stylistic pastiche which range from the early *Überbrettl* hack-work and the occasional kitsch of *Die Eiserne Brigade* (1916) to his orchestrations of Bach and Brahms[35] and the recomposition of works by Monn and Handel (1932 and 1933).[36] He also assisted with the many arrangements of modern works which were rehearsed at the Society for Private Musical Performances (between 1918 and 1921) and encouraged his pupils to make reduced orchestrations of compositions for the purpose of workshop study. Some of these, for example Webern's arrangement of his teacher's Chamber Symphony, op.9, for the ensemble used in *Pierrot Lunaire*,[37] have found a place in the present-day repertoire as pieces in their own right – as has the same composer's orchestration of the Fugue (Ricercata) from the *Musical Offering* which is as personal (and valid) a reinterpretation of Bach's contrapuntal model as Stravinsky's arrangement of *Vom Himmel hoch*.

The use of arrangement to provide an aesthetic commentary is nowhere better illustrated than in Busoni's 'Concert Interpretation' of Schoenberg's Piano Piece, op.11, no.2, which was published with Schoenberg's approval in 1910 at the same time as the original Three Pieces, op.11.[38] The two composers had started an intermittent correspondence in the Spring of 1903[39] and Busoni conducted Schoenberg's orchestration of Heinrich Schenker's *Syrian Dances* in November of the same year. He subsequently expressed an interest in performing the Chamber Symphony, op.9, but the proposed concert-series in 1909/10 was cancelled and Busoni turned instead to the newly-composed Piano Pieces.[40] It is clear from Busoni's letter of 26 July, 1909,[41] that he admired the musical content of the first two pieces but had reservations about their pianistic idiom:

> The first doubts about your music 'as piano pieces' arose because of the small span of the writing in the circumference of time and space. The piano is a short-breathed instrument and one can't help it enough.

and, in a postscript:

> I have now had your pieces with me for five days and have worked on them every day. I understand your intentions and have tried, after some preparation, to produce the sounds and moods which you expect. However, the task is made more difficult by your too great conciseness – that is the word.

Busoni then included a short example (op.11, no.2, b. 40) of how he might revise Schoenberg's score to make it more pianistic. The outcome was the complete rethinking (*Konzertmässige Interpretation*) of this movement in terms of the sort of pianism that Busoni himself favoured. In doing this, he extended the piece by twelve bars – not by adding new material or by changing Schoenberg's sequence of ideas, but by repeating phrases in different registers and arpeggiating chord sequences. What is particularly revealing is that it is the sections which contain the most challenging harmonic progressions that Busoni felt drawn to repeat in this way.

A comparison between the two versions above indicates the extent to which Busoni edited Schoenberg's piano writing – indeed, Schoenberg responded to Busoni's criticisms by composing the third Opus 11 piece in a quite different style which sets far more taxing technical problems for the performer. However, the real significance of the arrangement is that it reflects something of the difficulty that even a sophisticated musician experienced in coming to terms with Schoenberg's highly concentrated and increasingly dissonant idiom. It is clear that Schoenberg (a reasonably competent but unpretentious pianist) used the piano as a workshop instrument when he was experimenting with new procedures and techniques.[42] Busoni's reaction to Opus 11 is an indication of a more general problem in the reception of new music – although he is said to have been amused

Ex. 6   Schoenberg: Piano Piece, op.11, no.2, bb. 4–13.

by Schoenberg's suggestion that he had not understood his pieces. This is not the occasion to dwell on the two composers' theoretical and aesthetic writings, but it is worth noting that Busoni defended the processes of arrangement and transcription against the charge of disreputability in his *Sketch of a New Aesthetic in Music*[43] which was first published shortly after the appearance of The Three Piano Pieces. Schoenberg owned and annotated a copy of Busoni's treatise and referred to it in his own *Theory of Harmony* (1911).[44] In spite of their disagreements they shared a common vision of the nature and purpose of music and a contempt for the pedants – the 'lawgivers', as Busoni termed them. As a transcriber and editor of Bach's works, Busoni continued in the Lisztian tradition he so much admired; it is ironic that this approach to editing, which did so much to popularise eighteenth-century music, in due course provoked a reaction which led to the publication of fresh *urtext* editions and an obsession with that peculiarly twentieth-century concept of authenticity.

Ex. 7   Busoni: Concert Interpretation of Schoenberg's Piano Piece, op.11, no.2, bb. 4–15.

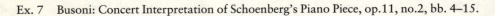

It is one of the great paradoxes of our times that a century which has witnessed more than its fair share of artistic revolutions and radical innovations should also have coincided with a period of (perhaps excessive) reverence for earlier cultures. In some cases, the two currents have flowed on independent courses, but in other instances they have been linked by tributaries which have combined past and modern material in a fertile way. The use of baroque and classical techniques has already been mentioned – as has the quotation of musical ciphers and other symbolic references – but perhaps the most significant development of the twentieth century in this sphere has been the composition of works which have been directly inspired by much earlier works or have responded to specific historical stimuli such as a building's cultural heritage (as in *Canticum Sacrum*) or a notational device (as in Peter Maxwell Davies's *Prolation* of 1957/58). What might be termed 'composition around' or 'composition upon' an existing piece has been a feature of Davies's output – most obviously in works based on Taverner's *In Nomine*,[45] Monteverdi's *Vespers of 1610*,[46] and Dunstaple's *Veni Sancte Spiritus*.[47] The list of sources for Davies's works includes Gesualdo, Buxtehude, Purcell, Bull, and Bach as well as plainsong and medieval polyphony; the influences on his style are equally diverse.[48] Writing of his references 'from Handel to Birtwistle' in *Eight Songs for a Mad King* (1969), he says:

> In some ways I regard the work as a collection of musical objects borrowed from many sources, functioning as 'stage props', around which the reciter's part weaves . . .[49]

Such a kaleidoscopic use of musical extracts goes well beyond the emotive quotation of a folk-song and a Bach chorale in Berg's Violin Concerto, for example, just as Davies's use of more substantial source material exceeds the normal conventions of variation-writing (as in *St Thomas Wake*, where Bull's eponymous pavane and foxtrots by the composer himself provide the basis of a 'confrontation between commercial music and serious symphonic argument').[50] Although some of Davies's transcriptions of earlier music are fairly literal, most demonstrate a considerable progression away from the original – often over several works. Parallels with the layering techniques used in Berio's *Chemins* series are revealing, as is a comparison with his use of the scherzo from Mahler's Second Symphony in *Sinfonia* (1968/69).

The constraints of a survey such as this preclude more than passing references to the outstanding folk-music research and editions by composers such as Bartók and Kodály, to Britten's arrangements of music by Purcell and Rossini, to the increasing concern shown by composers for self-editing (Schoenberg's invention of *Hauptstimme* and *Nebenstimme* signs, for example), or to the many editorial completions of works such as Berg's *Lulu* (Cerha) and Mahler's Tenth Symphony (Cooke and others). As I write, the composer Anthony Payne is reconstructing Elgar's Third Symphony, John Pickard is scoring *The Battle Song* (a piece for brass band) by Havergal Brian,[51] and the young musicologist Agusti Salvado is editing some recently discovered manuscripts of juvenilia by Roberto Gerhard.[52] All of these activities will undoubtedly contribute to our insight into the compositional procedures of those concerned – and all require specialised combinations of notational, editorial, and composing skills. Greater historical awareness has led twentieth-century composers to capitalise on the multifarious associations embedded in canonical works and to exploit the potential of earlier composition techniques such as isorhythm and plainsong paraphrase in new contexts (for example, the organ music of Messiaen). The interrelationship between composing and arranging has been strengthened and music's ability to comment on other music has been reaffirmed. Although editing of early music has become more of a musicological specialism, where composers have worked in this way (as with Webern's transcription of Isaac's *Choralis constantinus*)[53] the results have enriched composition as well as musical scholarship.

Notes

1. The name given to the troubadours, for example, is derived from the langue d'oc verb *trobar* (to find). Marcabru (one of the earliest troubadours) claims in his verse, *Pax in Nomine Domini*, that he *made* the words and the notes (*Fetz Marcabrus los motz e'l so*). As the first phrase of music appears to be based on plainsong, this statement seems to imply craftsmanship (constructing the tune) rather than original composition in the modern sense. In the transcription in the *New Oxford History*, vol. 2 (1954), pp. 229–30, however, the editor (J. Westrup) credits him only with writing the words.
2. See Rob C. Wegman (1996), 'From Maker to Composer: Improvisation and Musical Authorship in the Low Countries, 1450–1500', *Journal of the American Musicological Society*, vol. XLIX, no. 3, pp. 409–79, for a detailed consideration of such interrelationships.
3. This motet is located in the Bamberg MS (f. 52v.) and the Montpellier Codex (ff. 292r.–293r.). A modern performing edition with translations is available in Wyndham Thomas (1985), *Robin and Marion Motets*, vol. 1, Newton Abbot.
4. See *Alleluia – Dulce lignum* in *Liber Usualis* (Tournai, 1961), p. 1456. The melisma on *sustinere* is identical with *portare* (its alternative title).
5. Quoted in translation in Oliver Strunk (1981), *Source Readings in Music History*, London, vol. 1, p. 82.
6. Rob C. Wegman, op. cit., pp. 461–79 especially.
7. *John Dunstaple: Complete Works*, ed. M. Bukofzer (Musica Britannica, vii, no. 32, 1953); rev. edn., eds M. Bent, I. Bent and B. Trowell (1970).
8. Margaret Bent (1981), *Dunstaple*, Oxford, p. 55. Bent's preferred spelling of the composer's name has been adopted in this text.
9. *Dufay: Opera Omnia*, ed. H. Besseler (1966), Rome, vol. 1, no. 16.
10. Charles Warren (1973), 'Brunelleschi's Dome and Dufay Motet', *The Musical Quarterly*, vol. xliv, pp. 92–105.
11. Craig Wright (1994), 'Dufay's Nuper rosarum flores, King Solomon's Temple and the Veneration of the Virgin', *Journal of the American Musicological Society*, vol. XLVI, p. 395 *et seq.*
12. Modern editions of these two pieces can be found in Bernard Thomas (1981), *Music from the Buxheim Organ Book*, London, pp. 19 and 26–27.
13. See Beck, S. (ed) (1959), *Morley's First Book of Consort Lessons of 1599*, New York.
14. Gustav Reese (1954), *Music in the Renaissance*, p. 559.
15. J.J. Fux (1725), *Gradus ad Parnassum*, Vienna – a treatise on counterpoint. English trans. by A. Mann (1943), *Steps to Parnassus*, New York.

16. Norman Carrell (1967), *Bach the Borrower*, London.
17. Basil Lam, Foreword to Carrell, op. cit.
18. Mozart arranged *Acis and Galatea* (1788), *Messiah* (1789) *Alexander's Feast* and *Ode for St Cecilia's Day* (both 1790).
19. E. de Coussemaker, *Drames lituriques du moyen age* (Rennes, 1860, reprinted New York, 1964). Coussemaker's edition of *Adam de la Halle* (Paris, 1872, reprinted New York, 1964) has been superseded by Nigel E. Wilkins, *The Lyric Works of Adam de la Hale* (sic), CMM 44 (1967).
20. Brahms's Symphony 4, Finale, bb. 113–128.
21. See Charles Rosen (1996), *The Romantic Generation*, New York, p. 486.
22. Rosen, op. cit., p. 512.
23. Rosen op. cit., pp. 528 and 530.
24. The passacaglia-like variations (1862) are constructed on the bass of the *Crucifixus* from Bach's B Minor Mass which itself originates in the cantata *Weinen, Klagen, Sorgen, Sagen sind der Christen Tranebrot*. The work was occasioned by the death of Liszt's daughter, Blandine Ollivier.
25. Berg used the German spelling (Schönberg) to produce his cryptogram. Elsewhere in the text the composer's adopted English spelling (Schoenberg) has been used.
26. Constant Lambert, *Music Ho!* (London, 1934 and 1948), p. 43 *et seq*.
27. Constant Lambert, op. cit., pp 47–54.
28. These include orchestrations of Chopin's *Nocturne in A flat and Valse Brillante in E flat* for *Les Sylphides* (1909), and a new version of Mussorgsky's *Khovanschina* (1913/14) in which he composed a chorus for the finale. See also Stravinsky's own comments on the project quoted in E.W. White (1966), *Stravinsky*, London and Boston, p. 545.
29. These categories are not mutually exclusive but significant examples include the Concerto in E flat (*Dumbarton Oaks*) (1937/38), Symphony in C (1938/40), and *The Rake's Progress* (1948/51).
30. Quoted in E.W. White, op. cit., p. 457.
31. Stephen Walsh (1993), *The Music of Stravinsky*, Oxford, p. 216.
32. Stravinsky's arrangement uses basically the same forces as *Canticum Sacrum*, including a mixed chorus which sings the chorale in Variations 2–5. He prefaces the arrangement with a six-part setting of the original chorale for trumpets and trombones.
33. See score (Boosey and Hawkes 18284) and E.W. White, op. cit., pp. 547–49 for details.
34. Stravinsky is not specifically cited in 'The New Classicism' but the implications of Schoenberg's satire are made clear in his appendix to op.28 – quoted in full in René Leibowitz, *Schoenberg and His School*, trans. Dika Newlin (New York, 1949 and 1975), pp. 106–8. It would be strange, indeed, if the leading figure of neo-classical music were not the be-wigged *poseur* depicted in Schoenberg's text.
35. Schoenberg orchestrated two chorale preludes by Bach: *Komm, Gott, Schöpfer, heiliger Geist* and *Schmücke dich, O liebe Seele* (1992), and the Prelude and Fugue in E flat, BWV 552 (1928/29). Brahms: Piano Quartet in G minor, op.25, was orchestrated in 1937.
36. Monn's Clavicembalo Concerto in D (1746), was recomposed as a Cello Concerto (1932/33) and Handel's Concerto Grosso, op.6, no.7, was turned into a String Quartet Concerto (1933). See Joseph H. Auner (1996), 'Schoenberg's Handel Concerto and the Ruins of Tradition', *Journal of the American Musicological Society*, vol. XLIX, no. 2, pp. 264–313, for a critical evaluation.
37. Scored for flute (or violin), clarinet (or viola), piano, violin, cello.
38. Both works published by Universal Edition (1910): Schoenberg (UE 2991); Busoni (UE 2992).

39. See H.H. Stuckenschmidt (1977), *Arnold Schoenberg – His Life, World and Work*, trans. Humphrey Searle, London, pp. 219–31 for full details.

40. Schoenberg sent the first two pieces only in response to a letter from Busoni dated 16 July, 1909. See H.H. Stuckenmschmidt, op. cit., p. 221.

41. Quoted in full in H.H. Stuckenschmidt, op. cit., pp. 221–22.

42. See also Schoenberg's use of the piano in Six Little Piano Pieces, op.19, and Five Piano Pieces, op.23, for exercises in miniature forms and serialism respectively.

43. Ferruccio Busoni, 'Sketch of a New Aesthetic in Music', trans. T. Baker (1962), in *Three Classics in the Aesthetics of Music*, New York, pp. 84–86.

44. Arnold Schoenberg, *Theory of Harmony*, trans. Roy. E. Carter (1978), London, 1978, pp. 25 and 395.

45. John Taverner's *In Nomine* is used in Davies's *Seven In Nomine* (1963/64), *Second Fantasia on John Taverner's In Nomine* (1964), and the opera, *Taverner* (1962–68).

46. Montverdi's *Vespers* was the starting point for String Quartet (1961), *The Leopardi Fragments* (1961), and Sinfonia (1962).

47. Dunstaple's motet is used in *Veni Sancte Spiritus* (1963) and arr. with new *Veni Creator Spiritus* (1972).

48. The composer's own account of the composition of his First Symphony, for example, acknowledges the influences of Sibelius, Schumann and Boulez. The second movement uses the plainsong, *Ave Maris Stella*, and Davies ends by declaring his debt to Dante and St Thomas Aquinas. Quoted in Paul Griffiths (1982) *Peter Maxwell Davies*, London, pp. 157–62.

49. Quoted in Paul Griffiths, op. cit., p. 148.

50. Paul Griffiths, op. cit., p. 67.

51. Havergal Brian's short score, entitled 'Symphonic Poem: The Battle Song' (dated 1930–31), was purchased at Sothbey's in 1996 by the Havergal Brian Society. The compass of the writing and the manuscript's provenance (it was previously owned by R. Smith and Co., the publishers of Brass Band music) suggest that the piece was intended for brass band. The Havergal Brian Society commissioned John Pickard to make a performing edition with a view to a première in 1998. I am grateful to John Pickard for providing me with this information.

52. Agusti Salvado (a doctoral student at Bristol University) discovered these youthful works by Gerhard during the course of his research into Catalan Music in Barcelona. They include a charming Piano Sonatina dedicated to the composer's brother.

53. Webern's D.Phil. at Vienna University (1906) was on Isaac. His edition of *Choralis constantinus* (part 2) was published as *Denkmäler der Tonkunst in Österreich*, Graz, 1909, vol. xxxii, Jg.xvi/I.

4   A Performer's Responsibility
Susan Bradshaw

We are, it seems, only now beginning to emerge from a fog of nineteenth-century editorial influence that all too frequently leads performers still to opt for the first available – preferably the cheapest – copy of no matter what piece of music without stopping to wonder whether the notes they see before them may (as is more likely than not) have been 'pre-interpreted': that is, encased in an editorial espressivo which is often grossly misleading. Take, for instance, Mozart's A major Piano Concerto, K.488. Setting out to restore the composer's original markings 'which, as is always the case, are absolutely clear', the scrupulous Dr Friedrich Blume was horrified to find that 'the arbitrary mistakes and adaptations of the nineteenth century' included 'nonsensical phrasings, incorrect dynamic signs and even quite a number of wrong notes – all of which have been passed on uncritically from hand to hand'. He was, incidentally, writing in 1936.[1] Small wonder then that we as performers have learnt generally to disregard what we see by way of articulation and phrasing; supposing it to be arbitrary, we have learnt to take it, leave it, or exchange it for equally arbitrary ideas of our own. This view of articulation as something imposed upon the notes from outside and after the compositional event has become so ingrained a performance habit that, faced with an original text, it seems to us just another version – which we have likewise learnt generally to disregard.

My point here is a straightforward one, my purpose to draw attention to the structural evidence so readily communicated by music *as originally notated* and not as, 'passed on uncritically from hand to hand', confusingly overlaid with editorial encumbrances, however well intentioned. In its pristine state, the score has to be regarded as custodian of some original truth, however elusory; for since it alone stands as a unique record of a particular compositional undertaking it must also stand as the single unadulterated starting point for interpretation. It is in any case the sole means of access to a whole collection of contributory truths which are there for the gathering; yet much of this richly communicative musical evidence is lost when relayed to the listener in performances of a kind that can at best be described as superficial.

The performance of any piece of music must none the less include a degree of unwritten emphasis; it goes without saying that the committed performer – in the ongoing search for some particular portion of this ever-elusive truth – may from moment to moment decide positively to focus more on this aspect, less on that. But it is when such expressive choices are made without repeated reference to the quite specific checks and balances contained by the score that they become misleading distortions which, 'passed on uncritically', evolve into inarticulate half-truths deprived of any real perspective. And it is an awareness of musical perspective, of the ever-fragile balance between background and foreground (between melody and harmony, rhythm and metre), that has continually to be renewed if the trust assumed to exist between composer, performer and listener is not to be betrayed.

Tucked away in parenthesis at the top of page 34 of his book *The Classical Style*[2] Charles Rosen makes the supremely important point that 'The greater the composer the larger the terms of his control over the significance of his ideas'. It is how this compositorial control of ideas may be said to communicate itself (initially to the performer, eventually to the listener) that is of all-consuming interest to us here, even as we are emphatically reminded that the greatest composers reveal as much by what they do not need to specify (Bach) as by what they choose specifically to articulate (Haydn, Mozart, Beethoven).

It ought also to go without saying that the significance of musical thought is conveyed not by notes alone but by the countless ways in which those notes may be fashioned into articulate ideas; and that with music, as with words, punctuation – the linking or separating of elements – is a fundamental requirement for meaningful communication. It should then be safe to conclude that those composers who punctuate most effectively are those least in danger of being misunderstood. But alas, if performers fail even to notice the carefully positioned articulation slurs that serve to change the melodic emphasis from repetition to development in Example 8, then it is of little avail for the composer, Beethoven, to insist that his articulation is an obligatory pointer to structural intent.[3]

Ex. 8   Beethoven: Sonata in F minor, op.2, no.1, first movement, bb. 1–22.

(Ex. 8 concluded)

Let us pause for a moment on this extract from the opening page of his first piano sonata. Supposing the reader to be seated at the keyboard, score in hand, it should quickly become obvious that to play the passage beginning at the upbeat to bar 15 with an imaginary phrase mark extending from one barline to the next, even across the two bars 15–16, would be to focus on the rising 6th G–E flat; obvious too that this would be totally to contradict the fact that the six bars 15–20 feature *not* the rising sixth but a descending melodic sequence that each time ends with the cadential resolution from A flat–G. Beethoven not only marks it thus but shortens the G with a staccato dot for good measure. Then, as an additional guard against any possible misunderstanding, he puts a new slur at the start of each ensuing step-wise descent – whether of two, four, or three notes. If, as performer, I am to play this passage with due regard to its articulative sense, I must first observe the presence of these punctuations, then attempt really to hear as well as physically to feel the effect of incorporating them. By now I ought also to be curious enough to wonder what such instructions may signify relative to the structure of the movement as a whole.

Experience tells me that Beethoven's motivic articulation is cumulative, always harmonically goal-directed; so it is at this point in my questioning that I should be led to ask whether he may have other plans for the rising 6th he has evidently been at such pains to disguise. This in turn prompts me to see what manner of punctuation may be attached to the next appearance of a similar sequence of notes and there, towards the end of the exposition (Example 9, bar 41ff.), the same falling phrase returns recognisably intact – despite hints of a minor-mode slant to the melodic line (now expressed in terms of the dotted-note rhythm established earlier). But the real surprise here is to find the phrase ending one note early (on the A flat, now *not* included within the melodic slur of bar 15ff. or even the rhythmically matching one of bar 22); this change features both the rising 6th (G–E flat) and its cadential conclusion (the falling 5th E flat–A flat), so that each element needs to be separately articulated rather than linked across the barline as convention (and the rhythmic relationship between the two E flats) would more usually dictate. Moreover, the delayed resolution of the third and last of these cadences includes an affirmative response that seems finally to underline the essential purposefulness of these separations.

Ex 9.   Beethoven: Sonata in F minor, op.2, no.1, first movement, bb. 41–48.

If all this suggests an approach to performance that borders on the analytical, then so be it. Scores need urgently to be wiped clean of idle assumptions, and it is with this in mind that I choose deliberately to write in the first person. For it is by adopting the stance of an analytically observant performer that I hope to discover whether it may perhaps be possible to begin to narrow the great divide between written analysis (necessarily conceived before or after the musical event) and time-defying performance.

In any case, where does a naturally observant musicality end and analysis proper begin? As professional musicologists we can write all we like about matters that ought to be of equal concern to professional performers; but unless our communications can be made to relate to the time in which music unfolds, academic analyses – however imaginative and far-reaching in themselves – can scarcely hope to exert much of an influence on practical music making. Some kind of performance-adapted analysis could and certainly should stimulate performers to become more acutely aware of a multiplicity of enriching relationships (relationships just as important for composers to define as for performers to interpret), but only if it can be devised less with the purpose of laying down laws or prescribing easy answers and more with the aim of provoking performers first to observe and then to ask their own questions of the text confronting them.

As if for the benefit of the proverbial person from outer space, such a musical text might be defined as 'instructions for the recreation of an imaginary sound edifice which, dreamt up in the mind of its composer, starts to disappear even as it begins to be heard'; and furthermore that, 'like moving film, such a sound edifice has no existence in time except insofar and for as long as its succession of disappearing moments remain in the memory'. It is this inescapably evanescent quality of musical structures that has always led the greatest composers to take such painstaking care to establish connections between the just-past and the shortly-to-come.

But however seemingly explicit the notational instructions, it is the unavoidable intervention of the third-party performer that is ultimately responsible for the many slips that can come between original communicator (the composer) and the eventual communicatee (the listener). In a *Times* profile of conductor Bernard Haitink, critic Richard Morrison observed that 'Every music-lover carries around mental maps, however sketchy, of cherished pieces of music'; he might well have gone on to add that almost as many performers are seemingly content to perpetuate equally sketchy, generally second-hand, impressions of the pieces they play and (presumably) cherish. But while there is little reason to chide the listener for clinging to a mental map that takes scant account of detail, when the performer does likewise the result is akin to a map drawn from ill-founded memory. Anyone who has ever tried to map the surroundings of the locality in which they live will know how difficult it is to visualise precisely the angles at which the various pathways intersect relative not only to each other but to such apparently unmissable landmarks as the tower block or the mountain peak. Walking the same way on a daily basis, we know them well – but only as they relate to ourselves as figures in the same landscape; asked to place them to scale, let alone to fill in the detail that gives each its particular character, and we would have to admit less to having forgotten than to having failed ever to notice.

This kind of half memory is of course a vital ingredient in our human survival kit: too much fully remembered detail would become an obsession in itself – preventing us from functioning on any level other than that of mere remembering. Most of us can afford subconsciously to reject much of the visual information that town planners and cartographers must note and carefully measure on our behalf – so providing instant access to plans or maps that will enable us to plug the memory gaps as and when occasion demands. In the unlikely event that these plans were to be drawn up along the lines of the amateur sketch map we would have every right to accuse the perpetrator at worst of professional incompetence, at best of an idle unconcern for the precision and richness of detail we'd been led to assume we could take on trust.

But what about the trust placed in us performing musicians? Isn't this the level at which we so often fail to provide the listener with the properly balanced aural information needed to fill the gaps in his personal repertoire of half-remembered pieces? Have we perhaps become purveyors merely of half-remembered impressions? To quote Dr Albert Schweitzer only marginally out of context: 'the impression a work makes on the hearer depends on the player communicating the broad outline and the details simultaneously, both equally clear and equally full of life'. That a musical outline lacks substance without its contributory detail should be self-evident; yet it is the unthinking acceptance of copycat 'interpretations' gleaned from hearsay or from recordings that has blunted almost to extinction any idea of the score as documentary communication direct from composer to each ensuing performer, who is in turn responsible for relaying the message with all its articulative detail as far as possible intact. This is not to suggest that the composer can or even should attempt to predict every eventuality within what we must seemingly agree to call the 'real time' of performance, but simply to insist that musical notation offers a wonderfully precise yet infinitely flexible means of communicating ideas in terms of a musically specific articulation. But the difference between what we see (in the score) yet often do not hear (in performance) can be quite profound – at worst suggesting that the punctuating elements crucial to the sense of a particular message have been carelessly discarded along the way.[4]

Even at the risk of seeming to overstate the case, it is worth repeating that the particular character of a piece of music depends on context; and that merely to play the notes without regard for their surroundings or for the manner of their articulation (in terms of rhythm, metre, harmonic pacing, and so on) is so to weaken that context as to leave certain aspects altogether unremarked. It is almost as if, like the painting in need of restoration, the score as communicative artefact had become so smudged by time as to render much of its detail scarcely decipherable. It remains my contention that no detail is too small, no contributory factor too unimportant to the preparation of each and every performance for the player first to uncover and then to recreate the layer-upon-layer richness of their interlocking relationships.

But to proceed. My self-questioning as to the directional purpose of Beethoven's motivic punctuation of course represents only the first and most obvious line of enquiry – a preliminary step towards an investigation that must now take account of the vertical as well as the horizontal, the metrical as well as the merely durational. The precisely detailed articulation of the syncopated development noted earlier (Example 8, bars 15ff.) has for instance now to be set within the sentence-defining structure of a thrice repeated harmonic ostinato – a non legato cadence figure that not only paces out the 2-in-a-bar metre but whose static repetitions control (and must be *felt* to control) the length of the phrase. Even when the roles are later reversed (Example 9, bars 41–48), with the now staccato chording assuming the syncopated role, the insistently duple melody the metrical one, it is again the threefold cadential repetition (together with an equivalent octave transposition the third time around) which ought to ensure that the rhythmic momentum remains within the span of a single phrase.

Lest I begin to suggest an obsessive concern for these few bars, this exposition, this work, a different but not altogether dissimilar example of harmonic phrasing may help to make the case for what I hope to define as no more – and certainly no less – than an open-minded and entirely non-specific vigilance.

Unlike Beethoven, Chopin seems to have suffered from a lifelong uncertainty as to how best to articulate his elegant melodic lines. Searching for ways that would stand the test of time, he changed his mind frequently, mostly to confusing effect; he was, on the other hand, markedly more precise when it came to establishing the character of his harmony-bearing accompaniment figures. Related as they often are to the wide-spaced chord dispositions characteristic of the Viennese waltz, these accompaniments frequently occupy the whole register from low bass to high alto, and likewise support a bass line that is both responsible for and independent of what nearly always features as a subsidiary melody (outlined in the middle register above). Even in youthful pieces like the op.9 *Nocturnes*, the imaginative flexibility of these quasi-ostinato accompaniments is such as to allow for entire pieces to be based on the same figurative idea – a figuration whose harmony-defining substance generally spans a rather narrow register band within a middleground pitch area far removed from either melody or bass. To look behind (beneath) the top-line focus that so often seems set to cast Chopin merely as a supremely eloquent melodist is to discover an approach to harmonic rhythm that is much more sophisticated and noticeably more confident than is usually supposed.

Take the harmonic figuration from the second of his op.9 *Nocturnes*, the one in E flat major (see Example 10). As performer, one of my first practical tasks must be to ensure the melodic connection from one pizzicato bass note to the next – separately scanning the low-lying contours of what amounts to a true bass line. It would seem logical then to pursue the harmonic cohesion of the accompaniment as a whole by collating the harmonic content of each dotted crotchet – playing each as part of a phrased succession of complete chord formations (four chords to the bar, much in the manner of a chorale harmonisation) before restoring the independent bass line to its rightful position in support of a legato voice-leading that connects the two upper elements. With the relationship between harmonic background (the bass line) and middle ground (the chording) well heard and properly balanced, the melodic foreground (the true melody line) should in turn begin to focus downwards in search of a harmonic depth and a hitherto unsuspected rhythmic poise. But it is above all the pacing of each 4-bar phrase described by the explicitly directional bass line that will determine the melodic span of each long bar; for it is this movement-controlling horizontal dimension – determined by the arrival of the next bass note, the next distant downbeat – which has ultimate charge of any vertical freedoms that may be imposed upon it.

Ex. 10   Chopin: Nocturne in E flat major, op.9, no.2, bb. 1–8.

I must of course also take account of the fact that speed of harmonic movement will affect rhythmic impetus, and that the suddenly increased rate of change in bar 3 of this same *Nocturne* will of itself suggest that the serene pace of bars 1 and 2 has unaccountably quickened before just as suddenly relaxing into the seemingly slower cadential context of bar 4. The effect is that of an aural illusion – in kind not unlike the more extended one engineered by Beethoven at the start of his op.2 Sonata. Here (see Example 8), while the actual speed is very fast, the harmonic rhythm begins rather slowly, appearing to accelerate as the rate of change increases from one chord spread across two bars, to one every bar, to one every half bar – along with a rising bass that adds to the effect of rushing towards the cliff-top ending of a silent pause at the end of the phrase (bar 8). To make this progression clear, I shall have to carry the harmonic image through the rests, rehearsing the off-beat chording in as purposeful a manner as would any good string quartet, and avoiding any inclination to pre-empt the surprise ending by slowing in anticipation of its soundless arrival. The structure of the phrase itself suggests that any yielding of the tempo at this point should arise out of the very struggle to maintain it – through the fortissimo spread chord and the following steep diminuendo towards the grace-note inversion and abrupt cut off of the motivic triplet from bar 2.

The foregoing observations are, of course, to be understood as no more than a preliminary, toe-in-the-water investigation, as a few examples of the kind of performance-related observations that might be gleaned from a widely-based analytic alertness. I hope it therefore goes without saying that the examples of articulative purpose noted above (relative to a couple of quite specific, if randomly-chosen, extracts) are but pointers to an approach designed to enhance the perception of musical structure as received and understood in its entirety. As a third and penultimate example, it may be interesting briefly to imagine ourselves starting out as potential performers of Alan Berg's op.1 Sonata – if only because this is a piece whose interlinked structure is all too often made to seem dangerously loose-limbed and inconsequential.

Again using myself as guinea-pig, and assuming the reader still to be seated at the piano by my side, I will of course aim to start not from some already tainted version but from scratch: that is, from what can be read in the score. Knowing, with hindsight, that all music written during the first half of the twentieth century – and much of it thereafter – relates in some degree to one or more classical norms, I am already alert to the fact that a sense of historical perspective is now more than ever an essential tool in the search for an understanding of style. The more so since the richness of the stylistic palette at Berg's disposal in the early years of the century was such as to enable him to switch instantly, and with immediate effect, from the mainly harmonic to the mainly contrapuntal, while remaining everywhere and always concerned with a system of melodic voice-leading used not only to connect and to clarify an abundance of motivic development, but to underpin a long-term harmonic purpose not so different in kind from that of Beethoven. In other words, this is a work that leans heavily on the past even as it moves precipitately towards a yet-to-be-defined future.

Its youthful composer could perhaps be accused of failing to resist the temptation to overload the communicative space of this one short movement; as performers, we will nevertheless have little excuse for failing to notice that, even as he attempts to keep all his motivic ideas independently intact (no matter how complex the tangle of cross references in which they are embedded), Berg has had perforce to sacrifice a degree of more explicitly harmonic continuity. It is from this observation point that the final phase of our initial performers' challenge might well choose to set out. For even to begin to trace some of the often slender threads of its implicitly harmonic framework could also be to focus on the particular structural dimension that makes this sonata such a fascinatingly relevant subject for communicative research.

I will meanwhile have remarked a conspicuous flexibility in Berg's approach to both pulse and tempo – a rhythmic flux so immediately striking as to suggest that some kind of articulative control may be operating across the board from smallest intervallic motif, to phrase, to harmonic paragraph; and, moreover, that since an internal elasticity serves from the outset to endorse a rubato phrase articulation, it seems likely that external tempo alterations may prove to have a parallel function relative to the articulation of form. In any case, since some idea of tempo, however notional, is an essential prerequisite to definition of musical character, my initial enquiries ought certainly to concern the largest of these articulative categories.

Signalled as they are by the introduction of new or newly transformed material, the four 'thematic' tempi established by the end of the exposition must be presumed crucial to the structural identity of a one-movement work which nevertheless includes, at least in essence, the four different movement characters associated with classical sonata form. But by giving the opening tempo in large letters and in a bold type that is never re-used (see Example 11), the publishers seem seriously to have confused the issue, perpetuating the ill-founded notion that the work unfolds at the same moderate tempo throughout. It will be more interesting by far to accept the composer's instructions at face value and as they occur, using them not only to promote the particular rhythmic character of each 'movement' as an integral part of the structural whole but so as to establish which of these characters will later in the work be heard to infiltrate the tempo band of another. Because, although Berg's expressive rubato serves constantly to moderate whatever tempo is proposed for each ensuing section, such fluctuations can only be meaningful if securely attached to a recognisable norm from which to deviate and to which to return.

Despite his apparent insistence on a quasi-contrapuntal voice leading (designated by up or down-facing stems), I notice that, for most of the time, he purposely divides his mainly four-part harmony into three rather than four distinct lines – writing, as it were, for string trio with double stopping rather than for string quartet. The notion of a single harmonic voice set above, below or between two (sometimes three) purely melodic ones seems to suggest a sustained in-filling which, when played as such, gives a quite special substance to the mostly middle-register chording. While one ought of course to question the point at which the textural ambiguity of bars 1 and 2 starts to anticipate the partially contrapuntal outcome of the harmonic close in bars 3 and 4, the fact that Berg left the matter open to conjecture has itself to be regarded as a clue to horizontal connections that are best thought of as positively acknowledged rather than actively promoted in terms of a falsely linear independence. And since I have already seen that he is meticulous with regard to punctuation (of phrases, motifs, or phrases with motivic subdivisions), I shall proceed, as with Beethoven, to pay the utmost attention to his articulating intentions: by joining only what the composer joins, I may begin not only to unravel his motivic purpose but to let air into a rhythmic texture too often deprived of rests or registral contrast and – most importantly – to uncover a more explicitly harmonic sostenuto by giving longer notes (wherever they occur) their full durational weight.

For instance, following on from the textural thinning from three to two parts at

Ex. 11   Berg: Sonata for Piano, op.1, bb. 1–19.

the end of the second system (bars 7–8), the re-entry of the third part – now as an independently supportive bass line – should have real harmonic impact; and if the slowing down indicated here is so paced as to take account of the evidently cadential role of this bass (E–A, A–D), the composed ritenuto of the middle-voice thirds should more easily fall within the bounds of a harmonically goal-directed phrase. I begin to sense that the fleshing out of such longer-term relationships is likely to prove of ongoing importance if the kind of structural contrasts Berg seems already to be advancing are to make themselves properly felt. Looking back over the retrospective evidence of this one page, I begin to understand that the shift from chromatic to wholetone thirds at the end of the second system marks a turning point between the rhythmically restless, mainly chromatic, mainly middle-register linearity of the opening section and the bass-oriented stability of its harmonic close.

But although ensuring the audibility of relatively long durations would in itself be to include a degree of harmonic continuity, it is none the less difficult to see how the de-emphasised goal of bar 12 may convincingly be reached by means of harmonic perception alone – particularly when the tempo is slowing and the dynamic weakening. It is then that my attention is drawn to what should perhaps have been obvious all along: that the persistently downbeat emphasis of a threefold rhythmic ostinato is being used deliberately to pace the metrical decline of the phrase as it unwinds towards the eventual take-off point of its pianissimo arrival.

Furthermore, if I trace Berg's phrase mark from the still slowing upbeat to the section just beginning (in bar 12), I find that it directs me from one repeated-note upbeat figure (at the end of bar 11) to another (at the end of bar 14); and that if the first of these figures is placed not as the uncomfortably slowed down ending it might otherwise have seemed but as the poised beginning to the longish canonic phrase that follows, then the reason for the faster tempo becomes readily apparent. Particularly when I also see that the canon breaks off one bar too soon in the lower voice so as to make way for an 'extra' bass entry (A–E–A, bars 14–15), which, just as before (bars 11–12), overlap the upbeat to reach for a connecting 7th chord across the barline. But while a scrupulous observance of motivic slurs and other punctuating elements will at the outset ensure a textural articulation that includes phrasing, it is important to remark that Berg is not always so specific; furthermore, that he frequently resorts to adding a second layer of quasi-editorial *phrasing* slurs – not, of course, to describe a wholly legato articulation (except in the very short term) but rather to delimit phrases that may or may not include legato elements. Confusing? Yes, but, as with Chopin, any notational ambiguities are at least of the composer's own making, so leaving no doubt that 'editorial' responsibility for their interpretative unravelling is being handed direct to the performer. Which brings us full circle to a point where we can perhaps begin to trust the evidence of what we see as the only reliable starting point for what will eventually be heard.

It is I hope clear that I have throughout been adopting an advocatory stance *vis-à-vis* what might be called 'the Boulez syndrome' – that is, an infinite capacity for taking pains when it comes to the business of translating what may be seen into what ought to be heard. And if the breathtaking clarity of Boulez's own early performances of symphonic masterpieces was the result merely of a sensational accuracy, then accuracy is clearly an exemplary way to begin when it comes to laying the foundations for interpretative performance. Accuracy must certainly have been the starting point for Aloys Kontarsky as he prepared to embark on his 1965 LP recording (recently reissued on CD by Sony Classical) of Stockhausen's Piano Pieces I–XI; yet in these remarkable performances precision is made to seem entirely coincidental to a concentration that evidently stems from a quite extraordinary ability to listen as well as to count, to listen not only to where and how notes begin but to exactly when and in what manner they cease to sound. It is in this concluding instance not the music itself I offer as example but Kontarsky's supremely musical attention to its structure-revealing detail.

Notes

1. Eulenberg pocket score no.736.
2. Charles Rosen (1971, rev. 1976), *The Classical Style*, Faber; new Expanded Edition (1997), Norton, New York.
3. See his letter to Karl Holz of August 1825 in A. Tyson (ed.) (1967), *Selected Letters of Beethoven*, trans. Emily Anderson, London & New York, pp. 233–35.
4. Eugen Lehner, violist in the Vienna (later the Kolisch) Quartet, remembers Schoenberg's oft-repeated dictum that clarity should be 'the alpha and omega of music making' and that 'you must play music so that the last person in the hall should be able to write up in the score what you do'. (In an interview with Joan Allen Smith, as quoted in her book *Schoenberg and his Circle – A Viennese Portrait*, Schirmer, 1986, p. 114.)

5 Freedom of Interpretation in Twentieth-century Music

Charles Rosen

It is not illegal to interpret a work of music against the express intentions of the composer. No jail sentence is imposed for playing a piece wrong. Nevertheless, we often feel that, if not illegal, it is in any case immoral deliberately to flout the author's indications, to play *forte* where the score gives *piano*, or *legato* where *staccato* was demanded. For one school of performance, any deviation from the authentic text is a sin, venial or mortal depending on the gravity of the transgression.

A strict adherence to this austere position creates numerous problems, but we can understand how and why the dogma arose. The opposing school of performance practice that proclaims the absolute freedom of the interpreter ends up in nonsense. Particularly incoherent, however, is an intermediate position that generally holds sway, the widespread belief that we ought not to change the actual pitches the composer has provided, but that we may feel ourselves less constrained by the indicated dynamics, or the phrasing or the pedalling: only pitch is conceived as primary, rhythm as slightly less fundamental, while dynamics, phrasing and tempo are demoted almost to the level of merely helpful suggestions by the composer, who may have miscalculated the dynamics or misjudged the effectiveness of a tempo, it is often felt. But why could not lack of judgement affect the pitches as well? On the most primitive level of argument, we must remark that composers frequently set down wrong notes – they miscount ledger lines and forget to put in the needed accidentals.

There is a place in Schoenberg's Piano Concerto where the composer has clearly not written down what he intended to write, and this in a way much less trivial than the dozens of missed accidentals and slurs which also occur in the score:

Ex. 12   Schoenberg: Piano Concerto, op.42 (piano part only), b. 294.

It is sometimes maintained that we need to check the row in order to discover the errors in Schoenberg, but in fact a sensitive ear and a little common sense are all that is required. Here there are eight three-note chords in both hands, and the first four chords in each hand correspond to the last four chords in the other – except that one note in one chord does not correspond. This is not simply a case of forgetting to put in an accidental: Schoenberg made a mistake in carrying out his plan. I am not sure how many musicians would notice the wrong note in performance, but in practising the work a pianist can easily hear that the symmetry is badly disturbed.

We find a similar mistake in all the editions that I know of the first movement of Beethoven's Sonata no.1 in F Minor, op.2, no.1:

Ex. 13   Beethoven: Sonata, op.2, no. 1, first movement, bb. 73–78.

The manuscript is lost, so we will never know whether Beethoven himself or the engraver wrote D flat instead of B flat in the right hand for the first note of bar 76, but B flat is obviously the correct note, whoever made the *lapsus*. The plan of the sequential harmony is clear enough. This mistake is paradoxically interesting for its triviality: it does not make a great deal of difference here whether we play the right note or the printed mistake. Playing the wrong dynamics in Beethoven, however, is generally a more serious matter, and accents in his works are often more important than pitch. He complained about the original printing of his Three Sonatas for Piano, op.31, that the engraver had often placed the dynamics inaccurately. This implies that following the original text of these works pedantically with great fidelity is a sure way to get it wrong.

With the interpretation of a classic text that has entered the canon, we need to juggle a certain number of elements to keep them in equilibrium: it is useful to know what kind of freedom was expected from the interpreter during the composer's lifetime; we also should know to what extent the composer himself objected to some of the so-called traditional liberties taken with his works (as Beethoven, Chopin, and Rossini, for example, did); the tradition of interpretation developed for a classic text over the years that followed its composition is not irrelevant, as the tradition, however mistaken and unfortunate as it often is, was a direct response to the work itself; finally, we ought to speculate about the frequent disparity between established traditions of performance and revolutionary changes of style. It may even happen that a composer may play or conduct his own works in an old-fashioned manner inappropriate for the new conceptions revealed in his works. It was already remarked in the nineteenth century that Wagner's ideas of staging were reactionary and unsuited to music of such originality. It was not until Appia suggested new ideas of staging based on lighting that a more adequate production of the last works of Wagner became possible, a development retarded for many years by the conservative management of Bayreuth during the decades after Wagner's death. Even more suggestive is the disparity between Bartók's music and his performance style, as Bartók was one of the greatest pianists of his time. The recording of the 'Kreutzer' sonata with Joseph Szigeti is one of the finest examples of Beethoven interpretation. Yet in the interpretation of his own works Bartók's pianism can seem old-fashioned to a point that many details of the composition are left unrealized. His own music demanded the greater clarity and incisiveness of accent developed by pianists in the generation that immediately followed, but in so doing they lost the relaxed grace that characterized the composer's own playing. It is only recently that pianists have been able to recover that grace and combine it with the greater precision called for by the music. A composer's performance may be an excellent guide to interpretation, but never an infallible one. Above all, a simple attempt to reproduce a previous execution leaves no place for the range of freedom of interpretation which is an essential part of all music, except, of course, electronic compositions. (It is curious that the only works of music in which text and performance are absolutely identical are electronic pieces and improvisations, like jazz.)

Constraint and freedom in the performance of new music play roles somewhat different from those in playing works of the past. We do not have to reckon with the weight of established performance practice, and we are at liberty to create our own. On the other hand, the frequent presence of the composer anxious to hear his intentions realized must often put a limit on the performers' caprice. On the whole, performances of recently composed works tend to be inhibited – if only because the performer's understanding of any radically new style is somewhat uncertain, and he is often unsure where the most significant aspects are found, what is to be set in relief, and, in short, how the work is supposed to sound. Following the text blindly is the most frequent solution, and this is perhaps why Schoenberg once said, 'My music is not contemporary, it is only badly played'.

Indeed, the composer today will often demand a certain freedom, and will, in fact, even tolerate performances that shape the work in ways that he could not have expected. The freedom demanded may not be explicit in the text. When I recorded *Constellation-Miroir* from Pierre Boulez's Sonata no.3, the composer asked me at one point to slow down more than I had done. When I pointed out that he had directed a ritardando going from 96 on the metronome to 72, and that I had already reached somewhere around 50, Boulez replied, '*Suivez la sonorité!*' In fact, a greater part of Boulez's music implies a tempo that fluctuates, not quite the same thing as a tempo rubato but not so very different after all. With relatively new works, what is crucial is to determine where an absolutely strict rendition is obligatory and where a greater freedom – of rhythm, tone colour and phrasing – is appropriate. One pianist who played Elliott Carter's Sonata for Piano, said to the composer, 'I have three kinds of piano and three kinds of pianissimo, and you must tell me which one you want where'. The composer himself remarked to me many years later, 'That's not how you interpret a piece, is it?'

In Carter's work, where strictness is necessary is at the junction of two rhythmic systems. In the Sonata for Cello and Piano, for example, the rhythm of the first movement invades the finale towards the end, making an accent every fifth sixteenth-note or semiquaver in the piano while the cello continues its pattern of four notes to the beat. The strictness here is imposed by the ensemble, and no other way of playing it is possible. In the Concerto for Piano and Orchestra, however, the strictness of the rhythm of the major seconds must be maintained in the following passage, or the passage loses its intelligibility and the scherzando quality becomes merely haphazard:

Ex. 14   Carter: Concerto for Piano and Orchestra (2 piano version), bb. 62–67.

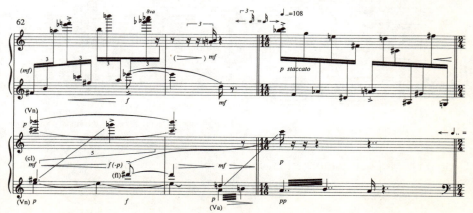

(Ex. 14 concluded)

The triplets in bar 66 are considerably slower than those in bar 62: the ratio is 5 to 7. It is the rhythm of the seconds that remains invariant and gives the character of the music. This demonstrates that if one tempo is basically altered in this concerto, all the others must be altered to preserve the relationships. Freedom of tempo, then, exists in Carter within the various sections, but not in the transitions from one section to another. There are many places in the concerto where a tempo rubato is welcome, but it is largely within the interior of the phrase.

In Carter's Piano Sonata, I have taken liberties of a different nature, which largely affect the sonorities so basic to that work. The sonata is based on the harmonics of equal temperament that characterize the sound of the concert piano. At one point, Carter suggests the reinforcement of these harmonics:

Ex. 15   Carter: Piano Sonata, p. 11, 2nd system.

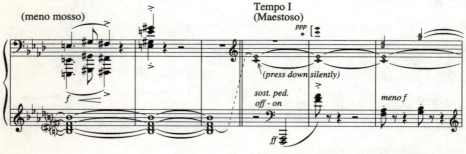

* Omit the notes in brackets if harmonics are audible

I continue, without authorisation, this reinforcement in the Meno mosso that follows:

Ex. 16   Carter: Piano Sonata, p. 11, 4th system.

and press down the harmonics two octaves or one octave above the right-hand staccatos, which I play with the left hand while holding the interval of the third in the lower part with the sostenuto pedal. I even contravene Carter's instructions to press down these harmonics silently: I actually play them, but so softly that the attack is drowned out by the two mezzo forte thirds.

Towards the end of the last movement, we find the harmonics of a fortissimo passage echoed pianissimo in a slower Andante:

Ex. 17   Carter: Piano Sonata, p. 40, systems 1 & 2.

Here, too, it seems to me desirable to hold down the bass with the sostenuto pedal, and to play the fortissimo marcato with the left hand, adding in the right hand the harmonics that will reappear two bars later. The pianissimo echo becomes more intelligible and more effective. This kind of freedom seems to me justifiable as it takes what is already implied in the score but is difficult to hear, and makes it easily audible.

A more radical liberty is one that may be taken very early in the first movement:

Ex. 18   Carter: Piano Sonata, p. 4, 4th system.

Here at the forte, the left hand follows the short accented chord by the harmonics of that chord. Following the invention of Schumann in *Carnaval*, one can play this with an entirely different sonority by putting the pedal down on the staccato accented chord, pressing down silently the harmonic third D sharp/F sharp that succeeds, and raising the pedal. The result is that the harmonics now seem to arise out of the initial chord and to become audible only gradually. When I performed this passage for the composer, his only comment was, 'I didn't realize that you could play it that way'. I am not sure whether this indicated approval or not, but at any rate there was no explicit protest, and I have continued to perform the passage as I have indicated. It gains an interesting and unusual sonority, and the technique also clarifies the structure of the material by demonstrating the importance for the work of the resonance of the overtones. Any liberty seems to me justified if it does not substantially alter the composer's conception but makes it more effective. I am aware that this opens the door to all kinds of strange alterations if the performer can convince himself that he knows the composer's intentions better than the composer himself.

A problem for performers is raised when the composer has, a considerable time after composition, added indications for performance of a nature not directly implied by the original text. The pedal indications in his Piano Variations that Webern added for Peter Stadlen are a good example. It may be that these indications (and the dramatic expression marks added as well) were a part of the original conception. It is also possible that, Webern, made uneasy in later years by the provocative austerity of the score, was trying to attenuate the strangeness of the piece, make it sound less idiosyncratic, more normal.

In this case, as in so many others, the performer has an astonishing freedom of choice. In interpreting a work of twentieth-century music, we can emphasize its radical nature, or we can try to indicate its nineteenth-century origins. I think that it has become increasingly obvious in our time that Schoenberg sounds best when his music is played as if it were by Brahms – it is indeed that aspect of his music that was attacked so polemically by the young Boulez in his article that created a small scandal, 'Schoenberg is dead'.[1] Stravinsky, on the contrary, does not benefit by trying to make his music sound as if it were by Rimsky-Korsakov. In any case, the most successful performances of contemporary works, as of the music of the past, are those that only give the illusion of remaining faithful to the text while they hide a genuine and deeply rooted freedom of interpretation.

Notes

1. Pierre Boulez (1968), 'Schoenberg is Dead' in *Notes on an Apprenticeship*, trans. H. Weinstock, Knopf, New York.

6   The Body in Performance
Eric Clarke and Jane Davidson

Introduction

In common with the dominant trend in modern cognitive psychology, a great deal of the psychology of music has adopted an almost entirely 'disembodied' approach to its subject matter. The preponderance of a radical mentalism has resulted in listeners and performers being regarded as information-processing devices, with inputs and outputs coming to and going from a central 'unit' which is located firmly in the head and which has little connection with anything as physical as an arm, a leg, a hand – or even an ear. If this slightly overstates the case even for the work of the 1970s and 1980s (where the more psychoacoustical end of the psychology of music was rather more aware of, and responsive to, physical realities), there has definitely been a growing awareness in the 1990s of the advantages of a rather more realistically corporeal approach (mirrored in some parts of psychology more generally e.g.: Harré, 1991; Varela, Thompson & Rosch, 1991; Shilling, 1993; Smith, 1996; Yardley, 1997). In particular, significant numbers of recent publications focusing on performance have incorporated a bodily element, or a concern with physical movement, and there is now the prospect of a rather less starkly dualistic approach to music (which for a long time has been elevated to a position of almost pure cerebral abstraction). The aim of this chapter is to explore some aspects of the role of the body in performance, focusing on the case study of two performances by the same pianist of a single piece of music.

Since Classical Greek writings on music, it has been recognised that there is a very intimate link between musical sound and the bodily movements involved in its production (see Barker, 1989). Certainly in the nineteenth century, many pedagogic texts refer to the essential interplay of musical features, expressive intention and the body. Baillot, for example, in his *L'art du violon* of 1834 (cited in Stowell, 1985) suggested that different types of movement are necessary to produce different musical tempi. He remarks that the Adagio tempo requires 'more ample movements' than the Allegro where notes are 'tossed off', whereas in Presto there is 'great physical abandon'. It is only quite recently that this relationship has been demonstrated empirically, however, and the full implications of such a relationship pursued. Nonetheless, in attempting to incorporate a greater recognition of the role of the body and of physical motion in musical performance, care needs to be taken to distinguish between at least three different levels or manifestations of these phenomena: truly physiological factors, cognitive representations, and the more metaphorical use of a physical or bodily language in talking about music.

There are undoubtedly physiological and anatomical factors involved in our understanding of musical performance, most obviously in motor control, but also in the sense of motion that is characteristic of our perceptual response to expressive performance (cf. Todd, 1994). A number of authors (e.g. Jackendoff, 1988; Lidov, 1987) have proposed that the somatic nature of musical experience, and the sense of motion that we attribute to music, is due to the mediating effect of a body *representation* – a cognitive structure by which we represent our bodies to ourselves, and which is instrumental in our response to any afferent information that has either an actual bodily origin (e.g. vestibular activation), or may be associated with such bodily origins (e.g. sounds or sights that convey a sense of bodily movement). Additionally, it is customary to use the vocabulary of physical motion in an essentially metaphorical fashion in relation to music – such as when we speak of a 'punchy performance', a 'flowing legato', a tonal structure 'moving back' towards the tonic, or more generally still in the cliché that music has 'the power to move people'. There may well be strong links between some of these different phenomena (tonal tension and changes over time in patterns of tonal tension may relate quite directly to muscular tension in a listener, thus linking tonal and physical motion), but there is a need to be wary of a premature physiological, or even physical, reductionism.

Motor programs in musical performance

As a physical skill, musical performance has attracted the interest of cognitive psychologists studying complex spatial and temporal skills. The origins of this interest go back to Seashore (1938/1967), who was one of the first to develop methods for recording the detailed features of performances, but the primary work on music as a skill has been that of Shaffer (1976, 1981, 1982, 1984), and more recently Palmer (1989); Palmer & van de Sande (1993; 1995).

An important theme in Shaffer's work has been the investigation of the structure and nature of motor programs in performance. A motor program, which is an abstract specification of movement, is conceived of as a hierarchical structure which translates an information input into a performed action. Shaffer's work has demonstrated in music that the specification of movement remains quite abstract until comparatively late in this translation process, the evidence of error data from piano performance indicating that performers carry out an unconscious parsing of the musical structure that filters down through the motor program, and exerts its influence even at relatively surface levels. For instance, Shaffer (1981) showed that a performer sight-reading a Bach fugue, who missed a clef change from one page to the next, produced a sequence of errors which preserved the underlying harmony of the passage, and were not simply the notes that would result from incorrectly assuming the continuation of the previous clef. It appeared that as soon as the performer became aware that something was wrong, and while he quickly took steps to discover what he had misread (he corrected the problem within two bars), he essentially improvised with appropriate rhythm and harmony. It is the availability of this structural information at the level of the motor program that provides the supporting framework for such emergency improvisation.

The theory of motor programming represents one significant attempt to understand how it is that abstract knowledge or understanding becomes translated into practical action. In a classic paper, Lashley (1951) recognised the central position this problem occupies in activities ranging from locomotion to language production. At one 'end' of a motor program are the muscle commands which directly control limbs, vocal articulators, the actions of the diaphragm and the whole apparatus of voluntary movement. At the other 'end' is the conscious or unconscious intention to produce some specified behaviour, and the aim of many researchers has been to try to explain how one gets from the one to the other. Although there is some recognition that information flows through the system in *both* directions (abstract intentions are formulated within the constraints of the available motor capacities of the organism), there is nonetheless a tendency to regard motor control as the handing down of a collection of progressively more concrete 'instructions' – i.e. as a predominantly top-down process strongly associated with the much-favoured generative approach to music performance, in which a mental representation of musical structure is seen as the primary, if not sole, source of performance expression (variations in tempo, dynamics, articulation, etc.).

However, a model which portrays performance simply as the flow of information from input through a set of abstract expressive rules to an output effector system is implausibly abstract and cerebral, and the reality is far more practical and corporeal. The body is not just a source of sensory input and a mechanism for effecting output: it is far more intimately bound up with our whole response to music – perceptual and motor – and needs to be recognised as having a far more central role than a simple generative model would suggest. A wide range of other factors, including the possibilities of the instrument, the acoustics of the performing environment, the nature of the audience, the mood and intentions of the performer, and even the performance ideology espoused (e.g. 'historically aware' performance practice) will contribute to the result, sometimes to the detriment of structure (as in the case of an indulgent or wayward performer), but preferably in accordance with an interpretation of structure. Movement, and the human body, are particularly significant in this complex set of relationships for all sorts of reasons – the most obvious being that music is produced by human and instrumental movement, and is thus indelibly stamped with its bodily and instrumental origins.

Movement and performance

The work of a German psychologist, Alexander Truslit, has recently been brought to light (see Repp, 1993). He empirically demonstrated in the 1930s that giving different kinds of movement instruction (or movement image) to performers resulted in measurably different performances. Truslit used these and other findings to claim that a very small number of general movement types, perhaps no more than three, underpinned the kinematic basis of performance. Independently of this, and more recently, other researchers have shown that the timing patterns of spontaneous performance follow the temporal curve of objects moving in a gravitational field (Feldman, Epstein and Richards, 1992; Sundberg and Verillo, 1980; Todd, 1992), suggesting that what sounds natural in performance does so because it mimics the behaviour of physical objects moving in the real world.

Todd (1992) has shown that a model of performance timing and dynamics based on the speed and force of objects moving under the influence of gravity can account rather well for the expression found in musical performances. In a similar way Repp (1992) compared a family of parabolic timing curves (which produce a close approximation to the constant acceleration function used by Todd) with other timing functions in a study that tested listeners' preferences for different versions of a melodic gesture from Schumann's piano piece *Träumerei*. He found that listeners preferred the parabolic curves over other timing functions, and amongst the parabolic curves themselves, preferred parabolas with a symmetrical shape. This is evidence to support the idea that expression in musical performance is in certain respects quite a concrete and physical phenomenon, whilst not denying the importance of more abstract and cultural factors: it simply suggests that we should see these as being overlaid upon, or intertwined with, a rather concrete physical and somatic basis.

Explicit studies of the body in peformance

Within the small number of existing empirical studies explicitly focusing on body movement in musical performance, Davidson (1993, 1995) has demonstrated that information about both structural features and expressive intentions is communicated to observers through body movement. For example, she showed that performances of the same piece of music with three different expressive intentions (to perform the piece without expression, with normal expression and with exaggerated expression) could be clearly differentiated by viewers who watched a video of the performers' movements alone. Indeed, when both aural and visual information were used as stimuli, non-musicians relied almost entirely on the visual information from the body movements for their judgements of the performers' intentions.

In two studies of the performances of a single pianist, Davidson (1994a) explored in detail the kinds of movement that may guide the perceptions of observers/listeners. The first study used a tracking technique to quantify the movements in two dimensions (up/down and forwards/backwards in relation to the keyboard), and showed the expected relationship between the movement size and expression – the more intense the expressive intention, the larger the movement. In the second study, observers' judgements were used to explore the extent to which different regions of the body were informative of the performance intention, demonstrating that the upper torso/head region alone was sufficient for an accurate perceptual judgement ('deadpan', 'projected', 'exaggerated') to be made.

In further studies, Davidson (1991) explored whether the movement information about the expressive intentions of a pianist was available to observers in a continuous stream, or whether it was limited to particular moments within a performance. On the one hand, observers reported a cyclical body sway that was continuously present and expressive, but on the other hand clips of only two seconds of visual material, whilst allowing accurate judgement of expressive intention to be made, revealed that some moments were more obvious indicators of expressive intention than others. These latter results also showed a significant link between the detectable intentions and musical structures, suggesting that the most obvious indicators of expressive intention coincided with important structural moments (a cadence point, for instance).

In Davidson's work, systematic observations indicated that the pianist's cyclical movements emanated from the hip region. Given the sitting position of a pianist, the hips represent the fulcrum for the pianist's centre of gravity, and therefore provide the pivotal point for the movements of the upper torso. This centre of gravity seemed to be the central location for the generation of physical expression. A parallel can be drawn between these findings and the work of Cutting, Kozlowski and Proffitt. Cutting and Kozlowski (1977) and Kozlowski and Cutting (1977) explored the nature of physical expression by examining walkers (in their work the 'expression' was the walker's identity and gender). Their studies showed that any part of the walking movement cycle, and any body joint, provides similarly expressive information. For example, any two-second excerpt from an isolated body part such as the ankle would reveal information about gender and identity. Cutting, Proffitt and Kozlowski (1978) explained these results by demonstrating that there is a point (referred to as 'the centre of moment') within the walker's body which acts as a reference around which movements in all parts of the body are organised. Clearly, the expressive information in piano playing is not equally distributed around the body for the simple reason that all parts of the body are not engaged to an equal degree in producing a performance. A centre of moment for expressive movements at the piano will inevitably be related to the sitting position and the player's centre of gravity, and is likely to be revealed in the large-scale swaying movements that Davidson's study revealed. The notion of a 'centre of moment' thus provides a framework within which to understand the perceptual importance of these swaying movements.

Cutting and Proffitt (1981) refined the description of the centre of moment by suggesting that different parts of the body convey similar expressive information at different levels. This explains the finding that in piano playing there was both continuously available expressive information (the swaying motion) and much more local information (for instance, specific information limited to just two seconds of the performance): that is, some areas of the body are global indicators of expression whilst other local parts of the body provide more specific information. In music, of course, there are many potential demands on the player, and simply coping with the demands of the music itself means that there will be differing technical requirements made on the body. This in turn will affect the presentation of expressive intentions, making some areas clearer indicators of expression than others. Additionally, key musical structures may be the individual points around which expression of the intention is most pronounced. Given the strong evidence that structure and expression are closely related, significant structural moments are likely to provide the focal points around which specific examples of expression will be organised, accounting for the very local nature of some expressive moments.

It would be short-sighted, and indeed misleading, to imply that bodily movement in performance can be accounted for simply in terms of the primary processes of physiology, sensori-motor coordination, and the cognitive mechanisms of expression. There is a powerful social component to the way in which we use and present our bodies – in musical performance no less than in other aspects of our lives. Gellrich (1991) explored how specifically learned mimetic movements and gestures furnish a performance with expressive intention, and suggested that these gestures can have both negative and positive effects on the production of the performance. In the positive sense, they can provide the observer with information which assists in understanding the performance since the gestures can intensify and clarify meaning, even when the movement itself is 'superfluous' to the production of the musical whole. In other words, there can be a 'surface' level of movement – a kind of rhetoric – which the performer adds to the performance. On the negative side, if these gestures are not consistent with the intentions of the performer, they can create physical tensions in the performer, inhibiting technical fluency, and disturbing observers with the incongruity between the gesture adopted and the performance intention.

Support for Gellrich's observations about the negative consequences of incongruous mimetic gestures is found in the work of Runeson and Frykholm (1983), who demonstrated that covert mental dispositions are specified in movement and can be detected by observers. Using the simple task of lifting a box, they asked observers to report what they could see, and discovered that the box weight, and how much that weight differed from the lifter's expectation about the weight, could be detected. Most relevantly, attempting to give false information about the box weight (i.e. by suggesting through movement that the box was heavier or lighter than it really was) as detected by the onlookers. Thus in this case, the lifter's expectation, the deceitful attempt and the real weight of the box are all specified in the movement information.

Clearly, 'surface' gestures may contribute significantly to the production and perception of a musical performance. Indeed, a further interpretation of the finding that some two-second excerpts of the pianist's performances were more richly informative that others could be that mimetic gestures are used at certain points during the performance, and that these movements heighten the expressive impact of a specific moment in the music. A fairly extensive literature on physical gesture in spoken language (cf. Ekman and Friesen, 1969; Ellis and Beattie, 1986) indicates that gestural repertoires emerge which are associated with specific meanings, and it seems to be the case that performers, such as the pianist in Davidson's studies, develop specific gestures for particular expressive purposes – a gestural movement repertoire. How much commonality there is between the repertoires of different performers remains to be investigated.

Having now established some kind of theoretical framework, we will proceed to a specific example, the Prelude in E Minor, op.28, no.4, by Chopin, which will illustrate the way in which the body is involved in performance. Our aim in this case study is to bring together three elements: a structural analysis of the music; expressive performance data from performances of the music; and movement data from the body movements of the performer. Since relatively detailed analyses of both the music and the expressive performance data have been presented elsewhere (Clarke, 1995; 1996), these two aspects will be considered only briefly, and more attention will be paid to the data on body movement, and the relationship between body movement, expression and structure.

Case study

Structure in the Chopin Prelude op.28 no.4

As analyses elsewhere have shown (Clarke, 1995; Schachter, 1994), the prelude (see Example 19) can be viewed either in terms of a binary A A' structure, or in a more singular and unified manner. The primary reason for adopting a binary view is the clear motivic parallelism between the first 12 and the following 13 bars, and the apparent absence of a conventional stepwise voice-leading structure in the upper voice binding the whole piece together. However, as Schachter has demonstrated there is such a unifying upper voice structure, though somewhat concealed within the piece. Thus the critical structural issues for a performer in distinguishing between these two readings of the piece might be:

i)   the amount of emphasis given to the return and potential 're-start' at bar 13;
ii)   the extent to which the first 12 bars are treated as a relatively closed and self-contained unit, as opposed to pushing forwards into the second half (bars 13–25), this in turn affecting the manner in which the first significant 'breaking out' of the melody (bar 9) is treated;
iii) the final cadence – understood as the goal of the whole piece, or as an almost parenthetical, though conventionally necessary, framing device.

Ex. 19   Chopin: Piano Prelude in E minor, op.28, no.4.

While there is much more that can be said about this prelude, the three points above provide some indicators as to how different performances may interpret the music.

The performance data

A professional pianist, RB, gave six performances on the same day on a Yamaha MIDI grand piano. He was neither encouraged to vary his interpretation in a conscious or deliberate manner, nor to stick rigidly to a single fixed way of playing the piece. Of the original six performances, two were selected for analysis, and three types of data were collected. First, MIDI data which permitted examination of expressive timing and dynamics. Second, tracking data for the head position throughout the performances, sampled five times per second. These data were collected from the video frame in which the pianist's fingers first made contact with the keys to the frame in which the final chord ceased to sound, and were obtained by taking horizontal and vertical measurements of the performer's head position in the picture plane of the video for the two performances. The performer sat in a right-side profile to the camera, so that horizontal measurements corresponded to his forward/backward position relative to the keyboard, while the vertical measurements corresponded to the up/down position of his head relative to the floor. Since the forward and downward movements and backward and upward movements are very highly correlated, rendering one set of data essentially redundant, only the horizontal data (forward/back) are discussed here. The third kind of data were expressive gestures, defined as discrete moments in the performances where a distinct gesture of some kind could be observed. These were identified and collected by the authors, who undertook repeated systematic observations of the performances. From these, specific selection criteria were developed which enabled all the distinctive individual expressive gestures to be characterised. These expressive gestures fell into two broad categories: head and hand movements. For the purposes of this chapter only the head gestures are discussed, again due to the very high correlation between the occurrence of head and hand gestures.

These data are shown in Example 20, the top and bottom panels providing information about each of the two performances (P1 and P2) in real time and musical location. The data comprise the dynamic profile of the right hand (top line), the note-by-note tempo track for the right hand (second line), the note-by-note tempo track for the left hand chords (third line), the expressive gesture locations (fourth line) and the head-position tracking data (fifth line). Within each panel, the top line shows the relative dynamic level of notes in the right hand (derived from MIDI velocity values); the second line shows the relative tempo for each note of the right hand; the third line shows the same tempo information for the left hand; the downward-pointing arrow heads indicate the location of expressive gestures; and the lowest line shows head position, recorded five times per second, with higher values on the graph corresponding to more backward positions, and lower values more forward positions. The location of the end of a number of

Ex. 20   Clarke & Davidson: Performance Graphs (authors' copyright).

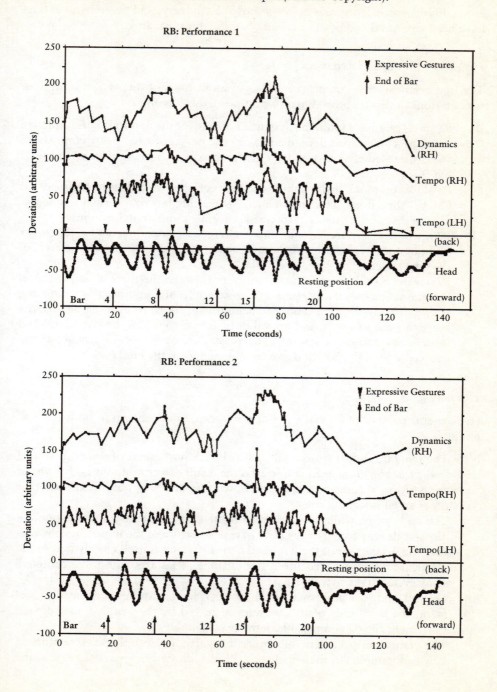

bars is shown with upward-pointing arrows on the x-axis to facilitate cross-reference with the score. All values on the y-axis are arbitrary, and the individual lines have been separated and positioned simply to facilitate reading.

Expressive timing and dynamics

The two performances contain a number of indications of the two structural interpretations outlined above (binary or unitary), these being:

i)   P1 starts relatively loud, the dynamic falling over the first four bars, and then rising to a significant dynamic peak in the passage at bar 9; by contrast P2 starts more quietly, and builds quite gradually to a lower dynamic peak at bar 9;

ii) P1 slows up more at the link/divide between the two halves of the piece (at bar 12) than does the second which, by making less of a formal boundary, achieves a stronger sense of forward movement and undivided unity;

iii) P2 introduces a more extreme and prolonged ritardando from bar 21 to bar 23 than does P1, heightening, almost to the point of collapse, the deferral of the final cadence;

iv) P2, as the corollary of iii) above, pushes through the three-chord cadence, maintaining a constantly *rising* dynamic profile, and significantly shortening (i.e. increasing the tempo on) the penultimate chord so as to emphasise the sense of push towards, and arrival on, the final tonic. P1, by contrast, has a more conventional constantly decreasing tempo through the cadence, coupled with a significant *decrease* in dynamic on the final tonic.

Tracking data

Five general points can be made about the tracking data shown in both parts of Example 20:

i)   The regular, almost sinusoidal forward/back movement of the head shown in the tracking data of Example 20 is the result of a continuous body sway in the performer, sometimes tracing a linear forward/back outline, and at other times an elliptical outline.

ii) The body sway, while maintaining a regular pattern, does not correspond in any simple way to the metrical or phrase structure of the music, nor the regular rubato pattern of the left hand chords (which is itself closely tied to the metrical and phrase structure). For example, P1 starts with three complete sway cycles in the first four bars.

iii) Overall, the two performances show very similar amounts of head movement, the amplitude of the 'waveform' traced by the head's forward/back movements being comparable in the two figures.

iv) The pianist adopts a generally more 'forward' (i.e. into the keys) posture in P2 (see Example 20) than he does in P1 as indicated by two measures: a) the mean head position is −32.2 in P1 and −38.2 in P2, and b) in P1 the head position moves 'backward' of the resting position (marked with a horizontal line in the two figures) on thirteen occasions, as compared with eight occasions in P2.

v)   P1 shows a more continuous and regular pattern of body sway than does P2: there are sixteen clear 'peaks' (i.e. backwards to forwards movement changes) in P1 and twelve in P2.

vi)   Although there are strong similarities between the tracking data for the two performances, the positions of peaks and troughs in the pattern are clearly not fixed in relation to musical structure: there are places where a trough in one performance corresponds to a peak in the other and vice-versa (see below).

We now proceed to a somewhat more specific comparison of the tracking data for the two performances section by section.

a)   Bars 1–4: P1 starts with a more emphatic initial forwards and backwards movement, and with a faster sway frequency over the first four bars (three sway cycles in P1 as compared with two in P2).

b)   Bars 5–8: a similar amount of body sway is present in the two performances, but in inverse-phase relation – illustrating point vi) above: troughs in P1 correspond to peaks in P2.

c)   Bars 9–12: P1 is more active in these four bars, with four complete sway cycles as compared with two and a half for P2.

d)   Bars 13–20: the two performances, though demonstrating differences in the position of the head at the same point in the music, show no difference in the overall amount of body sway.

e)   Bars 21–25 (end): while the periodic body sway continues in P1 (three complete sway cycles), it comes to a complete stop in P2.

Before attempting to understand how these body data relate to the structure of the music and the performer's expressive treatment of it as indicated in the performance data, we present a brief examination of the pattern of specific expressive gestures identified as described above.

Expressive gestures

i)   In the two performances RB uses very similar types of expressive gesture, comprising four distinct types of head movement: a head nod (repeating up/down movement), a head shake (repeating side-to-side movement), an upper body 'wiggle' (an emphatic sideways motion of the torso resulting in the head making a figure-of-eight movement), and a forward or backward surge (a fast and emphatic whole torso and head movement, usually contained within the cyclical swaying movement). These four expressive gestures appear in different sizes and at different speeds at the various locations marked in the two performances.

ii)   The two performances show some similarity in the locations of these expressive gestures, In the first 12 bars, for example, there are head nods/shakes at bars 5/6, 9/10, 10/11, and 11/12.*

iii)   In addition to the locations that are common to both performances, P1 has expressive gestures at 0/1, 3/4 and 12/13, and P2 at 2/3, 6/7 and 7/8.

iv)   P1 starts with a clearer expressive gesture at the upbeat at bar 1 (a head nod) than P2.

v)   The second half of the prelude (bar 13 to the end) shows a similar pattern of expressive gesture locations in both performances, with the following exceptions: a) the first performance begins the second half with distinct gestures at bars 12/13 and 14/15, both of which are absent in the second performance. Indeed, observations of the second performance reveal more of a continuous physical push which is not broken up by local gestures; b) while both performances contain a whole sequence of gestures which run into one another at the melodic climax of the piece (bars 16–18), P2 is somewhat more restrained in this respect than P1; c) at the final three-chord cadence, there are clear expressive gestures on the first and last of the three chords in P1, and only a single expressive gesture (a downward nod of the head that is integrated into the overall forward movement that the tracking data show at this point) on the second chord in P2.

Summary of results

Let us now evaluate these body-movement data in the light of the earlier analyses of structure and expression in the prelude. Expressed in the most simplified terms, the distinction between the two performances as shown by the MIDI data is between a performance that is more concerned with the binary motivic structure and arguably a more surface reading of the music and one which is more concerned with a goal-directed, unified interpretation. Much of the body-movement data is consistent with this distinction, as follows:

Performances 1 (binary, focused on surface) and 2 (unified, goal-directed) display three body-movement differences:

● P1 starts with a more emphatic body sway than P2, and a clear initial expressive gesture (absent in P2); both of these are consistent with the higher dynamic level of P1, and the consequent sense of the first half as a relatively self-contained unit.

● P1 makes more of the first-half climax (bar 9) than P2, as shown in more active body sway in bars 9–12.

● P1 makes more of the sense of 're-start' at bar 13 than does P2 by virtue of the expressive gestures at bars 12/13 and 14/15. The absence of expressive

*The majority of gestures in this passage, and in the piece as a whole, occur across the barline.

gestures in P2 helps to convey a sense of continuous forward motion, and of the unification of the two halves.

- P2 has more of a sense of moving continuously towards the final cadence than P1 by: a) using less body movement at the climax (bars 16–18); b) stopping the body sway in 21–25 (which, coupled with the very extreme ritardando in this passage, heightens the sense of expectation and impending arrival); c) using fewer expressive gestures in the second half of the piece, in particular minimising their appearance in the three-chord cadence so as to avoid breaking it up; d) arriving on the final tonic at the most forward (into the keys) position of the whole performance, and as the culmination of a continuous forward movement maintained throughout the cadence. Arguably, the more 'forward' (i.e. over, or into, the keys) average position of P2 conveys a sense of a more 'inner' or intense interpretation of the music.

Emergent issues

From this summary, and the whole approach adopted in this chapter, a number of themes emerge. First, there is the rather elusive matter of body sway. As we have seen from the tracking data, whilst being essentially periodic, body sway seems neither to have a simple relationship to metrical or phrase structure, nor to be random. It intuitively appears to perform a time-keeping role, whilst also having a linking function: a sway movement that goes on through a phrase boundary helps to keep continuity across sections of the music at the same time that the performer retains an awareness of a structural articulation. It is not unusual to find performers making highly controlled and temporally extended continuous movements between large sections of a work apparently to preserve a sense of continuity and sustained tension. Davidson (1994b) demonstrated just such an effect linking the prelude and fugue sections in a performance of part of Bach's *Well-Tempered Clavier*.

There is a further question here about whether the sway is a response to, or input into, the music – and perhaps the difficulty of answering this question is a reason for striking at the implicit dualism of action and perception that the question itself pre-supposes. The issue can be focused by considering whether a particular movement predicts or reflects a structural moment. We can imagine circumstances in which the performer shakes his/her head *in response* to a particular harmonic change, for example, just as much as we can imagine a *predictive* body movement (for instance a surge forwards of the upper body) which provides the impetus to generate and define a goal in the music. Not only are we dealing here with the vexed distinction between perception and action, but also with the contrast between a passive/receptive relationship between performer and piece, and an active/dominating one – an issue which is as much to do with different aesthetic attitudes and performance ideologies as it is with cognitive theory.

It is also a matter that relates to the issue of 'semantic openness' discussed by

Cook (this volume). A whole variety of sources of information, from the record sleeves and program notes that Cook discusses, to performers' movements (and facial expressions), can provide semantic closure. Audiences may have a range of responses to this: in the context of unfamiliar or confusing music the gestures of live performance may act as welcome pointers; in music that is regarded as being essentially ambivalent or indeterminate they may be intensely irritating and strait-jacketing; where the semantic closure seems directly motivated from within the music, it may be revealing and engaging; and where it seems to have been arbitrarily imposed it may be at best irrelevant and at worst disfiguring. Once again different aesthetic attitudes (this time on the part of members of the audience) are likely to be prime determinants of the acceptability of the degree and nature of physical gesture in performance.

Second, there is the relationship between body sway and the more local expressive gestures. A rather obvious interpretation of this relationship is that while sway conveys, and is a response to, the more global idiomatic and kinematic character of the music, the expressive gestures relate to more discrete and local features. This would, for instance, be consistent with the way in which RB suppresses sway in bars 22 to 25 in P2 as a means of achieving a focused and more strongly goal-oriented approach to the final cadential tonic. Nonetheless it is too simple to propose such a clear separation between the two body movement components when direct observation reveals both that local gestures develop as outgrowths of the body sway, and equally that the speed and direction of the body sway is adjusted so as to integrate with, and make possible, a particular local gesture. Todd (1994) has drawn attention to a distinction between two periodic kinematic components in the human response to music – one with a relatively long periodicity of the order of 5 seconds, the other with a much shorter periodicity of around 600 msec. These two are associated with the responses of 'body swaying' and 'foot-tapping' respectively, and with a functional distinction between a central and a peripheral motor system. This same distinction maps onto the relationship between sway and gesture that we make here, but with the complication that while foot-tapping (and the peripheral motor system) are associated with time keeping, the local gestures discussed here are not.

Finally there is an issue of causality: we neither want to assert that body movement determines the interpretation of structure, nor that a performer's conception of musical structure determines body movement. Rather these are co-determining features of the performance, and we are concerned to try to avoid the rigid mind/body dualism that the deterministic interpretation assumes. This is not a new attempt: Sudnow (1978), in a book concerned with improvisation, argues powerfully for a similar co-determination of performance by the hands and the mind, but in the context of an essentially introspective and phenomenological account. There are few precursors to adopting this kind of outlook within the quantitative tradition that the work reported in this chapter represents. This is not only true for the approach to research that we adopt here, but is a more general feature of our contemporary view of music. As Shove and Repp (1995) point out:

In many cultures this close connection of music and body movement is so obvious as hardly to deserve comment. In Europe, however, the remarkable development of musical notation and of complex compositional techniques over the last few centuries has encouraged a focus on the structural rather than the kinematic properties of music, at least of so-called serious music ... [T]he close connection between music and motion has receded from people's consciousness. (p. 64)

What, then, does the idea that performance is co-determined by musical structure and the body imply? First, it suggests that we are quite wrong to regard the body as under the rigid control of an all powerful 'executive controller' (the mind), with movements being no more than the contingent outcome of an abstract cognitive process. In any musical tradition in which improvisation plays a significant role it is far more obvious that the dynamics of movement may strongly influence (even at times determine) the sonic outcome. The jazz pianist Cecil Taylor is an example of a performer whose music is strongly influenced by the determining character of movement (Lockett, 1988). Second, co-determination suggests that we take rather more seriously the relationship between what might be called the ergonomics of performance (the inescapable physical demands of the interface between body and instrument), the dynamics of expressive movement, and the logic or constraints of interpretation. Ethnomusicologists have been quicker to recognise this relationship, and have taken it further, showing how even the development of the characteristic structures of a variety of musical styles can be traced quite directly to ergonomic factors associated with the instruments on which that music developed. For instance, Baily (1985) has shown how the music of the Dutar, a stringed instrument from Herat (a region of Afghanistan), evolved from music associated with a neighbouring instrument, and in the process acquired characteristics that were specifically related to the ergonomics of Dutar performance. In the classical-music culture of the West, a whole variety of ideological resistances to this kind of outlook (not least a belief in the inviolable nature of the logic of absolute music) have held the body firmly at bay. But if gesture and physicality play a much more integral role than has hitherto been recognised in specifying the character of a performance, and even of aspects of musical style, it opens up a fascinating field of enquiry in which the relationship between the intrinsic dynamics of the human body, the social codes of bodily expression – a kind of gestural rhetoric – and the practical interpretation of musical structure might be studied.

Bibliography

Baily, J. (1985), 'Music structure and human movement'. In P. Howell, I. Cross and R. West (eds): *Musical Structure and Cognition*, London: Academic Press.

Barker, A. (1989), *Greek Musical Writings, Volume II: Harmonic and Acoustic Theory*, Cambridge: Cambridge University Press.

Clarke, E.F. (1995), 'Expression in performance: generativity, perception and semiosis'. In J. Rink (ed.), *The Practice of Performance*, Cambridge: Cambridge University Press.

Clarke, E.F. (1996), 'The semiotics of expression in musical performance', *Contemporary Music Review*, 16, 325–41.

Cutting, J.E. and Kozlowski, L.T. (1977), 'Recognising friends by their walk: Gait perception without familiarity cues', *Bulletin of the Psychonomic Society*, 9, 353–56.

Cutting, J.E. and Proffitt, D.R. (1981), 'Gait perception as an example of how we may perceive events'. In: R.D. Walk and H.L. Pick (eds.), *Intersensory Perception and Sensory Integration*, New York: Plenum.

Cutting, J.E., Proffitt, D.R. and Kozlowski, L.T. (1978), 'A biomechanical invariant for gait perception', *Journal of Experimental Psychology: Human Perception and Performance*, 4, 357–72.

Davidson, J.W. (1991), 'The Perception of Expressive Movement in Music Performance'. Unpublished Ph.D. thesis, City University, London.

——— (1993), 'Visual Perception of Performance Manner in the Movements of Solo Musicians', *Psychology of Music*, 21, 103–13.

——— (1994a), 'What type of information is conveyed in the body movements of solo musician performers?' *Journal of Human Movement Studies*, 6, 279–301.

——— (1994b), 'A Case Study of PH's movements in the performance of J.S. Bach', Paper presented at a meeting of the Society for Research in Psychology of Music and Music Education, University of Sheffield, October 1994.

——— (1995), 'What does the visual information contained in music performances offer the observer? Some preliminary thoughts'. In: R. Steinberg (ed.), *Music and the Mind Machine: Psychophysiology and Psychopathology of the Sense of Music*, Berlin: Springer Verlag.

Ellis, A. and Beattie, G. (1986), *The Psychology of Language and Communication*, London: Weidenfeld & Nicolson.

Ekman, P. and Friesen, W.V. (1969), The repertory of nonverbal behaviour: categories, origins, usage, and coding. *Semiotica*, 1, 49–98.

Feldman, J., Epstein, D., & Richards, W. (1992), 'Force dynamics of tempo change in music', *Music Perception*, 10, 185–204.

Gellrich, M. (1991), 'Concentration and Tension', *British Journal of Music Education*, 8, 167–79.

Harré, R. (1991), *Physical Being: A Theory for Corporeal Being*, Oxford: Blackwell.

Jackendoff, R. (1988), *Consciousness and the Computational Mind*, Cambridge, Mass.: MIT Press.

Kozlowski, L.T. and Cutting, J.E. (1977), 'Recognising the sex of a walker from a dynamic point-light display', *Perception and Psychophysics*, 21, 575–80.

Lashley, K.S. (1951), 'The problem of serial order in behaviour'. In L.A. Jeffress (ed.), *Cerebral Mechanisms in Behaviour: The Hixon Symposium*, London: Wiley and Chapman & Hall, p. 122–30.

Lidov, D. (1987), 'Mind and body in music', *Semiotica*, 66, 69–97.

Lockett, M. (1988), 'Improvising pianists: aspects of keyboard technique and musical structure in free jazz – 1955–1980'. Unpublished Ph.D. thesis, City University, London.

Palmer, C. (1989), 'Mapping musical thought to musical peformance', *Journal of Experimental Psychology: Human Perception and Performance*, 15, 331–46.

Palmer, C. & van de Sande, C. (1993), 'Units of knowledge in music performance', *Journal of Experimental Psychology: Learning, Memory and Cognition*, 19, 457–70.

——— (1995), 'Range of planning in skilled music performance', *Journal of Experimental Psychology: Human Perception and Performance*, 21, 947–62.

Repp, B.H. (1992), 'Diversity and commonality in music performance: an analysis of timing microstructure in Schumann's *Träumerei*', *Journal of the Acoustical Society of America*, 92, 2546–568.

——— (1993), 'Music as motion: a synopsis of Alexander Truslit's (1938) *Gestaltung und Bewegung in der Musik*', *Psychology of Music*, 21, 48–73.

Runeson, S. and Frykholm, G. (1983), 'Kinematic Specification of Dynamics as an informational basis for person-and-action perception: Expectations, gender, recognition, and deceptive intention', *Journal of Experimental Psychology: General*, 112, 585–615.

Schachter, C. (1994), 'The prelude in E minor op.28, no.4: autograph sources and interpretation'. In J. Rink and J. Samson (eds): *Chopin Studies 2*, Cambridge: Cambridge University Press.

Seashore, C. (1938); *Psychology of Music*, McGraw-Hill. Republished by Dover Books, New York, 1967.

Shaffer, L.H. (1976), 'Intention and performance', *Psychological Review*, 83, 375–93.

——— (1981), 'Performances of Chopin, Bach and Bartók: studies in motor programming', *Cognitive Psychology*, 13, 326–76.

——— (1982), 'Rhythm and timing in skill', *Psychological Review*, 89, 109–23.

——— (1984), 'Timing in solo and duet piano performances', *Quarterly Journal of Experimental Psychology*, 36A, 577–95.

Shilling, C. (1993), *The Body and Social Theory*. London: Sage.

Shove, P. and Repp, B.H. (1995), 'Musical motion and performance: theoretical and empirical perspectives'. In J. Rink (ed.), *The Practice of Performance*, Cambridge: Cambridge University Press.

Smith, J.A. (1996), 'Beyond the divide between cognition and discourse: using interpretative phenomenological analysis in health psychology', *Psychology & Health*, 11, 261–71.

Stowell, R. (1985), *Violin Technique and Performance Practice in the Late Eighteenth and Early Nineteenth Centuries*, Cambridge: Cambridge University Press.

Sudnow, D. (1978), *Ways of the Hand*, London: Routledge & Kegan Paul.

Sundberg, J. & Verillo, V. (1980), 'On the anatomy of the ritard: a study of timing in music', *Journal of the Acoustical Society of America*, 68, 772–79.

Todd, N.P. (1992), 'The dynamics of dynamics: a model of musical expression', *Journal of the Acoustical Society of America*, 91, 3540–550.
—————(1994), 'The kinematics of musical expression', *Journal of the Acoustical Society of America*, 97, 1940–49.
Varela, F.J., Thompson, E. & Rosch, E. (1991), *The Embodied Mind*, Cambridge, Mass.: MIT Press.
Yardley, K. (ed.) (1997), *Material Discourses of Health and Illness*, London: Routledge.

7 Expectation and Interpretation in the Reception of New Music: A Case Study

Adrian Beaumont

It is surely self-evident that any listener's initial response to a piece of music must be conditioned by previous listening, and in some cases also reading and perform-ing, experiences. Such conditioning, moreover, is not merely applicable to music written in a contemporary idiom that the listener may find disturbingly advanced. How instructive it would be, for example, to be able to take a group of people who had never heard any music written later than Beethoven and have them listen to Berlioz's *Symphonie Fantastique*, some with and others without any prior knowledge of the 'programme'. What an interesting and illuminating discussion would surely follow. For the most part, however, the range of listening experi-ence, if not the extent of it, is likely to be fairly similar in the case of a group of people hearing a piece of nineteenth-century music for the first time and expecta-tions are unlikely to vary too widely in this circumstance. But in the case of a piece of new music, being heard for the very first time by anyone, the experience brought to bear by the audience will cover a very wide range indeed, with a con-siderable gulf separating the two extremes of those who have heard, perhaps also played, and been well impressed by other music from the same composer's pen and those who have persuaded themselves that they do not like modern music and therefore rarely permit themselves to suffer it. There are many circumstances in which persons in this latter category might find themselves listening to a new work, the most likely being that it is included in a programme which also features one or more pieces that are already known to them and very much to their liking. The expectations of such an audience will include at one end of the spectrum the anticipation of enjoyment, pleasure or intellectual stimulation and at the other an almost inbuilt resolve to dislike, hate and resist, together of course, with almost every position in between. When new works are heard in the context of other contemporary music the attracted audience as a whole will probably be more

93

sympathetic, though even here it is likely to include listeners who have been induced, for one reason or another, to undertake such an experience for the first time. In the case of a concert given by an ensemble whose unusual combination of instruments means that its repertoire is entirely contemporary and that its particular sound is neither widely known or easily imagined, even an audience of the committed and open-mindedly curious is likely to come with widely varied experiences and expectations.

This brings me to the subject of our case study: Jonathan Harvey's *The Riot* for flute, bass clarinet and piano. It was commissioned for Het Trio of Amsterdam,[1] a noted ensemble which not unnaturally specialises in the performance of new music, by the 1994 Colston Symposium of Bristol University which was devoted to 'The Intention, Reception and Understanding of Musical Composition'. The new work was not only to be heard for the first time at a concert given during the symposium but was to be the subject of a formal discussion scheduled within its proceedings. The new piece was in fact performed twice in the middle of the concert, once on either side of the interval, and the formal discussion took place the following morning. As chairman of this discussion I was assisted not only by the performers and the composer himself but by three other colleagues who were asked to formulate their immediate reactions to the work. Two of them, a young analyst and a composer, were also requested to remain totally innocent of the score until after the discussion had taken place. The third, a very experienced analyst, had the benefit of looking over the composer's shoulder at the score during part of the final rehearsal and, not surprisingly, contributed a very detailed and clear-headed response to the work which future experience may amplify but will probably modify very little. My concern in this essay, however, is with more basic responses, in particular with the way that not only expectation but also interpretation in the light of our own personal experiences play their part in the reception of new music.

In our case study the first point of speculation concerned the nature of the sounds that might be expected from a work composed for a combination of instruments which a considerable proportion of the conference members, let alone the audience as a whole, had not previously experienced. Those who had heard this striking ensemble before came with memories and therefore expectations of remarkable virtuosity and vitality. As to the rest, whether the fact that a new work is scored for an unimagined combination of instruments or uses instrumental or vocal techniques that the listener has not previously experienced, constitutes an additional barrier or provides an exciting and helpful stimulus is not easy to assess. Doubtless it varies from one individual to another and is closely related to a more general open-mindedness. In this instance the first two items in the programme, by the Dutch composer van Roosendael and the Italian Mario Garuti[2] helped to level the playing field and by the time the new piece was heard the basic sounds and sonorities of this unusual ensemble should have been well established in everyone's aural senses. Later, the composer was asked if he had been in any way influenced in the composition of his work by the context in which it was to be heard. The point was made that in this particular programme *The Riot* seemed to be a more traditional piece – not in the textures or the sounds but in the compositional procedures and the thinking behind them – whereas in a concert of really traditional works it would have stood out as *un*traditional. The composer replied that he had not composed with any sense of context and was inclined to think that it was not really possible since one must expect a piece to be heard in a variety of contexts. Nevertheless the question does raise interesting matters relating to expectation and interpretation, even if only on that basic level of perception of a work in more or less traditional, meaning more or less accessible, terms.

Expectations of a work may well begin with its title. As Schumann puts it in one of the string of aphorisms with which he opens his celebrated article on Berlioz's *Symphonie Fantastique*, 'we are accustomed to judge a thing by the name it bears: we make certain demands upon a "fantasy", others upon a "sonata" '.[3] Harvey called his piece *The Riot*, a title which would arouse quite different expectations if it were applied to a choral work or an orchestral symphonic poem. In those circumstances it would surely suggest some sort of revolution or at least the kind of lively 'demonstration' that the same composer conjured up in his *Ludus Amoris*[4] some twenty-five years earlier. In the context of an instrumental piece known to be scored for modest forces, expectations must be for a far less dramatic interpretation of what appears to be an evocative title, but they are aroused none the less. When it dawns on us that *The Riot* is a neat but quite uncomplicated anagram of Het Trio such expectations are further reduced but we are still wondering whether the title has any greater significance. The composer's programme note might be expected to throw some light on this question but we were deliberately denied access to it until the interval between the two performances. Asked, just before the concert began, whether the title had any significance beyond the anagram, the composer's rather enigmatic reply was that it was 'not inappropriate to the nature of the music'. Later he told us that it had occurred to him quite early in the composition of the work and that it 'seemed to encapsulate a direction which could be built on further'. But the programme note, when it arrived, made no mention of the matter: as far as the author was concerned it appears that the title had more or less served its purpose once we solved the pretty puzzle.

Yes titles and headings *are* important, particularly when the composer has something to suggest that is external to the purely musical concepts he is pursuing. Liszt was very much aware of this when, in the general preface to his symphonic poems, he referred to the programme as being intended 'to guard the listener against a wrong poetical interpretation' of the music. This notion was brought home to me very strongly on the occasion of the first performance of Raymond Warren's Third Symphony ('Pictures of Angels'). Having attended the first half of another concert half a mile away I had no copy of the programme. Seconds before the performance began I obtained a glimpse of the movement's headings: 'Nativity', 'Agony in the Garden' and 'The Opening of the Tomb'. Without that brief intelligence I would certainly have missed some of the secrets and treasures of a work that is as graphic as it is moving and as powerful as it is beautiful.

Another factor that sets up expectations in the mind of the listener is familiarity with other works by the same composer. One of our three reviewers, at that time a colleague of Harvey at Sussex,[5] observed that knowing the person and being familiar with his general philosophical ideas was part of the paraphernalia that conditioned *his* expectations, as of course did knowledge of other recent works such as the opera *Inquest* (In Quest – another crossword clue title) *of Love*. Those expectations had been further coloured by a lecture the composer had given on his *Ritual Melodies* and his identification in that work of no less than sixteen significant melodic ideas. How would the new work relate to these and should he be looking to spot a considerable number of melodies as he listened to it? Another reviewer had wondered beforehand whether the work would reveal the 'mystical' side of the composer's nature or whether he would be more concerned with exploiting the special effects available – microtones, multiphonics, Harry Sparnay's celebrated 'slap-tongue' and Harrie Starreveld's equally distinctive 'jet-whistle'.[6] Such speculations can only be indulged in by those whose experience of the composer's previous work and also of the ensemble concerned is considerable and will almost certainly be beyond the scope of the large majority of the audience.

It seemed not unreasonable that the chairman of the discussion should be one of those few who had previously seen the score and I therefore spent a couple of hours getting to grips with its intricacies. I should say that what I next present is not in any sense a studied analysis, but rather my initial reactions to (or interpretations of) the music as they occurred. With the aid of a few quotations, this exercise will also serve to establish some reference points that should help to make matters raised during the subsequent discussion easier to follow. Naturally I too brought experience and therefore expectations to the task. Familiarity with some of Harvey's previous music led me to anticipate three things in particular; first that the potential of the instrumental group in terms of colour and sonority would be exploited to the full; second that the basic material would be worked out with a high degree of technical skill and intellectual discipline; and third that all this would take place within a coherent and satisfying structure. My academic mind began by insisting that I seek out that structure. I saw at once that the lively opening statement, notwithstanding its clear reminiscence of the *Symphonies of Wind Instruments*, held out the promise that my first two expectations would be fulfilled (Example 21). Incidentally this identification with the opening of the *Symphonies of Wind Instruments*, observed by others too, including the performers, was acknowledged by the composer who 'wanted a ritualistic sort of theme and therefore allowed it to stand'. I very soon learned from the score that the entire piece is derived from the opening material. With the aid of a little imagination I was also able to gain a fairly accurate idea of the actual sounds, though I didn't always quite anticipate the *pace* of the music. (This of course can be a problem even for the composer himself, especially an inexperienced one, and is one of the commonest areas of misjudgement for the student.) The structure did not leap out at me on first or even second reading and I therefore began to look for possible points of

Ex. 21   Harvey: *The Riot* for Flute, Bass Clarinet and Piano, opening.

articulation. One or two particular moments had struck me quite forcibly and I
returned to them in hope. It seemed that the start of a flowing bass clarinet solo
(letter E in the score) and a senza misura flourish closing onto a firm F (letter J)
could be taken to subdivide the first, quasi-expository section of the piece and that
a second senza misura (letter L) could be seen as the start of a new section and
another way of presenting the material. This process begins with a passage for the
piano that came to be referred to, somehow inaccurately but not entirely unhelp-
fully, as the 'stride' passage (Example 22) and includes also, again on the piano, a
pattern of falling fifths that I immediately felt required some explanation and was
to attract a good deal of comment from everyone (Example 23). The arrival of the
music on a single and prolonged D (letter V) seemed certain to mark a point of

Ex. 22   Harvey: *The Riot*, 'stride passage'.

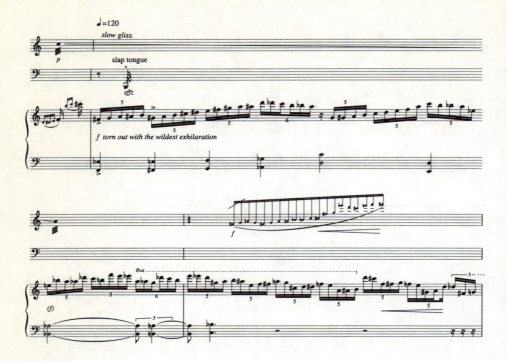

Ex. 23   Harvey: *The Riot*, 'falling fifths' idea (letter N).

significance in the structure but the more I looked at it the less certain I became of that and in the end I concluded that it was simply a moment of complete repose in the middle of a very busy section which then carried on where it had left off. Very soon afterwards a passage of multiphonics is underpinned by the piano's earlier material based on the low A and the three-note cluster around its octave (cf. Example 21 – letter A et seq.) and this suggested a recapitulatory element; again I became less sure of this later. Our with-score reviewer also mentioned it in the context of the inbred expectation that there might be some recapitulatory element but he too concluded that it was not especially significant in a piece that relied on one continuous process. The introduction of new 'jazzy' rhythms after letter AA (Example 24) clearly indicated another way of looking at the material and, equally clearly, the final phase of the piece could be seen to begin at letter HH where the music begins to dissipate its energy and the spacing of events is gradually widened with a beautiful sense of timing that was immediately apparent.

Ex. 24   Harvey: *The Riot*, 'jazzy rhythms' (after letter AA).

It is quite probable that other musicians, whether composers, analysts or performers, would have looked at this new score in a different way. I report here my first thoughts as they occurred. The result of my studies was, I think, that in listening to the first performance, still with score in hand, I was induced to concentrate too much on the notion of structure, trying to discover whether or not my ideas about it made sense. Had I not assumed a responsibility to examine the score and to formulate my impressions of it in advance of the performance I would almost certainly have thought this aspect of the work less important when the opportunity came to hear it. In the event, although I was very much aware of the excitement and the virtuosity of the piece, I listened to the second performance (without score) in a more relaxed way and found that the work's inner logic made my points of articulation far less significant aurally than I had thought them on paper. Our with-score reviewer commented that without it he would not have realised that there were as many as twenty-two changes of tempo in the piece. That is to say that many of the fluctuations of tempo are not easily detected aurally and we must assume that, in the case of so experienced and skilled a composer, we are not meant to detect them, that they are notational devices merely. To that extent again knowledge of the printed score alone could be somewhat misleading.

Performers too come to a new score with expectations and also with prejudices. Het Trio are, as they themselves point out, energetic performers who like to play lively and exciting music. They therefore look for 'happy, sunny' pieces, preferably by composers who also exhibit a sense of fun. Two of them had already recorded a work by Jonathan Harvey and expressed themselves delighted to hear of the commission because the style of that piece suited them so well that they had already had thoughts of commissioning a work from him themselves. A composer could hardly wish for a more congenial sense of anticipation of his music than this and, since he was equally aware of the group's qualities and style, Harvey's piece naturally enough was 'absolutely made for us and we were very happy with it'. Such an idyllic situation undoubtedly makes the first point of musical contact a great deal easier. Performers first have to interpret the notes they see on the page, not just as a set of pitches and durations but more particularly in terms of the intentions behind them, and that initial contact is sure to be less problematical when the expectations of composer and performers coincide so happily. At a workshop in the University of Bristol Music Department a few days earlier the same performers had played a group of very interesting new pieces by third year and postgraduate composers. The pieces were of a gratifyingly high standard but had nevertheless elicited a number of comments and queries from the players concerning notation and the expression of the composer's intentions. But for the assimilation of *The Riot* apparently very little of the composer's time was needed – perhaps five minutes' conversation to clarify a few minor details of balance, adjust the lengths of a couple of fermatas and sort out the precise meaning of an accelerando that led apparently to a slower tempo. This further underlines the close correlation between these particular performers' expectations of this particular composer and his understanding of and response to their needs and capabilities as players.

We turn next to the first performance, remembering that no programme note had been given to the audience at this stage and that for the 95 per cent or more who had not seen the score there could be no reasoned expectations concerning either the nature of the material, its textures, rhythms and melodic shapes or the structure of the piece. A short questionnaire was later completed by some sixty persons, more than half of whom were attending the symposium. Asked initially for first impressions, the audience used generally compatible words such as *exciting* (13), *lively* (8), *energetic* (6), *jazzy* (5), *fun* (4), *exhilarating* (3) and *vibrant* (3), with a couple of dozen others in roughly the same area – *playful, invigorating, colourful, vital, frenetic, humour, wit*, etc. – each appearing once or twice. At this stage only three people commented specifically on the ending – *lovely, moving, ultimate resolution* were the expressions used – so that clearly the more predominantly exciting and energetic aspects of the piece were what registered in the minds of the great majority of listeners. A few others commented that they were more aware of the ebb and flow of energy and of its final dissipation at the second hearing. Again only three people mentioned the difficulty of the work for the performers, perhaps because the level of their virtuosity had so quickly been established by the first two items in the programme. The handful whose reactions were less than sympathetic used expressions such as *bitty and disjointed, disconcerting, total shock*, and in two cases contented themselves with firing salvos at the *horrible* combination of instruments. Most of those who declared themselves unaccustomed to listening to contemporary music also tended to express surprise that the experience turned out to be more palatable than they had feared, which suggests that their expectations had been of a somewhat negative kind. More than half the audience admitted that the title had influenced the way they listened to the piece the first time, if only a little: as one of them put it, 'that's all we had to go on'. The composer's programme note, distributed during the interval, reads as follows:

> *The Riot* is a work in which virtuoso exhilaration is predominant. The game is to throw around themes which retain their identity sufficiently to bounce off each other sharply, even when combined polyphonically or mixed up together in new configurations. Each theme belongs to a distinctive harmonic field characterised by about two intervals; for example, the first is based on fourths and whole tones, creating minor sevenths and, as a further development, linear unfoldings in circles of fourths (or fifths).
>
> From time to time energy runs out and a mechanical repetition of elements takes over, dying away like an electronic 'delay'. Such a process in extended form provides the ending.

Fewer than half the responses received declared this to have been helpful at the second hearing. For some it confirmed that they had been listening in the way the composer evidently intended them to, but a number of others complained that it confused them, either because they could not understand its implications or else because it pushed them into listening in a way they did not wish to. Some hoped for programmatic rather than intellectual enlightenment about the work's puzzles, the 'stride' pattern, the D and, above all, the circle of fifths: expectations can extend to programme notes too. At all events most listeners, even some of the more hostile ones, evidently found reasons to enjoy the second performance more than the first. Some found the overall structure clearer and more coherent: some dwelt on details that they had missed the first time while others just seemed happy to confirm that their first impressions held good the next time round. Two felt that the piece seemed shorter while two more – I confess, I was one, the other being herself a very experienced performer – found the second performance itself more relaxed and perhaps a little less exciting. (The performers themselves were inclined to say that they felt happier with the second performance simply because they had been more 'on edge' in the first. Pressed as to whether this might have resulted in some loss of excitement they were, however, prepared to concede that, on listening to the tape, they might well find the first preferable after all.) As usual with this sort of exercise, one sees so much more clearly after the event how best a questionnaire should have been worded, but one other interesting point to emerge was that those people, whether musicians or non-musicians, who most strongly disliked the work were those who came to the performance not merely in the expectation but almost with the intention of disliking it. Those non-musicians who were apprehensive but at the same time prepared to open their ears to a new experience – which consisted of five unknown works in all – found it to be far more interesting and even rewarding than they had imagined possible.

Some more expectations came to light in the official discussion. Two of our reviewers expressed the dilemma of the listener who has been given absolutely no information about the work at all. For one the clear exposition of themes at the outset resulted in some feeling of disappointment when those ideas were never presented so clearly again. (It is revealing perhaps that even a modernist retains some expectation of a measure of recapitulation.) The other took the opening to suggest a dualistic way of proceeding – wind versus piano – but found that he was wrong. Later he wondered whether motivic development indicated a sonata-type structure and again found that he was wrong. But he confessed himself glad to have his predictions turn out to be unfounded, seeing that as an important part of the composition's make-up, and indeed the element of surprise, the confounding of expectations, has been a part of the composer's armoury for many generations, with Haydn and Mozart amongst its most skilled exponents. Similarly, another member of the audience expressed herself 'glad to have been surprised by the cycles of fifths'. The composer himself was to enlarge upon his question of surprise when given the opportunity to respond and indeed it became clear that the work's three little puzzles that exercised so many minds to so great an extent were regarded by him in precisely that light. The D that I had initially wanted to interpret as a point of articulation of structure when I came upon it in the score had the same effect aurally on one of our reviewers who instinctively wanted to attach a structural significance to it. Our with-score reviewer wondered if in the bareness of that D the work lived too dangerously, wondered whether indeed it was *too* bare. The 'stride' passage produced a rather different set of reactions, beginning with those of the performers. It appears that pianist René Eckhardt is given to playing musical pranks during rehearsals to mystify his colleagues and when he began to play this passage during the first run-through they thought he was joking – another, less straightforward example of expectations apparently being fulfilled. When they discovered that what he was playing was correct and they had fitted the passage together they pronounced it fun. The effect on our scoreless reviewers was similar. One found it a splendid expression of *joie de vivre*. The other agreed but nevertheless found himself wondering where it came from: he was able to satisfy his intellectual curiosity by making the intervallic connection during the second performance when he 'had a plan in mind and didn't have to worry about the overall direction'. It was the circle of fifths, however, that elicited most comment, largely because it was seen as stylistically alien. Even when many of us had made the intervallic/harmonic connection with earlier material, and in my own case that was before hearing the work, we felt that we had to find some other justification for it. Some wondered if it was a quotation, others if there was some extra-musical reason for its inclusion. The composer was pressed for an explanation.

In fact the circle of fifths is not a direct quotation, nor does it have any extra-musical significance, unless the composer's desire to surprise, to make a dramatic effect, is considered to be in some way extramusical. What Harvey had to say revolved essentially around one important point of balance, involving on the one hand the need to justify procedures academically and on the other the desire to surprise his listeners. Thus he had devoted a great deal of thought to the intervallic and harmonic workings of the thematic material and hoped that the various ideas were sufficiently strongly characterised to give structural depth when heard simultaneously or reheard in different guises after a short lapse of time. The discussion led him to the view that after only one hearing, and in many cases even after two, 'purely aural reception was unable to identify clearly the different types of (thematic) material and responded mostly to texture and the ebb-and-flow of energy'. Also 'the flattening out of *all* themes in swing-style, bringing to the fore the harmonic fields, was surely obvious to hear [see Example 24] but nobody commented on it as such. Curious!' He surmised that at the first or even the second hearing one is distracted by virtuosity, colour and energy, which is perhaps unsurprising since he owned that the first image in the compositional process was of the players, of their personalities, their energy and their exuberant virtuosity. Nevertheless he felt that the thematic working should become clear after a few performances.

This intellectual aspect of the composition is obviously very important for Harvey but at the same time he was at pains to emphasise that at certain moments in the work it is less important than the need to surprise. Hence the 'stride' passage which derives from the interval of the seventh (L.H.) and from the chromatic runs (R.H.). The thematic connection is clear enough and yet the passage stretches the contrast within this connection to the extent that its 'jazziness' is surprising. So also with the D: the composer could, he said, explain academically how everything leads logically to it, but he would rather not, for at the same time there is something irrational about it and that, for him, is the exciting part. The intellectual reasons for it are not so important as the irrational aspect, for it is that which occasions the surprise. The same is true even of the circle of fifths. It derives of course from the fourths and sevenths of the opening flute melody (Example 21) but at the same time sounds like another style and 'such an apparent change of style is what stimulates the musical nerves the most. I like that disruption, that challenge to the unconscious to make it belong to the piece. At least it pulls people up: they say "what's happening here?" It's a dramatic device: it's also a joyful, exuberant experience. I just love the effect in Mozart or elsewhere of this kind of collapsing of the music through some kind of abyss – this extraordinary experience of the ground falling from beneath your feet.'[7] This then was a moment, perhaps the ideal moment, when he could indulge his weakness for such a progression, knowing that on the one hand it was academically justified while on the other, and more importantly, it would make his listeners sit up and ask the kind of questions that we were asking – questions that resulted from the music's refusal to fulfil our ingrained expectations about the behaviour of a well-mannered composition. Knowledge of this fact will of course colour all our expectations concerning the next new Harvey work; but the question in our minds then may have to be 'By what means will he surprise us this time?'

I should like to thank Jonathan Cross, Geoffrey Poole, Christopher Wintle, Harrie Starreveld, Harry Sparnay, René Eckhardt and Jonathan Harvey, who provided much of the weft from which the fabric of this essay was woven.

Notes

1. With funds from South West Arts. The work is published by Faber.
2. *Kaida* by Jan Rokus van Roosendael and *Quando Diodoro declina lo sguardo Rivellando* by Mario Garuti.
3. Robert Schumann trans. Paul Rosenfeld (1946), *On Music and Musicians*, New York, p. 164.
4. Faber & Faber, 1969.
5. Jonathan Cross, now a lecturer at Bristol University.
6. On bass clarinet and piccolo respectively.
7. The composer's words, transcribed from the recording of the discussion.

8 The Domestic *Gesamtkunstwerk*, or Record Sleeves and Reception*

Nicholas Cook

The regime of absolute music, which lasted from near the beginning of the nineteenth century until near the end of the twentieth, led critics and scholars to look for the meaning of music in the notes (to the extent, that is, that they looked for it at all). Of course there was a general recognition that musical meaning came with a variety of optional accessories: words, gestures, pictures, and so forth. But they were seen as tangential to the music's real meaning, or even a distraction from it. The shift from a production-oriented conception of music to a reception-oriented one has, however, of necessity changed this perception, for listeners rarely if ever receive the notes alone. Notes are almost invariably accompanied by words; it is a striking fact that the analytical programme note developed just as words were expunged from absolute music, as if the words that were repressed in one place immediately came bobbing up in another. And when, with the advent of recording, the enjoyment of music migrated from concert hall to sitting room, the programme note was gradually transformed into the text on the back of the record sleeve. Here, however, a third artistic medium came into play, for the music was now literally sandwiched between text and image.

The history of the record sleeve is still to be written, but when it comes it will bear the hallmarks of the best historical narratives: a putative prehistory in the pictures on the front of popular and semi-popular sheet music around the beginning of the twentieth century;[1] an evolution that culminated in the glory days of

*The illustrations to this chapter comprise only a selection of the record sleeves included in the conference presentation on which it is based, and the text has been abridged and adapted accordingly; references to additional sleeves may be found in the endnotes. Reproductions are taken from the record library in the Department of Music at the University of Southampton (hence the library plates and other insignia). Thanks are due to all copyright-holders who gave permission for these reproductions (specific acknowledgements will be found in the Notes).

the LP; and a dwindling into the miniaturised art of the CD cover. Rather than telling that story, however, the present chapter has an analytical orientation, focusing on the means by which record-sleeve images contribute to the construction of musical meaning. For, as will become clear, record sleeves transcend their origins in packaging and become part of the product, or at any rate part of the discursive framework within which the music inside them is consumed. Seen this way, they function as agents in the cultural process, sites where meaning is negotiated through the act of consumption.

In the study of popular music there is general recognition of the role played by record sleeve imagery in the construction of the stars who, in David Buxton's words, 'anchor a chaotic aesthetico-ideological discourse and represent it in a "humanized" form by investing the human body itself'.[2] Identification with the star is the means by which fans represent and internalize these values. In this sense it is the star who is bought and sold, rather than his or her music, and so the record becomes the token of a vicarious possession; *In Bed with Madonna* merely makes explicit the aspect of possession that is implied in all star/fan relationships. Now the notion of the star (along with the correlative notion of the fan) is by no means the exclusive preserve of popular music; Kathleen Ferrier, for instance, was clearly marketed as a star in the 1950s and 1960s. On the front of an early issue of her recording of Brahms's *Alto Rhapsody* (Figure 1)[3] she appears elegantly and even glamorously dressed, as if in performance; she holds the score, which interposes between her and viewer and so creates a certain remoteness, an effect that is heightened by the artificial, metallic background against which she appears. Like Madonna, though less blatantly, Ferrier is presented as an icon rather than a woman; the emphasis, in other words, is on what she signifies rather than what she is.

In a bargain-price reissue of this recording,[4] however, the image is much enlarged; the score disappears and the background is no longer intrusive. We seem closer to Ferrier. But the glossy, painted sheen of her lips and skin – the photograph has been touched up with an airbrush – lend an air of unreality to the image. And of course, she still looks away, her attention directed elsewhere. Again, in a recording of Mahler's *Das Lied von der Erde*,[5] Ferrier looks upwards, her gaze apparently focused on the far distance; the light comes from above, touching her hair with fire and giving her an aura of other-worldliness. (As she is pictured singing, it seems clear that this other world is that of Mahler's music.) And something of this persists even in the apparently more intimate image on her recording of the *Kindertotenlieder* (Figure 2),[6] where the pearls, the evening dress, and the make-up have all vanished; this, surely, is the woman, not the icon. And yet Ferrier's gaze is disconcerting. She looks almost straight at the camera, but not quite. You have the impression that she is looking through you. It is as if she were not quite on the same plane as the rest of us. The effect is of a self-possession that borders on unattainability.

In this way, the image is ultimately a teasing one: like the musical masterworks that she brings to us, Ferrier is simultaneously available but unattainable, simultaneously a 'humanizing' presence (Buxton's word) and a sign. That is the equation that defines the star, endlessly deferring the fan's consumption of her or him. It is what prolongs the star/fan relationship and so makes possible the 'anchoring' function to which Buxton refers. And the principle is the same with male artists, even though the presentation may be different. Solomon was as big a star as Ferrier; his name (actually his first name, but used as a stage name, like Madonna's) often appeared on record sleeves in bigger letters than that of the music he played, or its composer. On a recording of Beethoven sonatas, he appears seated at the piano (Figure 3);[7] his head is slightly to one side and his gaze is diverted to the bass register of the keyboard. But his eyes are almost shut; it is as if he were looking not at the keys of the piano but at the music itself.

The effect is heightened in an illustrator's recreation of the same photograph that appears on a quite different recording (Figure 4).[8] Solomon is no longer at the piano (it now appears in the background, as a stylized element of the design). Because of this, his tilted head and closed eyes no longer have any functional significance; they speak of the imagination alone. The illustrator's pen has rendered his hair sleeker, given him lush, feminine eyelashes, and clarified what now appears as a quizzical, or even an ironical, smile. As with the images of Ferrier, we are brought close to the man, but at the same time cut off from him. And again the image seems to say something about the music; it is as if we were being invited into the cathedral of art, but as tourists only, cordoned off and excluded from the inner sanctum. Or maybe the inner sanctum is what lies within the record sleeve, the experience that it promises to those prepared to pay the price of admission. Seen this way, the image annexes to the product the qualities I described in relation to the star: the teasing combination of disclosure and concealment that at the same time proffers and defers consumption.

Perhaps the most famous image of Solomon is the one in which we do not see his face at all (Figure 5).[9] This radical image of the artist, in which Solomon's hands, his immaculately white cuffs, and the keyboard are eerily illuminated against a black background, carries several messages. At one level it speaks of technique, of manual dexterity (somewhat in the tradition of plaster casts of pianists' hands). But at the same time, I think, it suggests a penetration to the heart of the matter, as if Solomon's performance of the Emperor Concerto presented not his interpretation of it but the music itself. Like the images of Solomon's face but in a different way, the image of his hands exudes authority. It also exemplifies one of the things that characteristically happens as image tends towards icon: what might be called the fetishization of the artist. By this I mean the exercise of some visual attribute of the artist that becomes in effect autonomous in its signifying function, arbitrary in its relation to the referent. Thus the image of Solomon's hands entirely subordinates representation to semiosis (there is, after all, no way in which we can be sure that they are actually Solomon's hands at all).[10]

The image of Solomon's hands also exemplifies something else that happens as image tends towards icon, which I shall call visual fragmentation. A good example is a classic image of Toscanini that reveals nothing but his organs of expression

(Figure 6):[11] two hands and a face, with mouth wide open and eyes bathed in shadow. Everything else is swallowed up in the dark, creating an effect of over-powering concentration. Equally dramatic is an image of Karajan that again reveals nothing but hands and face (Figure 7);[12] the conductor's strongly diagonal gesture creates an effect of supreme authority, underlined by the upward camera angle. (It is perhaps no coincidence that both these images are taken from record-ings of the centrepieces of the canon, the Beethoven symphonies.) An image of another Beethoven conductor, this time Maazel, creates an equally strong diago-nal emphasis (Figure 8);[13] from his position at the top left corner, he dominates the entire picture space, and this is again underlined by the camera angle. All of these images are clearly designed to project the star to whose charismatic identity every detail of the interpretation must be subordinated; hence their tonal contrast, the fragmentation of the image into extremes of black and white.

Reinforcing the most stereotyped view of the conductor, such record sleeves tend towards banality. And so do many other images of conductors. Klemperer is pictured wrapped in thought, his head bent, apparently well away from the podium (Figure 9);[14] the lighting emphasizes his furrowed brow, but this time the photograph is full of grey shades. Bernstein is also shown away from the podium (Figure 10),[15] but unlike all the artists I've so far discussed he looks straight into the camera; this almost life-size image communicates frankness, authenticity, lack of affectation. Finally Melvyn Tan and Roger Norrington also look directly at us (Figure 11),[16] their asymmetrically-cropped double image communicating novelty, stylishness, and above all a sense of play. Compared to Solomon's Emperor Concerto sleeve, the Tan/Norrington image suggests a knowing, post-modernist awareness of the reflexivity of style, the intertextuality of all interpreta-tion. (This is quite ironical, of course, in view of Norrington's notoriously positivist stance on authentic performance.)

All these images conform to the simplest model of the record sleeve: what might be called the semiotics of packaging. Inviting but at the same time elusive, full of promise but without substance, they are conceived more or less exclusively in terms of the point-of-sale interface. They have no further burden of signification, or if they do, it is a signification that has to be read (so to speak) against the grain. In short, they don't really say anything about the music inside them.

The record sleeves I have discussed so far have not been designed to sell music as such; they have been designed to sell particular performances of it. Their logic, then, is one of differentiation; their function is to stand out against the back-ground of other recordings of the same repertory. But the scope for image man-agement is much greater when a record company markets a composer/performer whose music is not otherwise available, particularly when the association of artist and record company extends over a period of many years. A good example is Stockhausen, the vast majority of whose recordings have been issued by Deutsche Grammophon (DG). Early covers of Stockhausen's records are not particularly

1

2

3

4

5

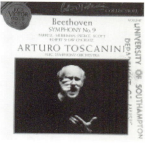

6

7

8

9

10

11

12

13

14

15

16

17

18

19

20

21

22

23

24

25

26

27

28

29

30

distinguishable from those DG used to package other composers. Around 1970, however, DG started to market Stockhausen in a quite different and much more individual manner.

I don't think the date is accidental. In 1967, the Beatles had included Stockhausen's likeness on the cover of *Sgt. Pepper's Lonely Hearts Club Band*; Paul McCartney reputedly listened to Stockhausen's music a great deal at that time. And the link between Stockhausen and the Beatles was reinforced over the following two or three years as both of them, along with many other popular musicians, flirted with oriental sound-worlds and philosophies. DG evidently saw an opportunity to market the guru of Darmstadt to the bead-wearing and joss-stick-burning youth market of the day. So they flaunted Stockhausen's Indian credentials, such as they were, on the full-size photographic cover of *Stimmung*, released in 1970 (Figure 12);[17] this is the record that took California by storm, selling by the thousand to hippies who found it the perfect complement to marijuana. (The sans serif typeface, long associated with Universal Edition and the European avant-garde in general, faces in the opposite direction.) And they decorated the back cover of *Opus 1970*,[18] released in the same year, with an electronic extravaganza unmistakably reminiscent of contemporary rock albums such as the Mothers of Invention's *Burnt Weeny Sandwich* (which also dates from 1970).[19] Perhaps it is significant that this time they left out the 'avant garde' label which had appeared under the DG logo for some time up to and including *Stimmung*.

The next landmark in the image-building process is *Aus den sieben Tagen*,[20] Stockhausen's monument to free (or being Stockhausen, not so free) improvisation. As a set of seven records, this clearly presented the designers with a challenge. They responded with a full-colour slipcase (Figure 13) bearing an appropriately blurred and multiplied image of the composer's face. Inside, the individual covers presented him in grainy, black-and-white close-up, in the manner of a motor-drive photo-opportunity, while the cover of the booklet combined these images into a single pattern (Figure 14). And from this point onwards the serial principle, if it can be called that, dominated DG's presentation of Stockhausen. The covers featured portrait photographs of the composer,[21] his eyes wide open or sometimes staring,[22] his gaze usually averted[23] but occasionally directed piercingly at the viewer.[24] And the new format was imposed on not just Stockhausen's latest compositions, but his earliest ones too; when *Prozession* was released in 1975 (eight years after its composition),[25] it was accompanied by a vintage photograph of the composer, complete with Mao suit, but subjected to the new designer image.

By now, the front cover represented only one image among many, particularly in the case of multi-record sets. As early as *Hymnen* (again released around 1970), DG moved away from the traditional boxed format, usually in black with a single illustration on the front of the box. Instead, they adopted what had by then become the standard format of the rock double album: a double sleeve folded in the middle, making much more space available for striking visual treatment. And that is not the only way in which DG emulated the packaging of rock. On the front of *Kurzwellen*,[26] released at the end of the 1970s, there is a photograph of Stockhausen's group perched slightly awkwardly on some steps behind a railing; this self-consciously wacky picture, surely intended to appeal to the student market, contrasts oddly (but I assume intentionally) with the traditional, full-size DG title plate. And on the back cover they printed a striking image that has nothing obvious to do with *Kurzwellen*, but much to do with the psychedelic art widely used for pop albums around 1970; similar artwork made it to the front cover of *Momente*, released in 1976.[27] What is revealing is that such psychedelic images were by now well past their sell-by date in the pop world. Like the cover of *Prozession*, their adoption suggests a consciously retro element in the image DG were crafting for Stockhausen.

Sirius dates from 1980 and may serve as a summary of the image-building process as a whole (Figure 15).[28] Another rock-format double album, its front presents a witty levitation of the composer; if you turn the sleeve the other way up you can see he is simply lying on a beach. (The printing of the DG emblem at the bottom, instead of its usual position at the top, adds to the effect of inversion – as, perhaps, does the association of sunbathing with a composition about the night sky.) On the back you see an absorbed Stockhausen at the sound projection desk, giving the recording the authenticity of a souvenir (Figure 16); the trailing leads create a wonderfully nostalgic look, considering that the record was released in 1980, just three years before MIDI hit the high street. And when you open up the inside, there are photographs of the performers in artfully choreographed poses (Figure 17). Over many years, DG's marketing of Stockhausen endlessly iterated and permutated images such as these. By doing so, it created a brand identity and positioned Stockhausen's music in the market, establishing it as a kind of niche product.

To this extent, the sleeves of Stockhausen's recordings fit into the standard pattern for marketing stars; they represent a longitudinal study in the semiotics of packaging. But they also represent something else. With its combination of realism and surrealism, its inverted symmetries and saturated hues, and its unusual use of silver, the cover of *Sirius* does not quite exhaust its burden of significance at the point of sale. As an accompaniment to the music – as its *only* authorized accompaniment, since no other recording is available – it colours and stabilizes the work's reception, just as DG's image management colours and stabilizes the composer's reception in general. You cannot quite imagine *Sirius* having any other cover. And to this extent, we can speak of an aesthetic interaction between sight and sound.

If a record sleeve with onion domes on it enters into the music-aesthetic process (Figure 18),[29] that is obviously not because Tchaikovsky's music is in any literal sense like onion domes.[30] It is because the onion domes and Tchaikovsky's music share an attribute that is of at least potential aesthetic significance: Russianness.

Whether that attribute is relevant to *these* works in particular is another question (record companies seem to insist on Tchaikovsky's Russianness almost to the point of marginalization). But it is certainly relevant to his second symphony, the 'Little Russian', the original version of which was only recorded fairly recently (Figure 19).[31] And this image, taken from a painting by the nineteenth-century artist S. A. Mokin, encodes not only Russianness but a number of other aesthetically relevant attributes: the evocation of a perhaps spurious national history; a flattened perspective that throws emphasis onto the picture plane; a pullulating surface of minute, calligraphic decoration, full of repetition and with a complete absence of *chiaroscuro*. All of these are attributes that translate meaningfully to the 'Little Russian' Symphony, and in a sense delineate just those aspects in which it deviates most strongly from the tradition of the Viennese classics.

Decca team Stravinsky's *Pulcinella* with an image that appropriately combines a pierrot figure with dancers whose dresses evoke the eighteenth century (Figure 20).[32] There is loosely neo-classical architecture in the background, and the composition as a whole has a symmetry and balance that matches Pergolesi's music. In all these respects the image efficiently parallels Stravinsky's work; it gives the impression of being painted to order. But it altogether lacks the lightness of touch without which *Pulcinella* would be intolerable. Its thick, encrusted textures look as if they have been laid on with a palette knife; with his exaggerated nose and forced grin, the figure in the foreground looks as though he has walked out of *Pierrot Lunaire*. What this image lacks is supplied by the Picasso drawing of 'Pierrot and Harlequin' that CBS reproduce on Bernstein's recording of the *Pulcinella* Suite (Figure 21):[33] the qualities of suppleness, spontaneity, and transparency. And yet this image, too, is unsuccessful by comparison with the one that CBS couple with Klemperer's recording of the *Pulcinella* Suite: Picasso's *The Three Musicians* (Figure 22).[34]

As the title indicates, this painting does not bear upon the story of *Pulcinella* at all (which is reasonable enough, since *Symphony in Three Movements* is billed as the main item). But it bears upon the principal musical issue of *Pulcinella*, which is the relationship between Pergolesi's music and Stravinsky's adaptation of it. In effect, it draws a parallel between the techniques of synthetic cubism and the recompositional devices that Stravinsky employs. It suggests an aesthetic whereby familiar objects are broken up into their parts and reconstituted in unfamiliar ways. It encompasses the juxtaposition of materials of extraneous origins and natures. It operates by allusion rather than explicit statement. And it subordinates all this to the overriding stylishness, the quality of *chic*, that characterizes both Picasso's and Stravinsky's work. Rather than reduplicating the obvious features of the music, in the manner of Figures 20 and 21, the coupling of Picasso and Stravinsky addresses the central issue presented by *Pulcinella*. Like the Mokin painting coupled with Tchaikovsky's 'Little Russian' Symphony, it sets out a way of hearing the music that is not only possible but also pertinent.

From this we can begin to draw out the basic principles governing the interaction of sound and sight instigated by record sleeves. In order to enter into an aesthetic relationship with the music, the image must possess qualities that are intelligible when transferred to the music. And this implies that what matters about the image is not its objective properties – what it represents – so much as its generic qualities: in other words, the *way* it represents. Strictly speaking, of course, there is no reason why a record sleeve should represent anything at all, and some don't. But just as music habitually presents its qualities raw, so to speak, rather than 'cooked' into the representation of a person, a story, or an idea, so images habitually congeal into representation. There is, then, a general complementarity, a relationship of inversion, between the two media. But this should not obscure the fact that the medium of exchange between them is the generic attributes that are transferred from the one to the other – that both, in other words, have in common.

So far I have only described the transfer of attributes from image to music. But the relationship between the two media operates in both directions, though unequally. No doubt listening to music can alter the way you see an image coupled with it, but it would be perverse to describe a record as a picture marketed together with some music to look at it by. What is of greater consequence is the way in which the images on record sleeves can come to stand for the attributes of the music with which they are coupled. The result of this is the formation of an iconographic vocabulary, a rudimentary discourse whereby the permutation and manipulation of images functions as a means of articulating critical ideas about music. Because we are dealing here with discourse, the focus of my analysis is not so much on individual images as on the clustering of traits within a group of images; in other words, it is the relationship between images that is of primary concern.

I can illustrate this by means of the cover of a recording of two of Mozart's Divertimenti (Figure 23).[35] It represents an idyllic scene on the sea, or perhaps on one of the Swiss lakes; the camera is looking almost into the sun and the water sparkles in the light. The tall piers, crowned with statues, convey the aristocratic ambience and perhaps the intrinsically aristocratic nature of Mozart's music, while the elaborate ironwork provides an analogue of its rococo decorative quality. All this is perhaps so obvious as to border on the banal. But an image like Figure 23 needs to be seen in the context of the other waterscapes that record companies regularly match with a vast diversity of music. For Brahms and Dvorak[36] and for Mahler,[37] for instance, Decca and CBS respectively turn to Caspar David Friedrich's seascapes, in which tiny figures are dwarfed by the sea and gigantic sky; their backs to us, these spectators are absorbed in the wonder of the scene before them. Lyrita couple Moeran with a similar, but this time photographic, image.[38] And on the cover of a Music for Pleasure recording of Tchaikovsky's 'Pathétique' Symphony,[39] there is no sign of human life at all; the empty sea is itself dwarfed by the sky with its dramatically backlit clouds.

What do the music of Brahms, Dvořák, Moeran, Mahler, and Tchaikovsky have in common? They all belong within or on the fringes of the Romantic tradition, and it is perhaps no accident that the music on these recordings is all instrumental.[40] But what this series of examples really shows is the generality of the association of music with sea and sky, and more generally with the sense of absorption in an impersonally sublime nature that Friedrich's paintings capture to perfection. It is easy enough to see why this should be so, in view of the oceanic qualities of music, its ceaseless motion, and its effect of being at once meaningful and devoid of human presence (that is why it is relevant that the music is all instrumental). And Friedrich's mute, absorbed figures could easily be musical listeners. But if the sea stands for music in the iconography of record sleeves, then the Mozart cover with its elaborate gates acquires an altered significance. Like Friedrich's figures, the statues on the piers face out to sea, but they are inanimate and insensible. The gates, seen absurdly from the wrong side so that they lead nowhere, cut off the viewer from the view, so serving to delimit the limitless. The rococo tracery chokes off the scene's potential for sublimity, transforming it into the merely pretty.

By itself, this is bound to seem like over-interpretation; I very much doubt that whoever designed the cover intended to convey the ambivalent impression of Mozart that I have read into it. Whatever plausibility it has arises by virtue of its relationship to the horizon of expectations defined by other record-sleeve images, and I hope at least to have established the *possibility* of reading such record sleeves for their critical content. But as I shall try to show, this is by no means the only area of iconography to suggest a strangely ambivalent quality in the reception of Mozart among the record-buying public.

Silhouettes were a fashionable form of portraiture during the period of the Viennese classics, so it's not surprising that record companies have made liberal use of them as a decorative solution to the record sleeve problem. Sometimes the images are original, sometimes not; a typical modern silhouette of Beethoven standing before his piano[41] is recognizable almost to the point of parody, with the composer's stocky figure and curly hair, not to mention the muddle of discarded sketches under the piano. Most characteristic, perhaps, is the fact that Beethoven is pictured alone, wrestling with his muse. Now silhouettes appear frequently on the sleeves of Mozart recordings, but they tend to be rather different in nature from those coupled with Beethoven's music. They tend to emphasize the decorative, the decorous, and the social; although DG appropriately couple Mozart's piano duet and two-piano music with a domestic scene (Figure 24),[42] it gives the appearance of being almost as much public as private, especially since the curtain at the right carries more than a suggestion of the proscenium arch. And while the piano and other furniture is seen in perspective, the floor is treated as a flat decorative plane; the whole thrust of the image is away from the inner experience conveyed, however epigrammatically, by the image of Beethoven standing before his piano, and towards the depiction of external appearances.

In another cover the silhouette technique remains, but the human figures have disappeared (Figure 25).[43] The instruments appear in a highly schematic perspective, with the cabriole legs and lyre box seen from characteristic but incompatible angles, in the manner of children's drawings; they become little more than elements in an essentially abstract decorative design. In a curiously inappropriate image to couple with Brendel (Figure 26),[44] which is put into repeat like a fabric design, the representational component is greater but the collage-based treatment of the surfaces is completely flat, again in a manner reminiscent of children's art. Nor is this the only child-like aspect of the design; quite apart from the image of Mozart on the piano lid, the performer's head has the shape and the far-apart eyes of a cartoon baby. Together with the flowers, these things give the image a kind of nursery innocence; it creates an effect quite different from the technically similar decorative treatment that Turnabout's designers gave Brendel's recordings of Beethoven.

The Complete Mozart Edition from Philips offers a much more up-to-date image, which could be loosely described as de Chirico by way of Benson and Hedges (Figure 27).[45] But behind the designer surface are the same old themes. Again we have the decorative emphasis on appearances; there is an air of theatricality that is almost surrealistic, mainly because of the disjunction of scale between the piano and the faded flowers (again flowers!) that are piled underneath it. The surrealism becomes overt in another Philips image (Figure 28),[46] with tiny people walking unsteadily past screwed-up fragments of sheet music and a giant wreath. Because we see the scene from the same height as the tiny people, the effect of the disjunction of scale is rather like that of the recent television adaptation of the classic children's story *The Borrowers*,[47] which was entirely shot from two or three inches above the ground. Familiar objects suddenly loom large and from strange angles; the world is defamiliarized, seen innocently, as if for the first time.

One of Peter Kivy's essays tells the story of 'Child Mozart as an Aesthetic Symbol'.[48] He focuses not so much on Mozart the child prodigy but on 'Mozart, *the man who remained a child*' (p. 201). And he links the enduring image of Child Mozart with the concept of aesthetic disinterestedness as it developed through Kant and Schopenhauer, for whom (as Kivy puts it) 'lack of experience – or, rather, the naive attitude of objective wonder which characterizes those who are not rich in experience – is a *necessary* condition of artistic genius' (p. 211). This, I suggest, is what lies behind the clustering of traits found on sleeves of Mozart's music: the disjunctions of scale, the emphasis on decorative appearance that tends towards children's art, and, of course, the explicitly child-like images (Figure 29).[49] Whether all this bears out Kivy's thesis that 'the "idea of Mozart" ... has replaced the "idea of Beethoven" as the dominating *musical* image of genius and creative intellect'[50] I am not sure; the image of Mozart as aging child (as in Figure 30,[51] with its incipient double chin) is hardly conducive to the aesthetic reception of his music, just as the ideology of aesthetic disinterestedness can itself be seen as contributing to the present-day marginalization of 'serious' music. But at any rate I think that these equivocal, and ultimately limiting, images of Mozart lend some credibility to the speculative reading I offered of a gate seen against sparkling water.

The text on the back of record sleeves (an element of the domestic *Gesamtkunstwerk* on which I have not touched) comes from a nineteenth-century tradition that aligns it with the aesthetic process: its source, as I said, is the descriptive or analytical programme note. But the image on the front has little in the way of genealogy; if, as I suggested, it has a prehistory in sheet-music covers, its immediate antecedents lie in the lettering on the front of boxes of 78s. Historically it is part of the packaging, not the product. But history teaches that this is a fragile distinction. When music videos were first introduced, record companies were very clear about what they were: a promotional tool. So they did not charge television stations for broadcasting them. But all this changed with the runaway success of MTV. A charging structure was introduced, and in this way the music video became as much a product as a promotion.[52] In the same way, the record sleeve (or nowadays the CD insert) is part of what is bought and sold; visual image and musical sound circulate indivisibly, and are consumed together.

The aesthetic interaction between image and sound is possible only because music possesses an intrinsic openness to semantic completion through the intervention of the image. To the extent that people assimilate what they see and what they hear into a composite experience, the everyday reception of music constantly gives the lie to the ideology of musical autonomy, according to which the touchstone of good music is that it is aesthetically self-sufficient. That ideology ruled questions of musical meaning out of court. Rejecting it does not, however, force us to maintain that music has discursive meaning in the way that language does. I would prefer to argue that music constructs in a kind of a semantic vacuum, attracting referents in the same sense that a magnet attracts iron filings.[53] The history of music amply illustrates this process; as autonomous instrumental music came to fruition in Beethoven's symphonies, a positive industry of musical hermeneutics developed, the purpose of which was to supply the referents that the composer had left out. The narrative structures put forward by critics like Kanne and Fröhlich helped listeners to represent what they heard to themselves and to others; to repeat Buxton's words, they anchored what would otherwise have been a chaos of subjective impressions.

The formal narratives of twentieth-century music analysis can be seen as serving very much the same purpose: stabilizing the reception of music through the formation of an intersubjectively comprehensible terminology for describing it. But of course formal analysis achieves this only for the small minority of musically educated listeners. Others must avail themselves of the potted biographies and analyses on the backs of record sleeves, or the iconography of music that appears on the front of them. I don't know how many people read sleeve notes, but everyone sees the picture on the front. And as I have shown, these images are by no means innocent; they are quite capable of reflecting and so perpetuating critical values, and perhaps on occasion modifying or subverting them too. As Peter Rabinowitz has observed,[54] we don't hear music innocently; it comes to us with its meaning largely predetermined by a range of what might be termed sub-scholarly discourses, of which the images on record sleeves are just one. I hope I have demonstrated that, sub-scholarly though they may be, these discourses need not be seen as beneath the notice of scholars.

Notes

1.   I owe this suggestion to Christopher Wintle.
2.   'Rock music, the star system, and the rise of consumerism'. In Simon Frith and Andrew Goodwin (eds) (1990), *On Record: Rock, Pop, and the Written Word,* New York, p. 434.
3.   Decca LXT 2850. Reproduced by courtesy of Decca Record Company.
4.   Ace of Clubs ACS 306.
5.   Decca LXT 5576.
6.   Columbia 33C 1009.
7.   Op.27, no.1 and op.110 (HMV ALP 1900).
8.   Bliss: Piano Concerto and Liszt: Hungarian Fantasia (WRC SH125). Reproduced by courtesy of EMI Records Ltd.
9.   Beethoven: 'Emperor' Concerto (HMV ALP 1300).
10.   In the original presentation I illustrated the fetishization of the artist in greater detail by means of a sequence of images taken from the CBS 'Stravinsky Conducts' series. In this series, which included both photographs and artists' interpretations of them, Stravinsky's spectacles gradually assume more and more visual significance, with the result that the representational qualities of the image are effectively supplanted by their iconic value.
11.   Beethoven: Symphony No. 9 (RCA GD 60256).
12.   Beethoven: Symphony No. 5 (DGG 138804). Reproduced by courtesy of Deutsche Grammophon Gesellschaft and Siegfried Lauterwasser.
13.   Beethoven: Overtures Decca LXT 6025). Reproduced by courtesy of Decca Record Company.
14.   Beethoven: Overtures (Columbia 33CX 1930).
15.   Mahler: Symphony No. 7 (CBS 72427/8).
16.   Beethoven: Piano Concerto No. 5 (EMI EL 7499651). Reproduced by courtesy of EMI Records Ltd.
17.   DGG 2543003. Reproduced by courtesy of Deutsche Grammophon Gesellschaft and Prof. Karlheinz Stockhausen.
18.   DGG 139461.
19.   Bizarre RSLP 6370.
20.   DGG 2720073.
21.   Inori, Formel (DGG 2707111).
22.   Kreuzspiel, Kontrapunkte, Zeitmasse, Adieu (DGG 2530443).
23.   Stop, Ylem (DGG 2530442).
24.   Drei Lieder, Sonatine, Spiel, Schlagtrio (DGG 2530827).
25.   DGG 2530582.
26.   DGG 2707045.
27.   DGG 2709055.
28.   DGG 2707122. Reproduced by courtesy of Deutsche Grammophon Gesellschaft and Prof. Karlheinz Stockhausen.
29.   Tchaikovsky: Serenade for Strings, Souvenir de Florence (Argo ZRG 584).
30.   Since this chapter was originally written, I have developed the argument of the following section at greater length in *Analysing Musical Multimedia,* Oxford, 1998 Chapter 2.

31. Chandos ABRD 1071.
32. Decca LXT 6230. Reproduced by courtesy of Decca Record Company.
33. CBS BRG 72040.
34. Columbia 33CX 1949.
35. Mozart: Divertimenti K 251, K 47 (Harmonia Mundi BAC 3017).
36. Brahms, Serenade No.2, op.16; Dvorak, Serenade for Wind, op.44 (Decca SXL 6368).
37. Mahler: Symphony No.4 (Columbia SAX 2441).
38. Moeran: Cello Concerto, Overture for a Masque, Rhapsody No.2 (Lyrita SRCS 43).
39. Tchaikovsky: Symphony No.6 (MFP 2007).
40. Apart from the final movement of Mahler's Fourth Symphony, of course.
41. Beethoven's Sketchbooks. Presented and illustrated by Denis Matthews (Discourses ABM2).
42. Mozart: Sonatas for Piano Duet K 358, K 381; Sonata for Two Pianos, K 448 (DGM 18455). Reproduced by courtesy of Deutsche Grammophon Gesellschaft.
43. Piano Quartets K 4478, K 493 (Decca LXT 2772). Reproduced by courtesy of Decca Record Company.
44. Mozart: Piano Concerti K 453, K 459 (Turnabout TV 34080S). Reproduced by courtesy of Decca Record Company.
45. Mozart: Piano Variations, Rondos, etc. (Philips 422518–2). Reproduced by courtesy of Philips Classics.
46. Mozart: *Il Sogno di Scipione* (Philips 422518–2). Reproduced by courtesy of Philips Classics.
47. Mary Norton (1952), *The Borrowers*, London; and (1955), *The Borrowers Afield*, London.
48. *Journal of History of Ideas,* 28 (1967), pp. 249–58, reprinted in Kivy (1993), *The Fine Art of Repetition: Essays in the Philosophy of Music* (Cambridge), pp. 200–13.
49. Mozart: *Il Re Pastore* (Philips 422535–2). Reproduced by courtesy of Philips Classics.
50. *The Fine Art of Repetition*, p. 4.
51. Mozart: Serenade No.9 K 320 (Decca LXT 2671). Reproduced by courtesy of Decca Record Company.
52. Andrew Goodwin (1993), *Dancing in the Distraction Factory: Music, Television and Popular Culture*, London, pp. 41ff. A similar story can be told regarding the relationship between sheet-music publication and performance in early twentieth-century England; see Cyril Ehrlich (1989), *Harmonious Alliance: a History of the Performing Right Society*, Oxford.
53. This observation is akin to John Corbett's description of pop music as 'a set of objects that produce their own visual lack' ('Free, single, and disengaged: Listening pleasure and the popular music object', *October, 54* [1990] p. 84; quoted in Goodwin, *Dancing in the Distraction Factory*, p. 49). See also my 'Music and meaning in the commercials' (*Popular Music* 13 [1994], p. 39) and, for a fuller account, Chapter 2 of *Analysing Musical Multimedia*.
54. 'Chord and Discourse: Listening through the Written Word', in Steven Paul Scher (ed.) (1992), *Music and Text: Critical Inquiries*, Cambridge, pp. 38–56.

9 Form and Forming: From Victorian Aesthetics to the Mid-twentieth-century Avant-garde

Bojan Bujic

Some forty years ago, in the mid-1950s, when I was a schoolboy in Sarajevo, coming one day to the rehearsal of my music-school string orchestra, we found on our music stands a piece by a contemporary Yugoslav author. The composition proved in the end too difficult for the school orchestra and we abandoned it after a couple of rehearsals. Nevertheless, the acquaintance with it offered me (for I cannot speak on behalf of the other members of the orchestra) an experience which has stayed with me ever since. Ideally, I should simply try to reproduce the piece and refrain from making any premature statements of a descriptive nature. As I cannot do this, I shall have to refer to the piece in terms which instantly place it in its historical and stylistic context. With hindsight I could say that the piece was written in an advanced atonal style, that it showed vestiges of Hindemith's language, but it was closer to the pre-serial Schoenberg. However, this contextual historical reference was not available to me at the time. All I had was my experience of the piece, as it was gained in the course of the rehearsals. I was deeply struck by it. The textures were new, the sense of phrasing and continuity unlike the predictable patterns one was exposed to in tonal music. It was difficult to play and called for additional concentration. In other words, it was a new musical experience and the strangeness of the texture could easily have had an adverse effect on a seventeen-year-old unaccustomed to advanced idioms. But the fact that, as I have said, 'I was struck by it' had to do not so much with my experience of single details of the composition – rather, the very nature of the experience seemed radically different from experiences which I hitherto associated with listening to and performing pieces of tonal music. I was struck by a totally new feeling of tonal space and integrity: after it was finished, the piece stayed in my

118

memory as a single indivisible entity. The details seemed deeply interconnected, forming a continuum and demonstrating, but only after the piece was over, the quality best summarised by the hackneyed phrase of 'unity in diversity'. However, the awareness of both the unity and the diversity were firmly controlled by my memory since the impression of the piece, the full realization of its existence, came as an after-effect of hearing it – an experience contiguous in time to the actual flow of the composition, but an after-effect none the less. A temporal hierarchy of experiences established itself very clearly, in that the 'cause' – the piece rehearsed – was overshadowed by the 'effect' – the feeling of a complete musical object after the piece stopped being played.

There is no easy way of proving whether my impression was either right or wrong. In order to do either it would be necessary to establish a definite set of conditions which determine the experience of a musical work of art – conditions which embrace not only the basic act of hearing but also elements of predisposition, and cultural and social factors. It is clear that in order to establish such a set of criteria one would have to arrive at one of those utopian and unwieldy all-embracing theories of experience which philosophers have from time to time dreamt of constructing.

I don't know what my preferred reading would have been had I, at that time, wanted to find some explanation for my experience, especially since the very notion of 'experience' would have led me to consider a theoretical work which operated with that concept in a prominent way. When only a few years later I first encountered German idealist philosophy my general interest in it was much stronger as a motivating force than any pragmatic need for explaining one isolated portion of my experience. I had, in fact, become overwhelmed by the concepts of cultural theory and philosophy and, in imitation of the predominant mode of thinking among aspiring intellectuals, I too pushed my experience somewhere onto the back burner. This ceases to be a personal confession for I believe that the process that I am describing here is a very common one and is reduplicated in countless cases of individuals whose thinking and reading is shaped by long-established patterns of education and progress from internal experiences towards grand schemes encouraged by historians.

Had I then been surrounded by a multitude of books offering a wide choice of possible orientations, had I been able to make intelligent choices and had my need to account for my experience of the work of music – completed and fully experienced 'after it was all over' – continued as a burning desire, it is very likely that I would have been attracted by a work which includes the phenomenon of experience as one of its starting points. Such a work could easily have been something from the repertory of the English psychological school since in any case it was only a few years after my experience of the atonal piece that I first read Bernard Bosanquet's *A History of Æsthetic* in which some attention is paid to the psychological orientation in aesthetics.[1] Yet Bosanquet, not unlike many philosophers of his generation, felt diffident when discussing musical matters and deferred to a better informed authority – Edmund Gurney.

'However rooted in the conditions of our environment be the enjoyment of the forms of concrete objects, it may be said, must not the pleasure in abstract proportions and forms be in some way a pleasure in order and regularity?'[2] No doubt, this sentence would have gone some way towards explaining my specific feelings after my listening/performing experience. Being an inexperienced philosophical reader I would not have recognized that this was not an original thought and that Gurney was merely reiterating Plato's position, varied so many times throughout the history of Western philosophy. In a passage that follows the one just cited, Gurney refers to music's lack of ability to represent anything in the external world and I may have easily taken him as someone providing me with a simple yet effective explanation of the powerful sense of inner unity and close and coherent musical argument which pervaded 'my' piece. I might have been so powerfully swayed by Gurney's thought that I would have failed to notice that Gurney was quite capable of subtly deflecting me from the line seemingly adopted in the quotation. He may have, indeed, reinforced my opinion that I was on the right track by asserting a very simple truth of the 'direct pleasure in rhythmic stimulation and in change of tone in pitch, the two factors of melodic form'.[3] Even if this was to be suspected of being too closely directed at the phenomena of tonal music, I would still have been capable of following him within the boundaries of my experience when he asserted that it was hard to establish the line between 'subsidiary organisms and larger combinations',[4] for this would have closely corresponded to the situation in which the close-knitted structures of 'my' piece refused to be separated into isolated phenomena governed by the grammatical rules pertaining to tonal music.

Imperceptibly, it seems, Gurney organizes his argument in such a way that the moment of hearing, the physical point of the auditory stimulus, becomes the centre round which all other aspects of his argument have to adjust themselves. The very notion of form, of the design which governs the totality of a work's appearance, becomes in Gurney coloured with uncertainty which pervades all his thought. Of course form is a given quality, and in recognizing its importance in music he accepts, or so it seems, some of the general notions of the 'givenness' of relationships of structure and symmetry that may be said to represent some basic organizations of formal nature. But then, anxious that it should be the given moment of hearing that governs the main act of experience, Gurney is driven into a position of suspecting any appearance of intentionality, and, in his opinion, intentionality, with the negative connotations he gives it, is embedded in any suggestion of a coherent formal plan since '[a] plan implies an end in view'.[5] An end also implies the projection of expectations towards a point in the future and thus detracts from the moment of hearing, or, this is at least a possible inference from Gurney's point. It was a minor point but its consequences are rather far-reaching.

It may be welcome to find an author who, when writing about musical processes, takes the temporal nature of music so seriously. Projection of expectations into the future implies an already well-formed knowledge of the intricacies governing the forming process of the piece so that, if listeners are sufficiently astute, they would through their own mental act prefigure the remaining portion of the composition, thus significantly depriving the work of the subtle interplay of appearances and expectations. But Gurney stops somewhat short of this kind of argument since his experiential mode is so much in the forefront of his argument that the moment of perception seems to exclude any other temporal dimension of a composition. He argues that 'pleasure in the whole has no meaning except as expressing the sum of our enjoyments from moment to moment'.[6] In this he is almost at one with another Victorian psychologist of music, his contemporary James Sully. Sully had already argued the existence of a tendency in larger and more complex musical structures to dispense with 'close organic unity',[7] by which he of course meant unity capable of being quickly recalled and reconstructed in the mind, although, on the other hand, he was more willing to assert the importance of large-scale patterns of organization. This, if anything, made him even more ambivalent than Gurney, since there is no clear sense of preference in Sully's argument – he tries to retain the middle position. Gurney, on the other hand, though mindful of general ideas about formal organization, eventually directs the main thrust of his argument towards establishing the pre-eminence of the moment of hearing. An additional reason for Gurney's need to establish the authenticity of the moment resides in his Darwinism – in reality nothing more than a positivist belief in the need to enquire into the origin and beginning of things. The real source of his atomism is in his naïve psychological belief of the uniqueness of the moment, asserting as he does, that in spite of the existence of extended musical structures, the important experience of music is to be fixed in short stretches, too short even to be 'actually presented alone' but 'in a way self-complete'.[8] Elsewhere he states that '[it] is characteristic of the whole apprehension of Music, . . . that the attention is focused on each part as it comes; and that we never get our impressions of a long musical movement, as we commonly do those of a great architectural structure, through views which sweep over and embrace the whole rather than dwell on the parts'.[9] His instinct is, however, not entirely negated by his professed belief in the supremacy of a moment and in almost the same breath with his insistence on the moment of hearing we may find a quick turning to another side, to an admittance of a different dimension of perception which seems to involve memory: 'It is an insult to the ear to treat it as if it could not spread its perception over these more extended reaches of form'.[10] This, however, is a rare example of Gurney's willingness to involve aspects of perception other than hearing and had I been forced to take Gurney as my sole guide in the attempt to explain my own listening experience I would have by now been in some considerable confusion: in spite of Gurney's claims to the contrary, the last-mentioned quotation would have gone some way towards establishing the possibility of there being a state of experience which allows a combination of actual hearing and memory, in which, if it is true to my experience referred to earlier on, memory of the whole had to have a higher degree of relevance than the act of hearing a moment or indeed a series of moments. Yet, Gurney was strongly pulling in the opposite direction.

It is obvious that, in spite of all the refreshing directness of Gurney, I needed some theoretical account of lived-through experience which would not require such constant recollective evaluation; or better, I needed a model of approach where both the pastness and the moment of accounting are discussed as closely related rather than as distinct phenomena. Had I been exceptionally lucky I might have come upon a discussion similar to the one that follows:

> Suppose a non-philosophical listener listening idly to a composition. To him we address the request, 'Give us a description of your listening experience', or 'How was it with you, auditively, during the preceding moments?' Uncautioned as to exactly what we want, he might reply in some such terms as these: 'I heard a composition of unusual density, where, instead of changing and definitely different patches and patterns of melody and timbre, I was confronted by so many strands of melodic lines that I was unsure of the points of distinction, of progress from one moment to another, being instead far too absorbed in the general flow of the composition . . .' and so on. So we explain to him. We explain that we want him to amend his account so that, without any sacrifice of fidelity to the experience as actually enjoyed, it nevertheless sheds all that heavy load of commitment to propositions about the piece which was carried by the description he gave. We want an account which confines itself strictly within the limits of the subjective episode, an account which would remain true even if he had heard nothing of what he claimed to have heard, even if he had been subject to total illusion.
>
> Our observer is quick in the uptake. He does not start talking about patches and patterns. For he sees that to do so would be to falsify the character of the experience he actually enjoyed. He says instead, 'I understand. I've got to cut out of my report all commitment to propositions about independently existing musical objects. Well, the simplest way to do this, while remaining faithful to the character of the experience as actually enjoyed, is to put my previous report in inverted commas or oratio obliqua and describe my experience as such as it would have been natural to describe in these terms, had I not received this additional instruction. Thus: "I had an auditive experience such as it would have been natural to describe by saying that I heard etc. . . . were it not for the obligation to exclude commitment to propositions about independently existing objects." In this way [continues the observer] I use the perceptual claim – the claim it was natural to make in the circumstances – in order to characterize my experience without actually asserting the content of the judgement. And this is really the best way of characterizing the experience. There are perhaps alternative locutions which might serve the purpose, so long as they are understood as being to the same effect – on the whole, the more artificial the better, since their artificiality will help to make it clearer to what effect they are intended to be.'

This act of unashamed plagiarism might help us towards understanding better the difficulties of describing the experience of a lived-through musical work. The indented paragraphs represent a close paraphrase of Peter Strawson's words, extracted for this purpose from a longer argument about aspects of A.J. Ayer's realism,[11] and adapted here to serve an account of an auditive rather than the original visual experience. Of course, the important difference between Strawson's account and this one is that the visual phenomena constituting the cause of the description continue, though only to a degree, in existence beyond the moment of the speaker's account, whereas our composition has by now terminated. It follows from this that a further distinction may be made between Strawson's original account and my alteration. In the original case the landscape which Strawson describes may be captured by the mind in an instant and accounted for as it were 'objectivitely', whereas the experience of a musical work implies an activity of the mind in sorting out and structuring, in participating in the creation of a totality. I shall return to this point a little later; now we can maintain that the difference is not so crucial as to make the borrowing impossible or pointless since further on in his essay Strawson argues in favour of perceptual judgements which presuppose objects existing independently of our 'relatively fleeting perceptions of them'.[12] This is applicable in our case since, with only a small adjustment to Strawson's description, we may say that the reference to the independently existing object provides sufficient foundation for security in assessing the finished composition as an integrated sum of impressions, so integrated, indeed, that there is no need to introduce Gurney's atomistic account, which strongly advocates a departure from a possible integrated experience and enslaves the perceiving subject in a web of identifiable moments, each of which would have to be regarded as a separate experience, if we are to follow closely Gurney's dictum that it is the succession of details that matters and not their integrated sum.

It is not necessary to lose Gurney's notion of moments out of sight in order to approach a mode of thinking in which both the moment and the larger unity retain their importance and are indeed brought into a relation rather more clearly than was the case in Gurney. Starting with Franz Brentano's analysis of time, Edmund Husserl remarked that '[t]he evidence that consciousness of a tonal process, a melody, exhibits a succession even as I hear it is such as to make every doubt or denial appear senseless'.[13] It is, of course, necessary to enquire further how this consciousness is to be thought of. The consciousness produces a 'pastness' modified by memory, since it is necessary to see that each segment of new experience pushes the previous one into a relative past, yet that relative past is causally connected with each new moment of appearance and it is fantasy that connects them into a meaningful succession. Gurney was troubled by the notion of a plan since, presumably, its existence implied a projection of expectations forward and, indeed, an establishment of a hierarchy of moments, since in the architecture of the piece crucial moments of architectonic importance would overshadow other moments, becoming, as it were, more equal than others, thus seriously undermining the existence of auditory perceptions which all arrive at the hearer as equally important components of a long chain. Both Brentano and Gurney started from a psychological point of view, with the important difference that Brentano was not committed to naïve atomism. The latter was also true of Husserl, who was able to introduce the notion of fantasy into his account of remembered experience, which in essence means the introduction of 'a new moment of presentation'. A musical work is therefore given in two temporal aspects, and this may sound like a trivial truism, but it has to be asserted since it is necessary if we are to move anywhere from Gurney's position. Gurney is interested only in the first moment of appearance, but, as Husserl asserts, the succession of moments does not make the past ones unreal. There is a possibility of conceiving a remembered content as a result of an experience which has lost its durational dimension and remains present in the consciousness as a given quality.

If we return to my modification of Strawson's narrative, we can observe that it would be practically impossible to give a running commentary in the moment of perception and remain truthful in respect of the 'now' of perception since the very act of description would be based on an impression which acoustically 'is not there', although we pretend that it is. Even in the circumstances similar to those described by Strawson, we may assume that the visual experience being accounted for exists but in a fleeting moment: that dark clouds, driven by a strong wind and moving across an otherwise bright sky, significantly alter the visual appearance of details, hitherto brightly lit leafy branches in an instant being transformed into darkened outlines. The description thus becomes tied to an instant and is no longer referring to an objective existence at the moment of speaking, yet we take it, as Strawson rightly does, as if it were true. Indeed, when we speak of our experience we must assume that the acoustical stimulus is not there but that in a different modus the work is there. It isn't even that we are constantly going to-and-fro, performing a series of excursions into the past by sampling moments of experience, then returning to narrate them, repeating the process, and so on. The statement about the experience itself is a different appearance of the formerly sonorous object, now remembered in its completeness which, having lost the attributes of temporal succession which it once had, re-forms itself into a coherent object of experience. It may therefore be that we are to be helped by looking into the process of forming, into the flow of procedures which, naïvely speaking, put us where we have once been in Gurney's company.

Gurney repeatedly asserts the lack of presentational, narrative content in music – in a phrase somewhat reminiscent of Hanslick, he speaks of 'ideal motion' and this may be responsible for parallels frequently being made between him and Hanslick. Hanslick is, however, very different from Gurney in that he does acknowledge intentional direction of a composition, moreover he is, in the tradition of German adulation of wordless instrumental music, clearly obsessed with the idea that a piece of music grows out of a small germ-cell which is endlessly varied by the action of the genius. There is but a small step between Hanslick's notion of the uniqueness of the original idea on the one hand and Schenker's conception of the unfolding of the 'arpeggiation' and Schoenberg's Idea on the other. Both Schenker and Schoenberg felt the need for a philosophical explanation of their ideas but in both cases we are dealing with conglomerates of more or less intuitive insights lacking a firm philosophical background. Yet an attempt to combine a discussion of structure with an account of the perceptual activity directed at the structures does exist in the work of Nicolai Hartmann.[14]

Hartmann starts from an assertion that the aesthetics of the nineteenth century were predominantly subjectively orientated. We should make up what has been lost in the analysis of the aesthetic object, but one should not disregard the analysis of the act, only in joining both types of the analysis may we hope to move away from the point of stagnation into which we have been forced by the singlemindedness of the past. There is in Hartmann much that still binds him to the German idealist philosophy of which, in a way, he was the last exponent. The reliance on idealist terminology should not blind us to the existence of perceptive analysis of the relationship between forming processes in music and the possibilities of the perception of such processes. Another possible stumbling block, not only for those approaching Hartmann but also for Hartmann himself, is his structural terminology of layers (*Vordergrund* and *Hintergrund*) and strata (*Schichten*) existing within the former. Although on the one hand this may be of some use in linking him with Schenker, it can easily side-track us into the Ingardenian terminology of stratification in works of art, into Ingarden's belief in the lack of strata in music and his somewhat petulant insistence that Hartmann appropriated his terminology and used it incorrectly.

Without entering too deep into Harmann's discussion of layers, it is possible to see the usefulness of his argument that the real foreground is represented by the succession and connection of sounding pitches (*Töne*). Now the question is whether there isn't something in a musical work which is above tones, something that the musical sense of hearing can comprehend as 'hovering above' the sonorous matter, something that is beyond it and shines through and in such a way that it forms the authentic musical content? That 'something' is not to be sought away from the sonorous matter but within it. Music is not only what is heard: what is 'musically' heard requires a different synthesis in the receptive consciousness – different, that is, from what pure acoustical hearing is able to offer. That 'other' is a larger whole which forms the background no longer perceptible through the sense of hearing. It is interesting that here Hartmann uses the term *Satz*.[15] The definition of *Satz* is elusive, since Hartmann did not define it precisely enough, having appropriated it too trustingly from the musical terminology of his time. We shall translate it for the time being as 'pervading structure'.

The pervading structure is not present as a whole in any given moment, and yet in musical hearing it is understood as completeness. The completeness is not established in actual hearing but through a synthesis. The uniqueness (*Das grundlegend Eigentümliche*)[16] of the musical work of art is in the temporal flow which enables the listener to hear in his mind the compositional unity of the structure, although the structure cannot be heard by the ear in any given moment. In musical hearing we witness the completion of the entire structure and in the last bars of a consistently and logically composed work we hear the completion of the process of composition.[17] It is perhaps fortuitous that here we see a parallel with Schenker's contention that in the transformational layers of the middleground in the closing bars of a composition we can clearly witness a reinforcement of the basic descent of, say, $\hat{3}$–$\hat{2}$–$\hat{1}$. Hartmann holds that we hear more than is possible to hear with the ear only, we hear a tonal structure of a different order.[18] The unity of the inner form determines the forming of what is acoustically hearable. Yet, and this is the detail which now nicely contrasts the psychological Gurney and the analytical Hartmann, the structure of the *Satz* is not conditioned by the motif. Are we then to infer that as such 'the structure' is a separate entity? Hartmann's answer is not unlike something that we may find in Schenker: deep levels contain the essence of motion to which the motivic material is added as it were, from the outside. As Hartmann puts it: if one would be rigorous one could say that it is possible to write the same *Satz* to a different theme. The *Satz* is thus a deeper constant and comes close to Schenker's *Ursatz*. 'But it contradicts the language accepted in the theory of music!' (*Das widerstreitet nur der in der Musiktheorie angenommenen Begriffssprache, . . .*)[19] says Hartmann despairingly, unaware how close he was to providing a philosophically well-formed argument to Schenker's analytical insight, something Schenker always lacked: when trying to philosophize, he tended to get hopelessly enmeshed in arbitrariness and theological explanations.

It has been mentioned that Hartmann was the last representative of German idealism. From the purely chronological point of view it appears slightly absurd that his *Aesthetics* was written when the function of tonal music was no longer that of a backbone to compositional practice. Yet the timing in no way differs from the type of interaction between musical practice and speculative thought that obtained in Europe throughout the late eighteenth and the nineteenth centuries. Philosophers, and here Nietzsche was an exception, rarely engage with the issues of the music of their time and therefore do not appear to offer immediate help to the composers, whose own intense engagement with the substantive issues of form and technique in any case seldom appear in the forefront of their thought. This is understandable, since issues of substantive and speculative nature are addressed primarily through the act of composition. Yet, in the twentieth century Schoenberg provided an example of a composer constantly searching for a better understanding of the process of creation, a process ultimately dependent on the relationship between the existing and the imagined – possible – methods of musical organization: a kind of quest which then draws into the web of thinking the question of a composer's own responsibility and introduces a certain moral dimension. There, too, an interesting parallel with Hartmann may be drawn since in his work, in a manner typical of the tendency towards completeness, inherited from earlier German idealists, details of aesthetic theory either derive from or lead into other areas of philosophical investigation.

The change of generations after 1945 signified a break with the tradition of theoretical thought in which completeness is upheld as a guiding principle, although in reality the break was not a clean one; rather, one may begin to see from the distance of some forty years how the elements of a dialectic process resiliently engaged in a trial of strength with each other. The possibilities for a show of strength existed within Schoenberg's and Webern's music: Schoenberg's desire to promote conditions for a unitary perception of unitary musical space was internally opposed by the surviving reliance on tonal procedures, the process so well documented in Boulez's and Adorno's polemical writings. Webern's striving towards the integration of musical material and the resulting generation of form is counterbalanced by the attention drawn to individual notes or strongly delimited complexes of notes, the attention inevitably resulting from Webern's desire to assign them a strong dynamic profile as an extension of the serial principle (e.g. in the Variations op.27).

The first phase of total serialism arguably still represents a desire to create unified musical space – something reminiscent of my experience with the composition which was meaningfully retained in my consciousness only once it was all over. But we did not have to wait long before the elements of the dialectic opposition were recognized for what they were. The unity of musical space, my instinctive reaction to a specific demand of hearing, was being challenged at that very time by Boulez (1954). And indeed it is a dialectic process which he was drawing the attention to, the dialectic between 'a strict global organization and a temporary structure controlled by free will'.[20] Although seemingly of different kinds, Boulez's demand for abandonment of continuous and homogeneous musical movements and a type of development which would result in a 'closed circuit',[21] and Gurney's praise for the primacy of the moment of hearing, as well as his reluctance to accept goal-directed motion, seem to belong to the same category of basic approaches to the issue of musical experience. I say 'seem to' for we may assume that in Gurney's case the dominant motivating force is his psychological orientation whereas Boulez may have components of history and tradition in mind when defining his position.

The use of the term 'moment' in connection with Gurney edges us inevitably towards Stockhausen. We need only recall Gurney's enthusiasm for the current moment of experience, as one of the vivid unique occurrences in a succession of points, to be struck by the similarity with Stockhausen's account of how in *Momente* it is precisely the uniqueness of an individual moment which acts as a point of departure for the construction of the whole:

> Instead of starting with something very homogeneous and then breaking the homogeneity, we start with completely separate instants: Now! Now! Now! Now! Now! – and then begin to determine how much memory or hope each Now may have – how much it may be related to what happened before or will happen next.[22]

Yet even here the similarity may be apparent since in quick succession Stockhausen singles out a moment and then, as if turning the tables on Gurney, acknowledges that it is important for a composer to determine 'memory or hope', thus progressing in the thought from the 'now' to a larger unified temporal structure.

Gurney is not precise on the nature of the origin of the moments, other than that they arise out of the nature of perception, and, as we have seen, his instinct is to believe in two possibilities at once: in the primacy of the moment as well as the ability of the ear to cover a wider span of musical duration. In this he is not troubled by an ideological position, something neither Boulez nor Stockhausen were able to get away from. Indeed, the process of 'getting away', of dissociation from an 'out-of-date' ideological position belonging to a seemingly different age, is very much the process with which both of them, but particularly Boulez, had to wrestle.

Boulez's critical attitude to the survival of tonal elements in serial music is, on the other hand, a logically argued position from the standpoint of technique only, but at the same time has a much deeper root in the desire to offer an alternative approach to musical perception, an approach which offers a chance of escaping from the tutelage of a philosophy of music initially formed under the influence of all-pervading systems of German idealism. That idealism, with its goal-directedness, must have been in Boulez's mind connected with Schoenberg's attempt at defining unified musical space and yet, initially at least, Boulez's own position remained an ambivalent one. Although total serialism for a time offered no change, since it too seriously tended towards such unified space, the new ideological position of open-endedness necessarily made the phase of total serialism a short one. However, the struggle between the positions of the idealist belief in the unity of space and purpose and the new reliance on the primacy of the moment leaves a residue which cannot easily fit into standard ideological categories. It cannot fit into them since any insistence on the quality and structure of perception inevitably minimizes the notion of a wide historical or social context. I am not denying the value of such contexts but by appealing earlier to the authority of Peter Strawson I wanted to stress the importance of the clarity and unambiguousness with which the act of perception has to be connected to the object of perception. Boulez seems to me to be instinctively aware of this issue, although in his utterances the awareness is hardly presented as an orderly progress from one set of ideas to another. His asides at Schoenberg and Webern, criticising the 'formalist utopia' of the former and accusing the latter's work as being 'an illusion, a formal phantasmagoria'[23] might at first appear to sit uncomfortably alongside his description of his own compositional activity as a long process of creating a single work with many faces, emanating from a single, central concept, where only the circumstances prevent him from elaborating the central idea broadly enough.[24] The former two statements date from 1986 and the latter was made some nine years earlier, though no great deal of significance should be read in the mere chronology of the statements. They are more an expression of a process of wrestling and signify an uncertainty in the face of one of the central problems of the philosophy of music – the problem of the relationship of the percipient to the status of the perceived object. Elsewhere in his paper, when talking of 'mature perceptual experiences' in the context of naïve realism, Strawson makes an extremely appropriate distinction between 'our seeings and hearings and feelings – our perceivings – of objects and the objects we see and hear and feel; and hence quite consistently accept both the interruptedness of the former and the continuance in existence, unobserved, of the latter'.[25] I shall permit myself a small adjustment to Strawson's distinction here and state that we can conceive of a possibility of the duality of experiences – the interruptedness and the consciousness of a complete object when we simply acknowledge the completeness of it – in other words, a state of mind in which the object resides in our consciousness as a completed past object achieving a new temporal dimension from the one guaranteed to it by the flow of physical time.

The two aspects of naïve realism have been competing with each other in Gurney's mind and they are still competing, nearly a century later, in Boulez's thoughts. Put differently, they appeared as elements of a sophisticated account of experience in Husserl's thought and represent the central issue in Hartmann's account of 'forming'. For this reason it may be said that Jean-Jacques Nattiez is erring on the side of caution when he says that it is only in the last thirty-five or forty years that music has been divided into two main tendencies, which he calls the 'poetico-centric' – that of Boulez – and the 'aesthesico-centric' – that of the American minimalist school.[26] The division is, in fact, much longer and runs much deeper since it does not relate so much to the music itself as to the ways the philosophers have debated the issue of musical perception and musical experience. In terms of an understated philosophical theory it even runs through the total complex of Boulez's ideas as a witness of a continuing polarization of the categories of naïve realism which in this case I have attempted to trace from Gurney but which may be traced much further back through the history of Western music. It seems that it was the strangeness of 'my' piece which clearly exposed me to the benefits of one of the components of the division and has had the continuing benefit of forcing me, years later, to address a thorny problem of musical experience.

In the recent philosophical aesthetics of music the problem of the emotions and expressiveness has enjoyed a phase of rejuvenation, as witness the writings of Budd, Kivy and Levinson,[27] and thus overshadowed the more important theme of experience. In addition, the school of the New Musicology has centred on the issues of narrativity which, unless handled sensitively, may give the upper hand to the notion of momentary experiences in the process of comprehending the supposedly hidden structures of narrative.[28] Although the ideas which the New Musicology espouses are not unimportant, we are witnessing here an uncritical lapse into one-sided naïve realism, deprived of that tradition of sophisticated argument towards which philosophers otherwise as unlike each other as Husserl and Strawson have helpfully directed us. *Pace* Raymond Monelle, we cannot easily dispense either with 'the "me" of phenomenology'[29] or with Strawson's account of the relationship of perception to its object without seriously undermining one of the central questions of the philosophy of music.

Notes

1. Bosanquet (1892).
2. Gurney (1880), p. 192.
3. Ibid., p. 194.
4. Ibid., p. 196.
5. Ibid., p. 199.
6. Ibid., p. 214.
7. Sully (1874), p. 218.
8. Gurney (1880), p. 227.
9. Ibid., p. 214.
10. Ibid., p. 229.
11. Strawson (1979), pp. 43–44.
12. Ibid., p. 44.

13. Husserl (1964), p. 23.
14. Hartmann (1953).
15. Ibid., p. 117.
16. Ibid., p. 119.
17. Ibid., pp. 119–20.
18. Ibid., p. 120.
19. Ibid., p. 234.
20. Boulez (1991), p. 17. The essay from which this quotation is taken ('Current Investigations') was originally published in 1954.
21. Ibid., p. 19.
22. Stockhausen (1989), p. 67.
23. Nattiez (1993), p. 190.
24. Boulez (1976), p. 50.
25. Strawson (1979), p. 48.
26. Nattiez (1993), p. 180.
27. Budd (1985); Kivy (1980), (1984), (1990), (1993); Levinson (1990).
28. Abbate (1991); Kramer (1990); Newcomb (1984), (1987), (1992). Some of the philosophical issues of the New Musicology are discussed in Bujic, 1997.
29. Monelle (1992), p. 58.

Bibliography

Abbate, Carolyn (1991), *Unsung Voices: Opera and Musical Narrative in the Nineteenth Century*, Princeton: Princeton University Press.

Bosanquet, Bernard (1892), *A History of Æsthetic*, London: Allen and Unwin.

Boulez, Pierre (1976), *Conversations with Célestin Deliège*, London: Eulenburg Books.

——— (1991), *Stocktakings*, tr. Stephen Walsh, Oxford: Clarendon Press.

Budd, Malcolm (1985), *Music and the Emotions: The Philosophical Theories*, London, Routledge & Kegan Paul.

Bujic, Bojan (1997, June), 'Delicate Metaphors', *The Musical Times*, 138, pp. 16–22.

Gurney, Edmund (1880), *The Power of Sound*, London: Smith, Elder & Co.

Hartmann, Nicolai (1953), *Ästhetik*, Berlin: Walter de Gruyter & Co.

Husserl, Edmund (1964), *The Phenomenology of Internal Time-Consciousness*, ed. Martin Heidegger, tr. James M. Churchill, Bloomington and London: Indiana University Press.

Kivy, Peter (1980), *The Corded Shell: Reflections on Musical Expression*, Princeton: Princeton University Press.

——— (1984), *Sound and Semblance: Reflections on Musical Representation*, Princeton: Princeton University Press.

——— (1990), *Music Alone: Philosophical Reflections on the Purely Musical Experience*, Ithaca & London: Cornell University Press.

——— (1993), *The Fine Art of Repetition: Essays in the Philosophy of Music*, Cambridge: Cambridge University Press.

Kramer, Jonathan (1990), *Music as Cultural Practice 1800–1900*, Berkeley, Los Angeles & Oxford: University of California Press.

Levinson, Jerrold (1990), *Music, Art and Metaphysics: Essays in Philosophical Aesthetics*, Ithaca & London: Cornell University Press.

Monelle, Raymond (1992), *Linguistics and Semiotics in Music*, Chur, etc.: Harwood Academic Publishers.

Nattiez, Jean-Jacques (1993), *Le combat de Chronos et d'Orphée*, Paris: Christian Bourgois, Editeur.

Newcomb, Andrew (1984), 'Once More Between Absolute and Program Music: Schumann's Second Symphony', *19th-Century Music*, 7, pp. 233–50.

———(1987), 'Schumann and Late Eighteenth-Century Narrative Strategies', *19th-Century Music*, 11, pp. 164–74.

———(1992), 'Narrative Archetypes and Mahler's Ninth Symphony', in Scher, S.P. (ed.), *Music and Text: Critical Enquiries*, Cambridge: Cambridge University Press, pp. 118–36.

Sully, James (1874), *Sensation and Intuition*, London: Longman.

Stockhausen, Karlheinz (1989), *Stockhausen on Music: Lectures and Interviews compiled by Robin Maconie*, London and New York: M. Boyars.

Strawson, Peter (1979), 'Perception and its Objects', in Macdonald, G.F. (ed.), *Perception and Identity: Essays presented to A. J. Ayer*, London and Basingstoke: Macmillan, pp. 41–60.

10 Stravinsky and the Vicious Circle: Some Remarks about the Composer and the Press

Stephen Walsh

'As for Brother Criticus, I do not wish to spoil my temper, and my book, by speaking of *him* here.'[1]

What is the use of music criticism? Nobody is asked that question more, I suppose, than the music critic himself, and no doubt it serves him right. But this is one of those cases where use and motive can easily become confused, since the reason a critic writes may have no bearing whatsoever on the use to which his writing is put. Historians know that journalism, of all kinds, is documentation, and not only of the factual, 'King Harold marched to Hastings' variety, but also a record of opinion, of the way people thought and reacted, an indispensable tool in the fashionable but not necessarily for that reason wholly idiotic study of reception history. Music being itself a kind of document which is performed, and therefore invites comment, but which also survives in a tangible, non-performance documentary form, responds particularly well to this process. A newspaper or journal review is a record of an event, but it is also a confession that blurts out the prejudices and intellectual limitations which it is precisely the nature of great art to challenge and which therefore tend to expose – albeit in a somewhat specialized form – the cultural context (otherwise hard to recover) to which that art was initially addressed.

As one might expect, some composers mind critics more than others. Benjamin Britten was notoriously – some might say pathologically – sensitive about them. Robert Saxton and Jonathan Harvey, it seems, are not.[2] In any individual case there may be a historical, identifiable reason for an extreme attitude. Perhaps Britten remembered the years in which he was routinely written off as 'too clever' by the English critical establishment, and continued to sense an element of condescension towards his supreme command of *métier* even in the laudatory notices

132

which greeted much of his later music. In the case of Igor Stravinsky – another confirmed critic-hater – there certainly are historical and psychological factors which we know enough about to be able to form a view on why he felt as he did.

The first and most important is that for almost his entire creative life he was an enforced exile, having, as it were, to justify his presence – and his standing – in alien cultures and societies. Stravinsky's basic insecurity was doubtless of much earlier origin and may have been connected with his small stature or the stiff, reserved attitude of his parents and elder brothers towards him and his gifts. It may or may not have been intensified by jealousy of his fellow Rimsky-Korsakov pupil Maximilian Steinberg, a more conventionally fluent composer who enjoyed a certain local success in St Petersburg and capped it by marrying Rimsky's daughter Nadya.[3] But in any case it wasn't proof against the conditions of social and intellectual nomadism in which Stravinsky led his life from about 1910 on. Unfortunately for him, the sword was two-edged. Not only was he an outsider in Switzerland, in France, in the USA; but from the moment of his first Parisian success, he became an outsider in his native Russia as well. His letters home after the first Russian *Firebird* of October 1910 are full of his longing to share his Paris success with his Petersburg colleagues and – what could be more natural? – enjoy their congratulations.[4] But nothing of the kind was forthcoming. He was like the Soldier in his Tale: an embarrassed silence, combined with something the soldier did not have to endure – a mixed and sometimes hostile press – was the sum total of the response to the prophet in his own country.

The question of Stravinsky's personal relations with Steinberg and the Rimsky-Korsakov family after 1910 is not directly relevant to the present chapter. It merely provides a context for the press notices themselves, some of which, nevertheless, were written by Andrey Rimsky-Korsakov, the composer's second son and hitherto one of Stravinsky's closest friends. But that context is important, because it was precisely the fact that Stravinsky's Diaghilev ballets appeared to supersede the work of Rimsky-Korsakov himself and succeed internationally where the master's own admired stage works had never achieved more than local fame that turned his family against a composer they saw as practically an invention of their own circle; and something similar was also at the very least a subtext in much of the published criticism of Stravinsky's new works. To put the point in general terms: Stravinsky fell victim to the jealous provincialism of a deeply conservative Russian musical establishment, but it was a jealousy that had its personal as well as professional aspects.

Anyone whose experience of music criticism is mainly based on a perusal of the comparatively genteel arts pages of the public prints of our own day might be amazed at the vicious and even hysterical abuse that some Russian critics saw fit to hurl at the early masterpieces of their young compatriot. Here, for instance, is part of a long review of *The Rite of Spring* by the most persistently antagonistic, the Moscow critic Leonid Sabaneyev, published ten days or so after the Paris premiere of late May 1913:

I have looked through the music of this new work of Stravinsky's. I will admit that I have never had a particularly high opinion of this writer's compositional (in the sense of 'musical') talent. In his music this young composer is as careful as a banker. Nothing with him has ever been spontaneous, inspired, intuitive. Everything is the fruit of mental toil – of apt and accurate calculations and constructions. His original creativity, if one can call Stravinsky's activities by this exalted term, was very like Rimsky-Korsakov's, but without his delicacy and fantasy. Later came a period of 'Frenchification'. Stravinsky began to copy the ways of Ravel and Debussy. But again the imitation was infinitely weaker than the original. In the end, with *Petrushka*, Stravinsky offers something that is in some sense 'his own'. But how antipathetic I find this 'his own'.

Ostentatious complexity, beyond which is inward poverty. The utter, irremediable absence of any 'innards' to the music, any hidden essence, any psychology. Stavinsky's music is a sort of spillikins in sound. Fake, moreover, contrived, confused. The harmonies seem unusual from lack of habit, and on closer inspection it turns out that this unusualness is a trumpery, behind which is concealed a poverty-stricken simplicity. They live no inner life, unlike the harmonic innovations of genuine talents; they are rickety and feeble. It is unbearable to spend long in this atmosphere of conscious falseness, built up so carefully and clinically. I cannot describe the feeling of hopelessness that reading through and studying the new ballet aroused in me....

And so on, and on. Sabaneyev admits that he has not actually heard the music. 'Is it possible,' he asks rhetorically, 'to judge Stravinsky's colouring without hearing it in the orchestra? ... But they told me the same thing about *Petrushka*. And I heard this *Petrushka* played superlatively by an orchestra under a first-rate conductor who seemed genuinely to like the work. And? The colouring remained colouring and the poverty of the conception remained poverty.' 'No,' he concludes,

> this is not a contribution to the literature of music. More decisively than ever, I can pronounce verdict on the sham, infinitely sham art of Stravinsky: an art of the temporal market-place, summoned to life by a chance concatenation of circumstances – it will die a natural and unattractive death when the need for it is past, when Diaghilev and the fashion for the Russian Ballet in Paris disappear, when the 'refined' Parisians are sated with barbarism and demand in their musical restaurants the classics or something yet else. Then Stravinsky will have to close down his factory of modernised luboks and occupy himself in some other way.[5]

Sabaneyev, an associate and proponent of Scriabin, had no particular brief for the Belyayev school. But those who had were not always more temperate. Here is the Latvian composer critic Jazeps Vitols, an older Rimsky-Korsakov pupil, reviewing Koussevitzky's St Petersburg performance of the original three-movement *Petrushka* suite, in the German-language *St Petersburger Zeitung*:

> ... [Stravinsky], a mixture of creative poverty and unbelievable audacity of sense and sound and form, with manifest nonsense in its artistic realisation. Like the Futurists, of whom such dreadful things are reported, Stravinsky seems richly provided with a flair for amusing himself at his public's expense; for the cabbage [twaddle] into which, in his ballet score *Petrushka*, he crushes a series of Russian folksongs with an unprecedented expenditure on sharp spices, is something never previously encountered in any musical kitchen. You can take it with the appropriate roast – the 'music' along with the hocus-pocus on the stage – the dancing nurses, the droshky drivers, the court-yard rag tag and bobtail, and other sweet-smelling apparitions, perhaps also to be explained as comestibles; if you spend an evening on a spree you may expect to have a bit of fun, and

modesty signifies lack of character. But in the concert-hall, alongside a symphony of Glazunov, this noise is mere tastelessness ... How noble Glazunov's art seems by comparison.[6]

'In all sobriety, I do not feel a particular urge to dilate on *The Rite of Spring*', Vitols wrote in a later review, 'my sphere of operations is the art of music, and in the present case the most competent critic would be a zookeeper.'[7]

Of course, there were hard words in the foreign press too, but nothing with quite the same sense of a hidden agenda – the same smack of personal animus. Andrey Rimsky-Korsakov's review of the St Petersburg premiere of the *Petrushka* excerpts in January 1913 is particularly significant in this respect:

> There is of course bottomless talent in this piece. The orchestral colours ... are exceptionally intense, rich and new. True, one can quite rapidly tire of the incessant stunts and conjuring tricks. There is, indeed, not even a 'monotony of luxury', but a kind of monotony of frenzied trickery. Sated with all these orchestral spices, you begin to dream of a crust of black bread ... If it weren't for the great gifts of Benois and Stravinsky, this piece with its vulgar tunes would be a monstrous crime. Yet, who knows, *Petrushka* might be the prelude to its own kind of musical futurism? If so, then perhaps it would be better if it had never seen the light![8]

The pre-history of this particular review is remarkable. It was Andrey Rimsky-Korsakov who in December 1910, at Stravinsky's request, had actually supplied two or three of the 'vulgar tunes' – tunes which Stravinsky had heard from Andrey's and his younger brother Vladimir's own lips.[9] Recalling this exchange half a century later, Stravinsky noted that Andrey sent the music, 'but with words of his own fitted to it, facetious in intent, but in fact questioning my right to use such "trash"'.[10] By this time, Stravinsky was already aware of a coolness in Andrey's attitude, a direct result of the *Firebird*, which Andrey had seen in Paris in July 1910, then heard again when Ziloti premiered the suite in St Petersburg in October 1910. Despite his urgent pleas from the south of France, where he was at work on *Petrushka*, Stravinsky could not get news from his close friends about Ziloti's performance or the impact made by the music, though he did read the guarded, when not openly hostile, Russian press.[11] When he did get a response, after the *Petrushka* premiere in January 1913, it seems to have been disagreeable.[12]

But by that time, the underlying dynastic reasons for Andrey's hostility were out in the open. Less than two weeks before the *Petrushka* concert, it had become known in St Petersburg that Diaghilev was planning a production of Mussorgsky's unfinished opera *Khovanshchina* with a newly composed ending by Stravinsky, effectively replacing the standard version by Rimsky-Korsakov. The Rimsky-Korsakov family had already made waves about Diaghilev's other Rimsky ballets – *Scheherazade* and the underwater scene from his opera *Sadko* – not only because the music was cut but because it was taken out of context and, perhaps the worst crime of all, subjected to that lowest form of theatre, the dance. One of the finest of all Stravinsky's surviving letters – written to Andrey's brother Vladimir in July 1911 – is a passionate defence of Diaghilev's approach to such transplants; and among many other telling points that emerge from this document is, precisely, the revelation that the Rimsky family despised ballet and placed it far below opera in their moral–aesthetic hierarchy.[13] Not a good starting point – we may now feel – for an appreciation of Stravinsky's early works.

The local reaction to the news about *Khovanshchina* seems quite amazing today, but it shows, first, what a provincial place St Petersburg was, and, secondly, how jealously the stature of a *petit maître* like Rimsky-Korsakov was guarded by an acutely touchy and protectionist priesthood. The *Stock Exchange Gazette* remarked sulkily that 'the Rimsky-Korsakov who edited and orchestrated *Khovanshchina* is now rejected. He has proved not good enough "for the West", and must be corrected.' And in the same columns, the old kuchkist César Cui affected incredulity at the news: 'Is it possible that Stravinsky will lift his hand to correct his own teacher? . . . I am inclined to think that Stravinsky will never agree to redo the final chorus for Mr Diaghilev's benefit.'[14]

That such issues tainted Andrey Rimsky-Korsakov's response to his old friend's meteoric Parisian success seems beyond doubt. But what is more striking is that *mutatis mutandis* the same reactions can be detected throughout the contemporary Russian criticism of the Stravinsky ballets. A sense of righteous indignation that this young upstart should presume to succeed with music so fundamentally different – in genre as well as style and technique – from that of his blessed teacher runs through all but the most thoughtful reviews, including many that are less openly hostile than the ones I have quoted so far. For instance, the reviewer of the *Stock Exchange Evening News*, A. Koptyayev, argues the commonly held view that *Petrushka* is a work that needs the stage to give it meaning. 'The fact is,' he writes, 'that Mr Stravinsky detests pure music, and in general gives his music only an insignificant role in the overall impression.'[15] In other words, the work's success can be explained away as a product of stage spectacle alone – precisely the aspect that Petersburg audiences were not being offered. This was a useful view for the orthodox Rimskians, since it preserved the virginity of those traditional musical values which Stravinsky seemed to be rejecting . Indeed, Steinberg himself had the nerve to make the same point in a postcard to the composer after the Petersburg premiere – failing, apparently, to see how uncomplimentary such an opinion would seem to Stravinsky, whether or not he was already nursing grievances towards the person expressing it.[16]

The essential absurdity of another version of this argument was publicly exposed by the most intelligent and sympathetic of all Stravinsky's early Russian critics, the composer Nikolay Myaskovsky, in his review of the piano score of *The Firebird* in the Moscow journal *Muzïka* in October 1911:

> When you talk to people, especially professional musicians, about Stravinsky, you invariably hear: 'Unusual talent for orchestration, amazing technique, rich invention, but . . . not music.' What a lot of rubbish! Talent, unusual, amazing talent, and yet not the thing which constitutes the substance of that talent; what is this but a mischievous muddle?[17]

Myaskovsky published perceptive, detailed and laudatory reviews of all three early ballets, as well as useful pieces on many of the smaller works of the time. Yet even he harboured doubts, which were more openly expressed in correspondence than in published reviews. For instance, to Derzhanovsky, the editor of *Muzika*, Myaskovsky wrote as follows:

> In general Stravinsky is alright, a splendid fellow, though his *Rite* seems to me sometimes extremely thin in invention: he gets into a sort of harmonic construct, from which there is no escape either backwards or forwards, and sometimes a whole number jumps up and down on the spot ... Incidentally, Prokofiev was in Paris for *Petrushka* and told me the very strong impression it made – [but] he noted a tendency on Stravinsky's part, alongside moments of real value, to devote too much space to padding, even at the most important moments – this is true.[18]

So Prokofiev, another (conservatoire) pupil of Rimsky-Korsakov, shared this view.

Myaskovsky soon developed a personal hostility to Stravinsky (whom he never met), partly because he disliked what he had heard about his mercenariness, partly because he was offended by Stravinsky's request to him, in August 1913, to proof-read *The Rite of Spring*, the E flat Symphony and *The Nightingale*. 'Why do I have to consider myself less busy than Stravinsky?' he wrote to Derzhanovsky in September. 'This whole business with him sickens me ... He obviously simply doesn't know how to proof-read ...'.[19] But there is no personal animus in the critical reservations, which express a serious problem with Stravinsky's work as art, and one which – as it turned out – Myaskovsky was to share with other, later critics whose musical credentials were also apparently above reproach and who also, unlike the St Petersburg pack in 1913, had no axe to grind.

For of course the whole point about *Petrushka* and *The Rite of Spring* is that, by the standards of their time, they were profoundly radical works, whose structural thinking was as new and powerful as their musical ideas. The fact that even intelligent contemporary critics tended to find a vacuum just at the point where the writing was most innovative, was a natural consequence of their prejudice in favour of a music in which profundity meant strongly directed harmonic growth allied to an intricate counterpoint of melodic motives. They had no vocabulary, and no artistic ethic, for a music whose discourse was rhythmic and colouristic – attributes which were regarded as secondary in turn-of-the-century academic circles. Hence the contradictory character of reviews which praised the vividness and vitality of a work like *Petrushka*, but ended up finding it shallow or unmusical. The contradiction strikes at the very heart of modernism; and since it led inevitably to the charge that Stravinsky could not do the 'important' things, like evolve a harmonic framework or develop a theme or even write a melody at all, it also struck *him* at the point where he was most vulnerable: the insecurity he had felt as the product of an essentially academic school of composition who was not himself a 'natural', purely gifted musician in the Steinberg, Glazunov, or indeed Myaskovsky/Prokofiev sense.

Stravinsky's letters of the time give out resonances of the criticism at home.

'Everyone here,' he wrote to Andrey Rimsky-Korsakov from Paris in November 1910, 'is amazed and furious at how, judging from the papers, my [*Firebird*] suite was received [in St Petersburg].'[20] 'As you're well aware,' he told Florent Schmitt in September 1912, 'I'm valued *at nothing* in my admirable country ... Critics annoyed by my success abroad declare me without originality, that I'm not at the head of the movement (that's clever ["malin"]) but that on the contrary I'm merely at the tail of the snob theories, and all this after hearing the works before *Petrushka* (which hasn't been played in Russia yet, even in concert).'[21] But interviews of the time show that he could be just as waspish as his critics. In February 1913 he told the London *Daily Mail* that 'Russian musical life is at present stagnant. They cannot stand me there. *Petrushka* was performed at St Petersburg the same day as here, and I see the newspapers are now all comparing my work with the smashing of crockery.'[22] By contrast, as he told another interviewer three days later, 'I frankly place London above the Continental cities in discrimination and appreciation ... I think the English are amazingly intelligent. Not that they plume themselves on it, but in their quiet, dignified way very little escapes their notice.'[23] It is perhaps not unduly cynical to note that *The Firebird* had been on the whole very amicably received by the London press the previous June – not only by music critics, admittedly, but in any case conspicuously without the griping animus against novelty to which Stravinsky was or would soon be getting used to in St Petersburg and Paris. At the time of these interviews, *Petrushka* had just had its London premiere, once more to an appreciative – and this time more musical – press.

Stravinsky seems to have been justified in his view that the London critics of the day were open-minded in the sense that they did not automatically write off new work which challenged their received ideas, however disagreeably. For anyone familiar with the later entrenched response of English critics like Ernest Newman and Frank Howes, the two long and carefully judged reviews of the first London performances of *The Rite of Spring* in July 1913 by *The Times* critic H.C. Colles come as a refreshing surprise. Colles attended two of the three performances and gave himself time to reflect on the significance of music which, it is clear from his review of the actual premiere, he found thoroughly disconcerting at first hearing – as indeed who would not have done? 'The music,' he had written,

> is unlike anything that has been given us either by the Russians or by anyone else, though one can trace its origin in much that Stravinsky has already written in *Petrushka*. Harmonically it is extraordinarily rough and strident ... There is much that is hideously and cruelly harsh, even to ears accustomed to modern music, and much, too, that is exceedingly monotonous.[24]

After a second hearing Colles began to grasp the music's mechanisms:

> The functions of the composer and the producer are so balanced that it is possible to see every movement on the stage and at the same time to hear every note of the music. But the fusion goes deeper than this. The combination of the two elements of music and dancing does actually produce a new compound result, expressible in terms of rhythm – much as the combination of oxygen and hydrogen produces a totally different com-

pound, water. .... M. Stravinsky has made the best use of his opportunities, and utilizes the most amazing and complex rhythms with the utmost skill. He is so preoccupied with them that he has made no attempt to please the ear. .... [But] it seems hardly necessary to consider it as a real foretaste of the music of tomorrow; for M. Stravinsky has already shown himself so adaptable as a composer that his next ballet is no more likely to resemble *Le Sacre du Printemps* than that itself resembles *Pétrouchka*.

It is true that several passages in the later work are to some extent explained musically by precedents set in the earlier, but there is little reason to suppose that its harmonic principles will be strictly adhered to in the composer's next production. *Pétrouchka* was a complete work of extraordinary beauty and colour. *Le Sacre du Printemps* is at best an experiment in another direction, and not an entirely successful one.[25]

And Colles ends with a remarkable intuition:

If M. Stravinsky had wished to be really primitive, he would have been wise to abandon his full orchestra and to score his ballet for nothing but drums.

Even here there is some veiled suspicion that the sheer impact of the work might be meretricious, got up, an empty piece of theatre. But it was only in the 1920s that this became a persistent theme of British Stravinsky criticism. The structure of the criticism is of the 'them and us' variety. 'Stravinsky's adherents assure us . . .', 'they tried to have us believe', and so on. In other words: a conspiracy theory. The chief exponent of this view was the great Ernest Newman, for nearly forty years the music critic of the *Sunday Times*, and a formidable opponent of modernism, because he both was, and presented himself as, a well-informed modern critic with a perfectly proper grasp of the elements of the new music. For instance, in his famous controversy with George Bernard Shaw over Strauss's *Elektra* at the time of its London premiere in 1910, Newman's central strategy was to insist on his own credentials as a paid-up Straussian and a careful student of his music.[26] Similarly with Stravinsky, Newman always protested his admiration for *The Firebird* and *Petrushka* and what he called 'the best parts of *Le Sacre du Printemps*'.[27] He thereby deflected in advance the obvious objection that he was fundamentally out of sympathy with Stravinsky, and so cloaked his actually unsympathetic remarks in a certain justifiably reproachful authority: King Mark remonstrating with Tristan.

Newman's review of the Massine revival of *The Rite of Spring* in London in June 1921 was decisively headlined 'THE END OF A CHAPTER' – a deliberate tease, presumably, at those who had described the work as epoch-making. 'For some years,' Newman wrote,

the public has been confused and harassed by a little group of musicians and journalists who have tried to bluff it into believing that much of the music that the world has hitherto thought great was rather poor stuff, and that a new revelation had been vouchsafed to a composer named Stravinsky, of whom they were the prophets. They tried to make us believe that they held the winning card, which would sweep the board when they produced it. Well, they have produced it at last, and so far from sweeping the board it has been laughed off the board. The bluff has failed.[28]

With characteristic guile, Newman points to a few pages in *Petrushka* – 'in the main, a masterpiece' – where Stravinsky's inspiration is starting to run dry, while in *The Rite of Spring* he is careful to admit that the composer 'still had some fine things to say'. Thus the attack cannot be construed – like the Petersburg reviews – as a vulgar, provincial rejection of something alien and difficult. Instead, Newman's technique is to reduce Stravinsky to the level of a mere talent in decline. Stravinsky, in this view, is a pretty good composer, but in no sense a major genius. There is here nevertheless an echo of the early Russian tendency to want it both ways, about which Myaskovsky had complained: to praise every aspect of the music then end by dismissing it as unmusical. But Newman is too clever to fall into this trap without first circling round it a bit. He is perfectly aware of Stravinsky's importance, but is sincerely disturbed by aspects of the music which seem to him wilful, ugly and exaggerated. How else can one explain the fact that when the composer conducted two BBC performances of *Oedipus Rex* in May 1928, Newman – like Colles with *The Rite of Spring* – reviewed it twice, on consecutive Sundays.[29] He even let slip (in his first article) why he might later have felt the need to do this:

> The work is the strangest mixture of styles, and much of the music is insignificant. Yet as a whole it leaves us decidedly impressed: there may be little that can be called great, or grand, or searching, in the sense in which we are accustomed to apply terms to certain other works, but again and again we feel that the music is well on the way to deserving to be so characterised.

This may sound like arrant nonsense; but it is not quite. Newman can feel the power of *Oedipus Rex* as well as the next man, even without the help of the stage picture, as he himself admits; but his understanding of what constitutes musical profundity prevents him from admitting that Stravinsky has achieved his effect by musical means. And yet, since the performances were broadcast, what other means can there have been? Newman has a good deal to say about the value of such broadcasts in permitting a detached, objective hearing of difficult new works. Perhaps the idea is that enough of what we experience in the theatre or concert-hall comes through for us to record an impression but not enough for us to be over-excited by irrelevancies, so that – in an objective kind of way – our assessment of our own response is more likely to be truthful. Newman, we know, believed that it ought to be possible to judge works of art objectively. Even so, it is hard to escape the impression that at such times the critic is unconsciously looking for an excuse not to have to admit that the work at hand is a major phenomenon.

If Stravinsky had been in the habit of reading British press notices – which he might have been if he had known English well enough – he would certainly have seen Newman's reviews as a systematic attack with, probably, some ulterior motive. With his St Petersburg background and his more recent experience of the facetious Parisian press, that would have been a perfectly natural reaction. Yet Newman, though often maddeningly polemical in his way of pushing an absolute argument to the brink of absurdity, was rarely I think gratuitously, or at least improperly, malicious. Nor are his contradictions evidence of shallowness or laziness or ill-will, as they often seem to be with lesser critics.

It is interesting to compare Newman briefly in this respect with one of his main American opposite numbers, Olin Downes. Downes was critic of the *New York Times* from 1924 until his death in 1955, and acquired during that time a prestige which in retrospect seems out of all proportion to his merits as a musical thinker or even as a reliable chronicler. Certainly Stravinsky and his circle came to despise Downes. On one occasion in 1943 Nicholas Nabokov asked Stravinsky to send him 'any particularly stupid reviews that you may happen to have, Downes's for example'.[30] But Downes, though captious, temperamental and sometimes ill-informed, was not at first openly ill-disposed. His notice of the first New York concert performance of the *The Rite of Spring*, in January 1924, was unqualifiedly friendly if not strikingly penetrating, in which respect it is comparatively rare among early reviews of *The Rite*, which tended to combine lack of penetration with more or less open hostility.

But as with so many other Stravinsky critics, the contradictions soon began to creep in. Reviewing the composer's own US premiere of the Concerto for Piano and Wind in 1925, Downes mused that 'it does not appear ... to be of really authentic inspiration. This is just one of the amazing things Stravinsky can do.' In Paris 'he has developed the restlessness, the lack of spiritual poise, of the artistic alien'.[31] The latter remark is perceptive in a slightly uncomfortable way, if not enough so to make sense of the preceding non-sequitur. But Downes's most spectacular intellectual somersault came in his twin reviews of *Persephone*: its US premiere in Boston in March 1935, and its New York premiere eleven months later. The twins, alas, are far from identical. The Boston review is warm and appreciative, in the same kind of way as Downes's *Rite of Spring* notice. *Persephone*, he writes, 'is a music more integrated and consistent in style than perhaps any other score of Stravinsky's late period', and he praises it as 'one of the most distinguished and inspired of Stravinsky's compositions since *Le Sacre du Printemps*, and in a large measure a vindication of his later tendencies'.[32] But by the New York performance things are looking a bit different. Now the distinction and inspiration

> do not suffice, at a second hearing, to palliate the aridities and banalities which encumber all too many pages. And not only aridity; some of the musical figurations are excessively trivial or directly cheap. For example, the orchestral part of Eumolpe's 'Tu viens pour dominer' is one more instance of Stravinsky the unbelievably futile and trite. Here is the old story, true of so many modern masters of increasing technic and decreasing inspiration, of a lack of invention which not all the technic and style in the world can conceal....[33]

One could almost imagine that Downes had meanwhile come across a clipping of Ernest Newman's vitriolic review of the British premiere of *Persephone* just over a year before, and become ashamed of his too ready enjoyment. 'With each new work of Stravinsky's in recent years,' Newman had remarked by way of conclusion,

> I have felt that he had drawn on the last depreciated franc of his modest resources for our benefit, but always he has proved to us that behind one void there can be yet

another. So it is quite probable that a year or two hence we shall again be sitting as his guests in Queen's Hall, where once more he will permit us to share with him the abundance of his musical penury.[34]

Venom like that is seldom wasted on an unworthy victim. Newman's abuse, no less than Downes's patent and somewhat pathetic anxiety, may well look like covert evidence of an underlying respect for their object. But why did it have to be covert?

It is possible to explain away the Russian hostility to Stravinsky's early Paris success as the simple jealousy of outraged provincials, and in some cases as straight personal vendetta; but there is already plenty of the kind of contradiction and confusion so noticeable also in later western criticism. Of course, such things are to some extent the common currency of all hack reviewing. But they rarely reach such bizarre levels as with Stravinsky. It may be, on the contrary, that they represent a particular response to something in the music itself. Perhaps, as I have already half-suggested, it was Stravinsky's aggressive break with traditional syntax, combined with his irresistible brilliance and energy, which first triggered this highly volatile ambivalence on the part of his critics. And perhaps, later, it was his seemingly unruly and perverse handling of materials, his mixing of styles and genres – his misreading, in Harold Bloom's sense, of the classical tradition – that perpetuated the love–hate relationship so many critics seem to have felt towards a composer widely regarded as one of the greatest creative artists of his time. Indeed, a Bloomite might argue that misreading already lay behind Stravinsky's trouble with his compatriots, which brings us back – via the Rimsky-Korsakov family – to the issue of outraged provincialism and personal vendetta.

If we look at all this from Stravinsky's point of view, we may note that many of these attributes of his creative personality relate directly, if superficially, to his situation, first, as an outsider in a circle of traditionally trained and traditionally minded musicians, and later as an exile in foreign lands. Incidentally, the role of exile as a motif in Stravinsky's stage works has not, so far as I am aware, been properly studied: *The Soldier's Tale*, *Oedipus Rex*, *Persephone*, *Orpheus*, *The Rake's Progress*, *Threni*, are all in one way or another concerned with this issue, and (apart perhaps from *Threni*) their music is a classic expression of the décraciné, in that it draws on materials and resources that do not belong to the genealogy (or personality) of the technique with which they are 'composed'. If so, it is small wonder that Stravinsky reacted badly to a critique which took its tone specifically from his supposedly rootless handling of revered traditions. After all, if insecurity breeds over-assertiveness, we can safely say that rejection will redouble insecurity: a vicious circle that is matched all too often and all too well by vicious language.

Notes

(All translations in the text are mine.)

1. Igor Stravinsky and Robert Craft (1962), *Expositions and Developments*, London: Faber & Faber, p. 111.
2. I mention these particular composers as they were participants in the conference at which the paper was given which forms the basis of this chapter.
3. Richard Taruskin (1996), *Stravinsky and the Russian Traditions: a Biography of the Works through Mavra*, Oxford: Oxford University Press. See especially pp. 384–95 and 974–77. Since delivering the paper I have come to feel that Taruskin exaggerates Stravinsky's resentment against Steinberg. See my review in *Music and Letters* (1997), vol. 78, no.3, pp. 450–55.
4. See for instance his letter of 7/20 November 1910 to Andrey Rimsky-Korsakov, in L.S. Dyachkova (ed.) (1973), *I.F. Stravinskiy: stat'i i materiali*, Moscow: Sovetskiy Kompozitor, p. 450: 'I am puzzled not to have heard from you. After the performance of my *Firebird* suite, mother wrote to me that you would be writing to me in detail about it. I waited and waited – and lost patience. Apart from the general wild abuse in the newspapers, I know nothing. Even Ziloti has not written. I take it very seriously to heart. Not a word from anyone.'
5. Sabaneyev, 'Vesna svyashchennaya', *Golos Moskvï*, 8 June 1913. A lubok is a crude print in a comic or popular Russian style.
6. J. Wihtol, 'Theater und Musik: Fünftes Kussewizki-Konzert', *St Petersburger Zeitung*, 13 December 1913. Original in German. Reprinted in Russian in Vitol [*sic*], *Vospominaniya, stat'i, pis'ma*, Leningrad: *Muzïka*, 1969, pp. 249–51. The present translation is from the German.
7. *St Petersburger Zeitung*, 15 February 1914. Original in German. Reprinted in Russian in Vitol, *Vospominaniya*, p. 254. The present translation is from the Russian.
8. A. Rimsky-Korsakov, '7-y simfonicheskiy kontsert S. Kusevitskovo', *Russkaya molva*, 25 January 1913.
9. See Stravinsky's letter of 3/16 December 1910 to Andrey, in *I.F. Stravinskiy: stat'i i materiali*, pp. 451–52. English translation in Taruskin, *Stravinsky and the Russian Traditions*, p. 700.
10. *Expositions and Developments*, p. 135.
11. See his letters to Andrey of 7/20 and 26 November 1910, in *I.F. Stravinskiy: stat'i i materiali*, pp. 450–51. A translation of the second of these letters is in Taruskin, *Stravinsky and the Russian Traditions*, p. 646.
12. *Expositions and Developments*, p. 135. But Andrey's 'hostile letter' has not survived.
13. Letter of 8/21 July 1911, in *I.F. Stravinskiy: stat'i i materiali*, pp. 459–62. English translation in Taruskin, *Stravinsky and the Russian Traditions*, pp. 972–74.
14. M. Dvinsky, 'Restavratsiya "Khovanshchinï"', *Birzhevïye vedomosti*, 22 January 1913.
15. A. Koptyayev, 'Simfonicheskiy kontsert S. Kusevitskovo', *Vechernyaya birzhevaya gazeta*, 24 January 1913.
16. 28 January 1913. The postcard is in the Paul Sacher Stiftung, Basle.
17. S.I. Shlifshteyn (ed.) (1960), *N.Y. Myaskovskiy: stat'i, pis'ma, vospominaniya*, Moscow: Sovetskiy Kompozitor, vol. 2, p. 21.
18. Letter of 20 June [/3 July] 1913, in *N.Y. Myaskovskiy: stat'i, pis'ma, vospominaniya*, vol. 2, p. 326.
19. See Stravinsky's letter to Derzhanovsky of 12 [/25] August 1913, in *I.F. Stravinskiy: stat'i i materiali*, pp. 476–77; and Myaskovsky's letter to Derzhanovsky of 8 [/21] September 1913, in *N.Y. Myaskovskiy: stat'i, pis'ma, vospominaniya*, vol. 2, p. 521,

note 125. A full English translation of Stravinsky's letter is in R. Craft (ed.), (1982) *Stravinsky Selected Correspondence*, vol. 1, London: Faber & Faber, pp. 55–56.

20.   Letter of 26 November 1910, in *I.F. Stravinskiy: stat'i i materialï*, p. 451; *Stravinsky and the Russian Traditions*, p. 646.

21.   Letter of 18 September 1912. See F. Lesure (ed.) (1980), *Igor Stravinsky: la carrière européenne*, Paris: Musée d'Art Moderne de la Ville de Paris, p. 19, item 45.

22.   13 February 1913.

23.   *The London Budget*, 16 February 1913.

24.   *The Times*, 12 July 1913; facsimile in F. Lesure (ed.) (1980), *Igor Stravinsky: Le Sacre du printemps – Dossier de presse*, Geneva: Editions Minkoff, 1980, p. 67. But the book reverses the dates of Colles's two articles.

25.   *The Times*, 26 July 1913, facsimile in ibid., pp. 63–64.

26.   See 'The Newman–Shaw Controversy Concerning Strauss: 1910 and 1914', in Herbert Van Thal (ed.) (1962), *Testament of Music*, London: Putnam, pp. 115–62.

27.   See his review of *Jeu de cartes* in *The Sunday Times*, 24 October 1937.

28.   *The Sunday Times*, 3 July 1921; facsimile in F. Lesure (ed.), op. cit., pp. 74–75.

29.   *The Sunday Times*, 20 and 27 May 1928.

30.   *Stravinsky Selected Correspondence*, vol. 2, p. 376, note 32.

31.   *New York Times*, 8 February 1925.

32.   *New York Times*, 16 March 1935.

33.   *New York Times*, 5 February 1936.

34.   *The Sunday Times*, 2 December 1934.

11 Mobilising Our Man: Politics and Music in Poland during the Decade after the Second World War

Adrian Thomas

The study of Polish music since the Second World War provides us with a number of unusually distinctive periods shaped largely by non-musical events. Perhaps we should not be so surprised, given the country's turbulent history and anyone interested in delving further into Poland's past may nowadays do so in the excellent English-language studies by authors such as Norman Davies and Adam Zamoyski.[1] Chronologies of cultural–political events since the war have recently been compiled by Marta Fik and Jakub Karpiński, both of whom bring together facts and contemporary polemics affecting a wide range of artistic activities in post-war Poland.[2]

The ten years immediately after the Second World War – what may reasonably be termed the Dark Decade – are particularly rich in the intercutting of music and society, music and politics. What, in the particular circumstances of Polish composers, was composition – was it their own affair or did anybody else have a hand in it? Who was communicating what and to whom? And within what general context did they live and work? This chapter certainly does not pretend to present the totality of their experiences, but it does refer to totalitarianism, Polish style. It highlights the genres of the mass song and the cantata, with reference to some of the principal composers; it outlines the gist of significant meetings and conferences; and finally it discusses a number of ways in which composers developed away from officially encouraged outlets.

The principal fact of the post-war decade in Poland is this: that it saw the rise and fall of 'socialist realism', or *socrealizm* as Poles called it. This dogma was imported from the Soviet Union and started to take hold in 1947 and by the end of the 1940s was clearly controlling Poland's cultural policy. It was deliberately designed to manipulate society, to unite it behind the reconstruction of Poland (a laudable aim) and the monopoly of a socialist government. Its brief was mass communication, which was more easily controlled in the days before television, let alone fax machines, satellite dishes and the Internet. The focus was on the press, radio and film (few homes had telephones). The first four years of the 1950s saw the height of the policy's powers but, following Stalin's death in March 1953, its influence in Poland gradually waned and by 1956 it was thoroughly, although not entirely enfeebled. Today's preconceptions of socialist-realist music revolve largely around the idea of endless songs marching to glory in a relentless 4/4. But one of the most recent discoveries indicates that considerable variation and leeway were possible within the developing dogma of the post-war decade.

It has long been known that Witold Lutosławski (1913–94) composed a number of 'mass songs' in the early fifties.[3] All but one of these songs were published at the time. The exception was *Towarzysz* ('Comrade', 1952). A recording of *Towarzysz*, made in 1952,[4] was discovered by the present author in the archives of Polish Radio in February 1994, and it reveals, alongside the manuscript which became available for study when Lutosławski's musical materials were deposited at the Paul Sacher Foundation in Basel, that Lutosławski applied a degree of imagination unusual in the genre (Example 25). It has much more musical personality than the vast majority of songs to comradeship and socialist solidarity. It is in 3/2, rather than the usual 4/4, the baritone is halted twice by pauses, the second time coloured by an unexpected chord (a characteristic shared by one or two of Lutosławski's orchestral pieces of the time), and a similar event occurs in the purely choral response. The text is by one of the better Polish poets of the time, Stanisław Wygodzki (1907–92), and Lutosławski seems to have taken some care to provide a musical setting – including the pauses and dissonances – which mirrors the questioning of comrades in the struggle (second refrain and third verse):

> ... I w każdej krainie, o każdej godzinie
> Widzimy nasz sztandar nad nami on płynie.
> Od ilu już znamy się lat?
>
> Widziałem cię w boju,
> Od iluż to lat?
> Pieśń twoja jest moją,
> Towarzysz to brat.
>
> (... In every country, at every hour,
> We see our flag flying over us.
> For how many years have we known each other?
>
> I have seen you in battle –
> For how many years?
> Your song is mine;
> Comrade means brother.)

The popular as distinct from the polemical or military song was the most visible and the most durable of all the musical legacies of the post-war period. Some, like the most famous song to the rebuilding of Warsaw – *Na prawo most, na lewo*

Ex. 25   Lutosławski: *Towarzysz*, first verse and refrain.

most ('On the right, a bridge, on the left, a bridge', text by Helena Kołaczkowska, 1950), by Alfred Gradstein (1904–54) – are still popular songs. Gradstein's hit did have a message in 1950, but its lyrics were couched in a relaxed waltz tempo and used everyday language – 'I look around me at 8 a.m. as I go to work. Isn't the city wonderful: streets are being rebuilt, and the buses and trams are running. Soon there will be new bridges across the Vistula to left and to right' (Example 26). Gradstein was one of the main composers of vocal music after the war.[5] Like many of his colleagues – Edward Olearczyk (b.1915) and Władysław Szpilman (b.1911),[6] for example – he came from the world of light music and slotted quite happily into the new requirement for uplifting songs of many kinds.

Some composers did not write any music overtly for 'the masses' – the closest Grażyna Bacewicz (1909–69) came was by writing encores for her violin recitals, and the critic-composers Stefan Kisielewski (1911–91) and Zygmunt Mycielski (1907–87) were so closely identified either with outright opposition to or guarded accommodation of the government's cultural policy that they refused to con-tribute to such vocal genres. In fact – as an aside – there are many different permu-tations of genres in which individual composers worked and each found a balance, that he or she could live with, to keep body and soul together without too much heartache. Witold Rudziński (b.1913) reckons that over 1500 mass songs were written in the post-war decade[7] – an astonishing number, so why did so many composers comply? Two events, one from 1948, the other from 1950, sym-bolize the pressures faced by Polish musicians.

The concept of the mass song was introduced from the Soviet Union in July 1947 by Zofia Lissa (1908–90), the main Marxist–Leninist arbiter during the period, in an article in the weekly newspaper *Odrodzenie* ('Rebirth').[8] Eight months later, in March 1948, a group of writers and composers met outside Warsaw to discuss what constituted a mass song;[9] and Polish Radio, together with the Ministry of Culture, organised a mass song competition. The rules were straightforward: songs in stanza form, with a rhythmical and memorable refrain, a tonal melody and suitable for amateur performers. There were twenty lyrics to choose from and the songs had to be acceptable in the wider community, to the armed forces and the workers. With a prize of 25 000zł each for the successful entries, not surprisingly it attracted 408 entries. But the jury, which included Zofia Lissa, the composers Rudziński and Mycielski, and the Polish Radio conductor, Kołaczkowski, had problems in finding quality entries – only sixty-eight made the first cut and only seven top prizes were awarded. Both Lissa and Mycielski pub-lished articles on the outcome of the competition[10] and the polemic resurfaced periodically thereafter, as in Lissa's article in the first issue of a new, politically orthodox journal, *Muzyka*,[11] and in an article by Rudziński four years later when the genre was clearly on the wane.[12]

Although further competitions were held for mass songs, they did not always bring results and subtler pressures began to be applied to composers. The state had learned that arm-twisting, through professional organisations like Polish Radio and the ZKP (Polish Composers' Union) as well as private persuasion (not

Ex. 26   Gradstein: *Na prawo most, na lewo most*, refrain.

to mention financial incentives), more readily produced what it required. In a volume of conversations with the Russian musicologist Irina Nikolska, Lutosławski gave a personal insight into the power-play that went into the commissioning, composing and dissemination of such songs.

> During the 1st Congress of Polish Composers (1950), held in the building of the National Museum, Minister Sokorski took me aside, to a store-room (where brooms, buckets, litter-bins, etc., were kept), – he badly wanted to have a tête-à-tête with me. 'Do write,' he said, 'something like Shostakovich's "Song of the Forests" – we'll give you a State Prize'. My answer was to the effect that I could not do that for the simple reason that work of this sort did not interest me.[13]

Lutosławski went on to say:

> ... the fact is that I have never resorted to compromise. The only thing for which I can reproach myself is the circumstance that I have written several 'mass songs'. I could not help doing it, for I was the only bread-winner of the family (consisting of four persons). I had been instigated to this deed by Henryk Swolkień, a musicologist [and composer, 1910–90] on the staff of the Polish Radio. At that time I worked for the Radio – on the staff, too, – as a composer of incidental music for radio plays and children's programmes. One day Swolkień told me: 'Members of the Editorial Board are discontented with you: you are known to have written a few songs for the Armia Krajowa [Home Army] (during the war) – why do you write, they say, no mass songs today? Take my advice, do write some songs – otherwise troubles are in store for you'. In short, I selected some texts, in which there were no political implications whatsoever, and composed a few songs – alas, what's done is done.[14]

Lutosławski was horrified to find at a concert some time later that duplicated copies of one of his songs were being freely distributed, this time with a totally new text in praise of Stalin. And thirty years later, copies of this same 'cantata to Stalin' resurfaced mysteriously in Polish libraries during martial law in the 1980s as an apparent attempt to discredit Lutosławski, who was a firm Solidarity supporter. Writing the music was one thing – the composer had communicated with the Party and arguably the masses – but the communication path followed by the music after that was sometimes subject to further interference outside the composer's control. Small wonder that Lutosławski and many other composers were intensely wary of the Party and its propaganda outlets.

The second event, in 1950, was one of the first results of a new means the PZPR – Polish United Workers' Party – invented for regulating the output of composers. This was the *przesłuchanie* (peer-review listening session), one of which was reported, with photographs, from Polish Radio in the early summer of 1950.[15] Three months later, the ZKP instituted vetting procedures which were applied across the whole range of compositions, not just to mass songs. The first instance of a Composers' Union 'listening session' for mass songs was exceptionally well documented in the sixth issue of *Muzyka* (September 1950).[16]

On 6 September 1950, the Mass Song section of the ZKP held a peer-review listening session in Warsaw's National Museum. Edward Olearczyk gave an introductory address which included the exhortation that 'our songs are a mobilising agent in the struggle for peace, in the struggle for the implementation of the

Ex. 27   *Ankieta:* Table of nine Polish songs, based on *Muzyka* (5 September 1950, p. 70)

ANKIETA

Obok dyskusji zorganizowano także ankietę. Ankieta była anonimowa. Żadała tylko wskazania zawodu, wieku, rodzaju płci, wykształcenia oraz oświadęzenia, czy się posiada wykształcenie muzyczne.

Wypełniający ankietę miał odpowiedzieć, jaką ocenę postawiłby za muzykę i tekst wysłuchanego utworu, czy muzyka i tekst harmonizują ze sobą, czy potrafiłby zanucić daną pieśń po jej parokrotnym usłyszeniu.

Wyniki ankiety z I przesłuchania sekcji Pieśni Masowej:

	Utwór	Ocena muzyki	Ocena tekstu	Uwagi wybrane z niektórych ankiet:
1.	Z. Turski Piosenka 1-majowa (słowa Gruszczyńskiego)	4,3	4,3	Melodia, ładna, przystępna; marszowość psują wydłużenia 2-ch ostatnich wierszy zwrotki; masowa
2.	W. Rudziński Siedzi Maryś (sł. Sadowskiego)	4	4	Melodia ładna, ale trudna. Kontynuacja naszych najlepszych tradycji pieśniarskich. Tekst słaby ideologicznie.
3.	W. Rudziński Zrękowiny (sł. Kołaczkowskiej)	4	4	Piosenki estradowe.
4.	E. Olearczyk Piosenka ZMP-owców Warszawy (sł. Woroszylskiego)	3,8	3,5	Melodia chwytliwa, jednak zbyt szybkie tempo. Tekst słaby – poetycko. masowa
5.	Wł. Szpilman Wiatr wolności (sł. Winklera)	3,8	3,9	Melodia łatwa i dobra. Tekst patetyczny, nieprzeżyty. masowa
6.	Z. Turski Pieśń bojowników o wolność (sł. Bezymieńskiego – tł. Brzechwy)	3,3	3,9	Brak kulminacji melodycznej. Melodia trudna. – Tekst dobry. Niemasowa
7.	W. Lutosławski Nowa Huta (sł. Wygodzkiego)	3	3	Wspaniałe opracowanie muzyczne, ale bardzo trudne (zwł. refren). – Tekst nieaktualny. Niemasowa
8.	J. Maklakiewicz Pieśń o Stalinie (sł. Gałczyńskiego)	2,8	2,8	Melodia trudna, sentymentalna. – Tekst slaby, groteskowy. Niemasowa
9.	H. Swolkień Przyjaźni złocista (sł. Krzemienieckiej)	2,8	3,6	Konstrukcja mel. nieprzejrzysta. – Refren nie skontrastowany. – Tekst pogmatwany przez pytania, na które nie ma odpowiedzi. Niemasowa

Six-Year Plan'. Also present at the listening session were members of the ZMP (Związek Młodzieży Polskiej, usually referred to as Zetempowiec or Polish Youth Union), which was one of the Party's organisations from 1948 to 1956, and the ZHP (Związek Harcerstwa Polskiego or Polish Scouts' Association). First, the Polish Radio Choir sang seven mass songs, five Polish, one Russian and one Czech. The five Polish songs included Lutosławski's *Żelazny Marsz* ('Iron March'), one of his most popular war-time resistance songs and a song which was then hijacked by the post-war authorities as a mass song. None of these seven songs was up for judgement that day. There then followed discussions on nine other songs and a vote was taken on the success or otherwise of both music and text of each (Example 27). The report of the discussions is lengthy, but in the RH column of the 'Ankieta' ('Poll') there is a summary of comments made by the participating listeners.

Top of the list came *Piosenka pierwszomajowa* ('Song of the First of May', text by Krzysztof Gruszczyński, 1949) by Zbigniew Turski (1908–79). Its melody was described as 'lovely, accessible'. In fact, this song is a good example of a simple melody and accompaniment which, like many other marching mass songs, moves symbolically from minor to major for the refrain (Example 28). It has the classic, upright 4/4 metre, but it certainly does not measure up to Lutosławski's *Towarzysz*. Compared to many other mass songs, Turski's is very strait-laced, and yet, at this relatively early stage in the game, it seemed to fit the bill and was judged 'masowa', with ratings of 4.3 (out of 5) for both music and lyrics. But not all the songs were judged to be worthy of the name 'mass song'. Rudziński's two songs had ideologically weak texts and were deemed to belong more to the music hall or stage.

Then there was Lutosławski's hymn to Nowa Huta, a gigantic iron foundry and surrounding new town then being built on the outskirts of Kraków as part of the Party's plan to thwart any resurgent intellectual resistance in Poland's ancient capital. *Nowa Huta* had 'splendidly worked-out music, but was very hard, especially the refrain'. And the full report said:

> The discussion was pointed but sincere. Most of the speakers agreed that the song had been composed from spurious musical and poetic material and was beyond repair. Ms Legomska, a ZMP activist, said: 'I did not hear the voice of our foundry in this song. The melody is remote from us and the text sounds as if it had been written half a year ago! 9000 young people work in Nowa Huta and they sing their own songs. ... Come and see how we work, and then transplant our zeal into your new songs.'[17]

Nowa Huta was judged 'niemasowa' ('not a mass song'). And yet, not only was it published by PWM (Polish Music Publishers) that same month (Example 29) but Polish Radio's archives show that at least three recordings were made of the song, one of them a matter of weeks after this listening session.[18] This would indicate that such peer reviews were not all-powerful in authorising or denying life to a composition.

Perhaps the most interesting comments – and ratings – were addressed to the 8th-ranked song, the only one to Stalin. The text was by Konstanty Ildefons Gałczyński (1905–53), one of the state's main apologists and a fine poet in his

Ex. 28   Turski: *Piosenka pierwszomajowa*, first verse and refrain.

PIOSENKA PIERWSZOMAJOWA

ZBIGNIEW TURSKI

Vivo e gaio (♩ = ca 120)

Wzdłuz zie-mi swo-bo-dnej od mo-rza do Tatr, po nie-bie po-go-dnym prze-cha-dza się wiatr i zo-rzę ro-zwi-ja, jak ha-sło w pocho-dzie i śpie-wem się sta-je, gdy schwy-ta go mło-dzież. Pio-sen-ka se-rca nam u-zbra—ja i na-przód pro-wa-dzi nas, pio-sen-ka o pierwszym ma-ja, o świę-cie lu-do-wych mas. Pio-

Ex. 29   Lutosławski: *Nowa Huta*, first verse and refrain.

own right. In fact, Gałczyński was one of the first writers to issue a public self-criticism (not a common event in Poland),[19] a confession that also implicated two other important poets and song writers, Władysław Broniewski (1897–1962) and Wygodzki. In this instance, Gałczyński's text was described as 'feeble and grotesque' by the representative of the ZMP. The melody was difficult and sentimental. The ZHP representative thought there was a disharmony between the music and the text, a point taken up by the ubiquitous Zofia Lissa. She felt that a song about Stalin in the rhythm of a polonaise – a dance of the nobility – struck a false accent, even though she understood that Jan Maklakiewicz (1899–1954) had been trying to give the music a national character. Someone had shouted out during the performance 'Since when did the fancy-dressed Polish aristocracy build any new villages?' A pertinent point, commented Lissa.[20]

There are only a few such detailed accounts of listening sessions: they soon disappeared from public view (probably under pressure from the membership of the ZKP) and by 1952 only a bald statement of what was listened to at a particular session was given, this time not in *Muzyka* but in the ZKP's own internal type-written *Biuletyn informacyjny*, which had limited circulation. But this vetting system continued right through until the very end of 1955, when the last listening sessions were reported in the *Biuletyn* in five Polish cities other than Warsaw. On the whole, the activities of Polish 'socialist realism' in the arts, though often blunt and negative, rarely aimed to extract blood in public.

Of the 1500 mass songs mentioned earlier, about a fifth, some 300 and a mix of polemical and non-polemical, were published either by PWM, by the ZMP or other organisations like Samopomoc Chłopska (Peasants' Self-Help). Tracking these titles down can be difficult, but there are indications in Polish Radio catalogues that over 100 recordings of mass songs made between 1950–55 have survived (many more of course were broadcast live); 1950 was the high-point (with over two dozen surviving recordings), with a substantial drop by 1955, when only four appear to have been recorded.

How broad was the stylistic range of music for the masses? There was quite a variety of idioms, as has already been observed. But what about the much-vaunted mission to communicate with the people through their own music? Clearly, Maklakiewicz miscalculated in his use of the polonaise; other Polish dances, however, are much more clearly associated with the peasant or labourer, therefore with the Party and its leaders. Not surprisingly, to get young people on side, composers and lyricists bore in mind the lively krakowiak (2/4) and mazurka (3/4) when writing songs about and for young people. Gradstein and Olearczyk's songs about the Polish Youth Union, the ZMP, are good examples: snappy, well-written – the Polish equivalent of the knapsack song or 'I'm H-A-P-P-Y!'. For a well-composed song, sophisticated in its catchy use of real folk-rhythmic models (mixing it with duple and triple metres), it is hard to beat Witold Rudziński's depiction in *Po zielonym moście* ('Over the Green Bridge', text by Tadeusz Kubiak, 1951) of colourful young lads, armed with pick-axes and shovels, crossing the green bridge to build houses (Example 30).

Ex. 30   Rudziński: *Po zielonym moście*, opening.

The simple truth is that if the music is fun and memorable it survives. But it can also be reflective. Lutosławski's most popular mass song – measured by its print runs, radio recordings and appearances in 'Radio i Świat' – was *Wyszłabym ja* ('I would marry', text by Leopold Lewin, 1950). A young woman consults a clover leaf on whether she should marry the bricklayer, the weaver or the turner. Lutosławski's setting won him second prize (the first was not awarded) in a mass song competition held in 1950. Its success was due to a number of distinctive factors: it has a female protagonist, an unusually relaxed tempo of a slow mazurka, a strong folkloric melodic line, and an inverted formal structure – the unvarying refrain comes first, followed by three verses, although the song's alternating minor modality and tonic major key are conventional. Lutosławski neatly matches the woman's indecision by largely avoiding tonic resolutions in the verses (Example 31). Incidentally, this is the only mass song which Lutosławski appears ever to have performed, according to Polish Radio's archives.[21] Given that the song is his only truly non-political mass song, it is a pity that the tape has disappeared, even if it was for understandable reasons.

The subjects covered by mass songs ranged from peasants and the countryside to the workers and the city, although, with the exception of the Nowa Huta complex near Kraków, it is noticeable that urban attention was firmly centred on Warsaw. That, after all, was where the main action was. So we should not be surprised at Gradstein's *Na prawo most, na lewo most* nor that the construction of the main East–West highway through Warsaw should be celebrated by Maklakiewicz.[22] The highway was a major building achievement and its opening on 22 July 1949 was as important for Warsaw as the old Route 66 was in the United States.

By far the most unwelcome compositional task was the mass song in praise of the Party, of leaders like the General Secretary of the PZPR, Bolesław Bierut (1892–1956), or the Soviet leader, Stalin, or of army generals, even of songs to brotherhood or peace, because everyone knew that the underlying motivation was political. Furthermore, although Stalin or the desire for peace could be lauded in songs, there developed a parallel demand for more elaborate odes to socialism.

The burden of making the grand statement about lofty ideals fell to those composers prepared to write a cantata. It is noticeable that many of the prolific composers of mass songs did not make this step upwards. This was left mainly to the 'serious' composers. Cantatas could sometimes be as short as a mass song and were rarely much longer than twenty minutes. One short example by Lutosławski has resurfaced in the past couple of years. It is called *Warszawie-sława!* ('Glory to Warsaw!', text by Ewa Szelburg-Zarembina, date unknown). The manuscript – like those of most of his mass songs – is now kept alongside the bulk of his creative output at the Paul Sacher Foundation in Basel. A recording was discovered at Polish Radio in 1995, although it is of very poor sound quality, unlike that of tapes of his mass songs.

The text of *Warszawie-sława!* concerns the rebuilding of Warsaw and recounts, in general terms, the mythical beginnings of the city through to its horrendous struggle for survival during the Second World War:

Ex. 31   Lutosławski: *Wyszłabym ja.*

W. LUTOSŁAWSKI

Fa- le w Wi - śle pły - ną, szu-mi w ga - ju liść.

Za któ-re-go ko-ni-czy - no, chłopca za mąż iść, za którego, ko-ni-czy-no,

chłopca za mąż iść?

1. Pewien murarz chodzi do mnie, za je - go spra-wą do-my sto-ją,
2. Pewien włókniarz chodzi do mnie, na je - gokrosnach kwitnie wio-sna,
3. Pewien tokarz chodzi do mnie, i - skry to-kar-kę je-go sto-ją,

mó-wi, że ko-cha mnie o-gro - mnie jak mu-ra - rkę swo - ją. Wyszłabym ja za mu-ra-rza,
mó-wi, że ko-cha mnie o-gro - mnie tak jak swo-je kro - sna. Wyszłabym ja za włó-knia-rza,
mó-wi, że ko-cha mnie o-gro - mnie jak to-ka-rkę swo - ją. Wyszłabym ja za to-ka-rza,

(Ex. 31 concluded)

... Nad Wisłą, Biała woda, warszawscy dzielni ludzie
Z ruin dzwigają miasto w pięknym, radosnym trudzie

Nam pokój stanał na straży
Ten Wielki Budowniczy
Pod jego skrzydłami rosną mury stolicy.

(... On the banks of the Vistula, White Water, the brave people of Warsaw
Are raising the town from the ruins: beautiful, cheerful hardship.

Peace, the Great Builder,
Has mounted guard over us.
The walls of our capital are growing under his wings ...)

Given the various epithets attached to Stalin, it is possible that 'Peace, the Great Builder' is a covert reference to the Soviet leader, in which case the uncertain dating of *Warszawie-sława!* might be narrowed down to *c.* 1950; the cantata is conceivably related to Lutosławski's meeting with Minister Sokorski that year. But, given its short length (some five minutes), Lutosławski's cantata has more the feel of an extended mass song than anything truly elaborate. For the grander gesture, it is necessary to turn to the work of other composers.

The subjects of most cantatas were similar to those of mass songs: in 1951, for example, cantatas or symphonies to peace were composed by Andrzej Dobrowolski (1921–90), Andrzej Panufnik (1914–91) and Stanisław Skrowaczewski (b.1923), an ode to Stalin was written by Gradstein and a cantata on bricklayers by Kazimierz Serocki (1922–81).[23] There was also a backwards historical glance in Maklakiewicz's celebration of the Paris Commune (1949) and some doffing of the cap to things like the new Constitution of 1952 in *Karta serc* ('Charter of the Hearts') by Tadeusz Szeligowski (1896–1963). Both Panufnik and Skrowaczewski disowned their 1951 compositions, not least because of their embarrassment with the texts. Panufnik, however, having fled Poland in 1954, re-used music from his Symphony in his post-defection *Sinfonia Elegiaca* (1957) and in his later *Invocation for Peace* (1972).

Panufnik's text was provided by Iwaszkiewicz, the librettist of Szymanowski's opera *King Roger* thirty years earlier. It consists of three connected movements, marked 'Lamentoso', 'Drammatico' and 'Solenne', the first two being inspired by prose fragments without actually using them, the last one being a setting of a four-verse poem. Sentiments typical of such works are contained in the unheard words behind the central movement:

> Ale wybucha bunt przeciw biernemu cierpieniu. Prawo do życia i walka o życie jest moc-niejsza od lamentów. Czasami walczyć – to żyć. Lament i walka słabych – niewiele, aby przeciwstawić potworowi wojny. Music się zrodzić wola pokoju, walka pokoju, obrona pokoju.
> (But revolt bursts forth against passive suffering. The right to live and fight for life is stronger than lamentation. Sometimes to fight – is to live. Laments and the resistance of the weak – too little this with which to oppose the horrors of war. To fight for peace, to defend peace, the will for peace must be born!)

Whatever the Party's motives for encouraging such sentiments – and they were the same motives that prompted the International Congress of Intellectuals in the Defence of Peace, held in Wrocław (Breslau) in August 1948, at which Panufnik was one of the Polish representatives – it should be borne in mind that Poland and Eastern Europe had gone through the sort of terror that most today would have nightmares about and there was understandable paranoia. Certainly, the Party whipped up such fears for its own ends, but the desire for peace, especially when the Korean War started in June 1950, was very real. So songs and cantatas on the subject did have a certain rationale and sometimes some fine music, as in Skrowaczewski's *Cantata for Peace*.

The third movement of this cantata is affectingly lyrical, and Skrowaczewski incorporates a well-known ancient Polish melody, 'Chmiel' ('Hops'), collected by the nineteenth-century ethnologist, Oskar Kolberg. The setting, for solo soprano, has its roots in Soviet music and in the folk-based compositions of Szymanowski such as his *Stabat Mater* (1926), which served as an important model for a number of Polish composers. The ensuing finale with its concentration on the Polish word for peace – 'pokój' – is an uncomfortable and unconvincing contrast in its pastiche of an eighteenth-century fugue.[24] In fact, 'Baroquerie' was very common in the early 1950s, probably because it provided uncontroversial but varied technical support for composers at a time when the norms were hackneyed memories of classical procedures. Back-to-Bach fugues also occur in the cantatas by Dobrowolski and Jan Krenz (b.1926),[25] for example, but the extent of Baroque influence was even wider. Bolesław Szabelski (1896–1979) wrote a *Concerto grosso* (1954) and Lutosławski's entire *Concerto for Orchestra* (1954) – rightly held up at the time and since as the towering achievement of the period – is based on Baroque techniques and forms:

> It is a neo-baroque composition, in a sense. The opening Intrada is played *détaché à la* Bach and Handel. There are Passacaglia, Toccata, Capriccio. But all these baroque genres are folklore-tinctured, which results in fairly novel patterns.[26]

The significance is that Lutosławski's expertise and imagination surmounted without destroying the prevailing ethos of the time and the *Concerto for Orchestra* came towards the end of the period in question. He also had two decades of composing behind him (he was forty-one when he completed the Concerto), and along with other mature composers he coped more ably with socialist-realism's ambiguous pitfalls. When a younger composer stepped out into the limelight, he either played very safe – as did Tadeusz Baird (1928–81) when, aged twenty-one, he wrote his *Sinfonietta* (1949) – or made a brash attempt at programmatic composition, as did Krenz when, aged twenty-four, he composed his *Conversation of Two Cities*. Krenz's cantata, like Skrowaczewski's, illustrates how ill-signposted were the stylistic norms of socialist realism. It is scored for orchestra and two choirs, one representing the Soviet capital, one the Polish. It begins in operatic fashion with the equivalent of 'Halt! Who goes there?' from the citizens of Warsaw. There then follows an orchestral interlude (shades of Fauré) and the main section in which there is much bragging about building schools (We are building schools – 'Budujemy szkoły') before Krenz launches into a fairly undignified if upbeat Baroque fugue (I am happy – 'Jestem wesoły'). The final two sections move from a nineteenth-century pastiche of Renaissance music to a full-blown mass song *à la marcia* via a spoken choral fugato. Not until more recent times (as in the case of Alfred Schnittke) has a composer attempted such polystylism, but no work can survive such crassly obvious texts or disparate musical styles as used by Krenz. Despite its gaucheness, his tribute to the friendship between Warsaw and Moscow received a major spread by the musicologist Józef Chomiński.[27] The textual tail (short and stumpy though it was) was wagging the dog (unfortunate mongrel that it was). Composers understandably approached this Soviet import with apprehension.

The Skrowaczewski and Krenz cantatas illustrate, however crudely, that the arbiters of socialist realism had no clear idea of how to control large-scale forms when their political ambitions outstripped composers' ability to realise them. So we can hardly be surprised that young composers in particular floundered around in trying to please the authorities.

Although the likes of Zofia Lissa and the principal man from the Ministry of Culture, Włodzimierz Sokorski, spared no effort in exhorting composers to 'mobilise our man' (Lissa's phrase), they were short on specifics. The major attempt by Sokorski to set the socialist-realist agenda had taken place in August 1949 at a country castle called Łagów. Its proceedings were fully reported in the October 1949 issue of *Ruch Muzyczny*, which in recent months had been stinging the authorities with outspoken articles by Kisielewski. His article challenging the ideological foundation of socialist realism and its much denigrated opposite, 'Can formalism exist in music?' (November 1948), was answered in the next issue by Sokorski, on 'Formalism and Realism in the Arts'.[28] The last straw was when, in September 1949, *Ruch Muzyczny* published a quasi-scientific analysis of one of the most experimental pieces of the late 1940s – Panufnik's quarter-tonal *Lullaby*.[29] *Ruch Muzyczny* was then forced to publish an article, translated from the Russian, called 'Arnold Schoenberg – Liquidator of Music'[30] and by the end of the year Kisielewski's main musical outlet against the government was closed down to be replaced by the more tightly controlled *Muzyka*.

Sokorski's conference at Łagów was not as vitriolic as the infamous General Assembly of Soviet Composers held in Moscow eighteen months earlier, and the account published in *Ruch Muzyczny* was more open and argumentative – again, a crucial difference between the Soviet totalitarian and the Polish democratic spirit over the centuries. Łagów is the subject for a full paper on its own, but here three points are worth making: first, only a quarter of the ZKP membership was present (attendance was not compulsory – Bacewicz and Panufnik were not there, although Lutosławski was); second, peer-review listening sessions took place – Baird's light-music *Sinfonietta* was highly praised, Turski's prize-winning *Olympic Symphony* (1948) was damned as pessimistic and formalist by Sokorski and Lissa, but not by some of the leading musicians present. And, last, three composers in their twenties – Baird, Serocki and Krenz – formed 'Group 49' to carry out the goals of the socialist-realist policy. They had swallowed what Czesław Miłosz (b.1911) was shortly to refer to as the pill of Murti-Bing.

In Miłosz's penetrating essay on Polish socialist-realism *The Captive Mind*, written shortly after he had sought asylum in the West in May 1951, he recalls the pre-war fantasy novel *Insatiability* (1930) by Poland's wildest creative artist of the first half of this century, Stanisław Ignacy Witkiewicz (1885–1939). Witkiewicz foresaw the invasion of a decayed Western civilisation by a Mongolian army, an invasion facilitated by giving Murti-Bing pills to the unfortunate, degenerate citizens. These pills, named after a mythical Mongolian philosopher, imbued the citizens with peace of mind and freed them from any metaphysical concerns. As Miłosz puts it:

> Instead of writing the dissonant music of former days, they composed marches and odes. Instead of painting abstractions as before, they turned out socially useful pictures. But since they could not rid themselves completely of their former personalities, they became schizophrenics.[31]

The three composers of 'Group 49' set about their task with a will, but each had separate trajectories. Krenz wrote *Conversation of Two Cities* (no mass songs) and a good deal of orchestral music. Serocki wrote mass songs, a cantata, two symphonies, a piano and a trombone concerto (he was capable on both instruments) and made an isolated foray into the unknown, in his *Suite of Preludes* (1952). Baird also did his bit for the cause – an ill-fated cantata – *Ballada o żołnierskim kubku* ('Ballad of the Soldier's Cup', text by Stanisław Strumph-Wojkiewicz, 1954) – and an earlier, untraceable 'Pieśń o rewolucji' ('Song to Revolution', 1951), but at the same time he wrote a piano concerto (a popular genre), two symphonies, and much pastiche work.

All three were involved in music for the radio and for films. Serocki wrote the score for the most famous film of 1952, Aleksander Ford's *Młodość Chopina* ('Chopin's Youth'), whose closing scene has the composer waving the red flag and marching hand-in-hand with the revolutionaries. In such ways was history purloined to give credence to the Party. Incidentally, so powerful was the use of Chopin's music in this film that the fledgling composer Henryk Mikołaj Górecki (b.1933) went to see it over a dozen times, trying to ignore its socialist evangelism.

This essay has concentrated on areas of little-known musical composition – the mass song and the cantata – genres that lent themselves to mass communication and to which state control was more easily applied. To borrow a term from the visual arts and considering what was going on in that field of creative endeavour at this time, these two genres (and to an extent, opera) may be regarded as figurative music. But most composers yearned to set their own agenda, to write what may be called abstract, or at least semi-abstract chamber and orchestral music. The most obvious example of the semi-abstract is Lutosławski's *Concerto for Orchestra*, with its folk-derived thematic material, but there are many others. Sometimes composers trod water with pastiche pieces, like Baird's *Colas Breugnon* (1951) or with arrangements of old Polish music – Panufnik's *Concerto in modo antico* (1951) is a lame example, Krenz's *Dance Suite from the Tabulature of Jan of Lublin* (1953) is an effective one.

Sometimes, if composers were so disillusioned with their inability to conform or adapt, they deserted composition altogether. Włodzimierz Kotoński (b.1925) was a vulnerable twenty-five-year-old when his *Mountaineer's Dance* was savaged at a listening session in 1950 and he turned for the next few years to annotating folk music instead; his four articles in *Muzyka* 1953–54 are important contributions to Polish ethnomusicology.[32] Some of the younger generation of composers turned to conducting after a while. 'Group 49' split up after only four years as Krenz succeeded Grzegorz Fitelberg (1879–1953) as chief conductor of the Polish Radio Symphony Orchestra in Katowice, then known as Stalinogród.

There are some abstract orchestral and chamber pieces which marginalise external 'tincturing' (to borrow Lutosławski's word), and yet, curiously enough, they are the ones that remain obscured even today by the obviously folk-based pieces. Notable among such works is Turski's strong-minded and harmonically independent Violin Concerto (1951).[33] But it is in the orchestral music of Tadeusz Baird that we find a Polish composer grappling with formal structures in a bold way. In his Second Symphony 'Quasi una fantasia' (1952) he tried to break away from the accepted norms. It has three movements, the shortest of which is the almost inevitable concluding 4/4 march (no Polish work could end quietly). The central 'Allegro quasi variazioni' is a Scherzo with a dark soul. But the first movement, lasting some fourteen minutes – over half the piece – is almost Mahlerian in its melancholic introspection. It foreshadows Baird's post-1956 reputation as Poland's foremost lyrical composer. And it avoided the serious charge of 'pessimism' and was hailed instead as romantic. It is long-breathed, and its sustained opening is a youthful and uncanny anticipation of the opening of Lutosławski's last major work, the Fourth Symphony (1992). But, for all the daring of that first movement, Baird's Second Symphony as a whole remains a schizophrenic hybrid, much as did other large-scale works by his immediate Polish contemporaries. Older composers like Szabelski, Turski or Lutosławski seem to have had the compositional experience and armoury to write works without destructive internal tensions.

Were Polish composers totally isolated from the outside world? Well, to all intents and purposes, they were between 1949 and 1954. Only a privileged few – like Panufnik in the thrall of the Party – went abroad. Did they have no knowledge about the world of Webern or Schoenberg? Did we in the United Kingdom at the time? Certainly, the outline principles of twelve-note composition were known – *Ruch Muzyczny* before its demise in 1949 had published some thoughts – but actual scores were hardly known at all. It is possible that composers heard music from foreign radio stations in cities like Vienna.

But some younger composers did dip their toes. In his *Music for Strings: Nocturne* (composed, it would seem, in 1953, but not performed until the late 1950s), Bogusław Schäffer (b.1929) used very basic contrapuntal layering of an all-interval row, in a language that already indicated that this most avant-garde Polish composer after 1956 already knew something about the Second Viennese School. The most unusual incident was the awarding of a state prize to Serocki in 1952 for his rather daring Suite of Preludes. That same year he won a prize for a soldiers' song[34] – schizophrenia was being officially recognised. The Suite has seven short preludes, five of them in toccata mode and loosely chromatic. But two of them – No.2 'Affetuoso' and No.4 'Teneramente' – are improvisatory in feel and, more importantly, explore the full chromatic range in twelve-note groupings. This is not twelve-note in the Viennese sense but closely allied to the harmonic applications Lutosławski was to reveal in his *Five Songs* (1956–57). The 'Teneramente' would seem to show that Serocki had heard of Berg's Violin Concerto (Example 32). And the 'Affetuoso' is indulgently jazzy in its harmonic language – and this at a time when jazz was officially banned as a sign of American imperialism.

Ex. 32   Serocki: Suite of Preludes, no.4, opening.

There was one composer who had teflon-like qualities in the post-war decade – no socialist-realist cantatas or mass songs, but admittedly a few Polish folk dances as encore pieces and several orchestral and chamber pieces with finales 'tinctured' by obereks (the fast cousin of the mazurka). But Bacewicz's tally of abstract compositions – just to mention three symphonies, four concertos and three quartets – is astonishingly high. And almost single-handedly she kept alive that most abstract of compositional outlets, chamber music.

There appears to be no ready explanation why Bacewicz evaded censure, except to say that she was also an active concert violinist and pianist at this time and made her obvious contribution to 'outreach' through performance. But she certainly was one of the foremost composers. Bacewicz was by nature prolific; her music is conventionally regarded as having not only drive but also a neo-classical elegance. But this view of her output in the early 1950s is barely a half-truth. In both her Fourth and Fifth String Quartets (1951 and 1955 respectively), she explores the medium with an individual imagination. Her Fifth String Quartet is a work of unusual emotional depth, harmonic dissonance and formal innovation. From the opening of the first movement, 'Moderato', it is evident that there is no reliance on accepted formulae. Bacewicz treats the customary sonata structure with a mixture of reverence and disregard. The introductory bars (Example 33)

Ex 33. Bacewicz: String quarter, no.5, first movement opening.

transcend their initial function to reappear at the climax of the development, in the recapitulation and at the final 'cadence'. Moreover, the descending semitone and minor third pervade the Quartet. Arguably the most significant aspect is Bacewicz's ability to achieve a dramatic balance between the kinetic energy of the first subject group and the remote stillness of the second. Bacewicz also showed a flair, matched only by Lutosławski at the time, for instrumental colour. The folk-style second subject emerges in artificial harmonics, counterpointed by ostinati, both arco and pizzicato, and a pedal natural harmonic (Example 34).

Ex. 34   Bacewicz: String Quartet, no.5, first movement.

This essay has scratched the surface of another world, a world where the traditional trio of composer, performer and listener suddenly became a quartet. We know who this 'other Party' was, and how it disrupted what it regarded as a cosy world of exclusivity. However laudable its intentions, however reprehensible its actions, did it change anything for the better? Perhaps not, but then would the Polish avant-garde explosion of the late 1950s and 1960s have happened without the repression and 'mobilization' of the Dark Decade? The difficult question remains: do the ends justify the means?

Notes

1. Norman Davies (1981), *God's Playground: A History of Poland*, Oxford; and (1984), *Heart of Europe: A Short History of Poland*, Oxford; Adam Zamoyski (1987), *The Polish Way: A Thousand-Year History of the Poles and Their Culture*, London.
2. Marta Fik (1989), *Kultura polska po Jalcie: kronika lat 1944–1981* ['Polish Culture since Yalta: A Chronicle, 1944–1981'], London; Jakub Karpiński (1995), *Poland Since 1944: A Portrait in Years,* Oxford.
3. See Adrian Thomas (August 1995), 'Your Song Is Mine', *The Musical Times* 1830, pp. 403–9.
4. Recorded (or possibly catalogued) on 5 March, 1952, Bernard Ładysz (baritone), the Warsaw-based Polish Radio Choir and Orchestra, conducted by Jerzy Kołaczkowski (Polish Radio Tape M.2636/2). At least one other recording was made (undated), by Eugeniusz Ostrafin, the Kraków-based Polish Radio Choir and Studio Orchestra, conducted by Jerzy Gert (Polish Radio Tape 6.331, apparently destroyed).
5. Gradstein's many other mass songs include *Pieśń jedności* ['Song of Unity', text by Wygodzki, 1949] *ZMP pomaga wsi* ['The ZMP helps the countryside', text by Kołaczkowska, 1950], and *Nasza ziemia* ['Our Native Land', text by Zbigniew Stolarek, 1951].
6. Olearczyk was one of the most popular composers of mass songs, which included *Miliony rąk* ['A Million Hands', text by Krzysztof Gruszczyński, 1950], *Piosenka Zetempowców Warszawy* ['Song of the Warsaw ZMP', text by Wiktor Woroszylski, 1950], and *Pokój! Mir! Frieden! Paix*! ['Peace!' (in Polish, Russian, German and French), text by Mirosław Łebkowski, 1951]. Szpilman's songs included *Do roboty* ['To Work', text by Stanisław Ryszard Dobrowolski, 1950], *Jak młode Stare Miasto* ['How Young the Old Town is', text by Bronisław Brok, 1951], and *Morskie orły* ['Sea Eagles', text by Tadeusz Urgacz, 1952].
7. In 'Pieśń masowa' ['The Mass Song'], Józef Chomiński and Zofia Lissa (eds), *Kultura muzyczna Polski Ludowej 1944–1955* ['The Musical Culture of People's Poland 1944–1955'], Kraków.
8. *Odrodzenie* 29, 20 July 1947, p. 3.
9. See, Zygmunt Mycielski, 'O drugim zjeździe poetów i kompozytorów' ['The Second Conference of Poets and Composers'], *Odrodzenie* 13–14, 29 March–5 April 1948, p. 7.
10. Zofia Lissa, 'Sprawozdanie z konkursu na polska pieśń masową' ['Report from the Competition for the Polish Mass Song'], *Ruch Muzyczny* [Musical Movement] 17, 15 July 1948, pp. 13–14; Zygmunt Mycielski, 'Kłopoty jurorów czyli konkurs na pieśń masową' ['Troubles for the Jury, i.e. The Competition for the Mass Song'], *Odrodzenie* 32, 8 August 1948, p. 7.
11. Zofia Lissa (April 1950), 'Raz jeszcze o polską pieśń masową' ['Once Again on the Polish Mass Song'], *Muzyka* 1, pp. 5–17.
12. Witold Rudziński, 'Pieśń masowa na punkcie zwrotnym' ['The Mass Song at a Turning Point'], *Muzyka* 7–8, July–August 1954, pp. 35–38.
13. Irina Nikolska (1994), *Conversations with Witold Lutosławski,* Stockholm, pp. 40–41.
14. Ibid., pp. 41–2.
15. 'O pieśń, która będzie mobilizować do dalszej pracy i do dalszej walki' ['For Song, Which Will Mobilize the People to Further Work and Further Struggle'], *Radio i Świat* ['Radio and the World'] 24 June 1950, inside front cover. This page of Polish Radio's listings magazine was exhibited as part of the exhibition 'Witold Lutosławski: The Hidden Composer and Polish Radio', organized and mounted by the present author as part of the BBC/Guildhall School of Music and Drama

festival, 'Breaking Chains', devoted to the music of Lutosławski, 13–19 January 1997.

16. Witold Rudziński, 'Z życia Związku Kompozytorów Polskich: Protokół z dyskusji na I przesłouchaniu Sekcji Pieśni Masowej ZKP' ['From the Life of the Polish Composers' Union: Protocol from the Discussion at the First Listening Session of the ZKP's Mass Song Section'], *Muzyka 5* (September 1950), pp. 64–67, 70.

17. *Muzyka 5* (September 1950), p. 67.

18. On 25 October 1950, by Tomasz Dąbrowski (tenor), Polish Radio Choir and Studio Orchestra, conducted by Jerzy Kołaczkowski; it is the only recording of the song still extant. *Radio i Swiat* also published the melody and text, no.47 (November 1950), p. 4.

19. *Odrodzenie*, 19 February 1950.

20. *Muzyka 5* (September 1950), p. 66. Curiously, in *Pieśni żołnierskie* ['Soldiers' Songs'], Warsaw, 1953, the first item is a song to Stalin, by the same composer and lyricist, and it too is in the rhythm of the polonaise. Is it possible that this much criticized song resurfaced three years later under a new title, *Stalin z nami* ['Stalin Is With Us']?

21. Recorded on 9 December 1950 by Janina Godlewska (mezzo) and Witold Lutosławski (piano), Polish Radio Tape M.2532/1.

22. *Trasa W–Z* ['East–West Route', text by Eugeniusz Żytomirski, 1950].

23. Dobrowolski *Kantata na cześć pokoju* ['Cantata for a Time of Peace', text by Biędrzycki], Panufnik *Symfonia pokoju* ['Symphony of Peace', text by Jarosław Iwaszkiewicz], Skrowaczewski *Kantata o pokoju* ['Cantata for Peace', text by Broniewski], Gradstein *Słowo o Stalinie* ['A Word on Stalin', text by Broniewski] and Serocki *Warszawski murarz* ['Warsaw Bricklayer', author unknown].

24. Although no score appears to have survived, a recording from 1952, in which the Silesian Philharmonic is conducted by Karol Stryja, is still catalogued at Polish Radio.

25. Krenz *Rozmowa dwóch miast* ['Conversation of Two Cities', text by Gałczyński, 1950].

26. Nikolska, op.cit., p. 40.

27. Józef Chomiński, 'Dwa miasta – Kantata Jana Krenza' ['Two Cities – a Cantata by Jan Krenz'], *Muzyka 3–4* (March–April 1951), pp. 8–12. A 1952 recording survives at Polish Radio.

28. Stefan Kisielewski, 'Czy w muzyce istnieje formalizm', *Ruch Muzyczny 22* (1948), pp. 2–6. Włodzimierz Sokorski (1948), 'Formalizm i realizm w sztuce', *Ruch Muzyczny 23–24*, pp. 2–5.

29. Anna Moskalukówna (1949), 'Kołysanka Andrzeja Panufnika', *Ruch Muzyczny 13*, pp. 25–26.

30. I. Ryżkin (1949), 'Arnold Schoenberg – likwidator muzyki', *Ruch Muzyczny 15*, pp. 24–31.

31. Czesław Miłosz (1953; Penguin edn 1980), *The Captive Mind*, London, p. 5 .

32. Włodzimierz Kotoński, 'Uwagi o muzyce ludowej Podhala' ['Notes on Podhalian Folk Music'], *Muzyka 5–6* (May–June 1953), pp. 3–25; 7–8 (July–August 1953), pp 43–58; 11–12 (November–December 1953), pp. 25–45; 1–2 (January–February 1954), pp. 14–27.

33. Turski's Violin Concerto is now available on Olympia OCD 327 along with his discredited 'Olympic' Symphony.

34. *Leśna marszruta* ['Forest Route', text by Henryk Gaworski]; see 'Kronika Krajowa' ['National Chronicle'], *Muzyka 1–2* (January–February 1953), p. 101.

Index of Names and Titles